*To the memory of
Bruno Minoletti
and
Lambert Schaus*

COMMISSION OF THE EUROPEAN COMMUNITIES

Transport and European integration

by Carlo degli Abbati

THE EUROPEAN PERSPECTIVES SERIES
BRUSSELS

This publication was prepared outside the Commission of the European Communities and is intended as a contribution to public debate on transport and European integration. It does not necessarily reflect the opinion of the Commission.

Cataloguing data appear at the end of this publication.

Luxembourg: Office for Official Publications of the European Communities, 1987

ISBN 92-825-6199-2

Catalogue number: CB-45-86-806-EN-C

Contents

PART TWO - ORGANIZATION AND INTEGRATION OF THE TRANSPORT MARKET

List of abbreviations

ACP	African, Caribbean and Pacific
AETR	European Agreement concerning the work of crews of vehicles engaged in International Road Transport
ASOR	Agreement on the International Carriage of Passengers by Road by means of Occasional Coach and Bus Services
Bull.	Bulletin (of the European Communities)
CAA	Civil Aviation Authority
CAB	Civil Aeronautics Board
CAP	Common agricultural policy
CCR	Central Commission for the Navigation of the Rhine
CIM	International Convention concerning the Carriage of Goods by Rail
CIV	International Convention concerning the Carriage of Passengers and Luggage by Rail
CMR	Convention on the Contract for the International Transport of Goods by Road
CNR	Italian National Research Council
Comecon	Council for Mutual Economic Assistance
CONI	Italian National Olympic Committee
Coreper	Permanent Representatives Committee
COST	European cooperation in the field of scientific and technical research
CSC	International Convention for Safe Containers
Doc.	Document
EAEC	European Atomic Energy Community
EAGGF	European Agricultural Guidance and Guarantee Fund
ECAC	European Civil Aviation Conference
ECE	Economic Commission for Europe
ECR	European Court Reports
ECMT	European Conference of Ministers of Transport
ECSC	European Coal and Steel Community
ECU	European currency unit
EEC	European Economic Community
EIB	European Investment Bank
EMS	European Monetary System
ERDF	European Regional Development Fund
ESC	Economic and Social Committee
IATA	International Air Transport Association
ILO	International Labour Office
IMCO	Inter-Governmental Maritime Consultative Organization
JAR	Joint Airworthiness Requirements
NCI	New Community Instrument
OECD	Organization for Economic Cooperation and Development
OEEC	Organization for European Economic Cooperation

OJ	Official Journal (of the European Communities)
u.a.	unit(s) of account
Unctad	United Nations Conference on Trade and Development
UTA	Union des Transport Aériens

'Nationalism runs counter to the very concept of the "nation"'

J. Ortega y Gasset

Introduction

Twenty-five years after the signing of the Treaties of Rome (and a few months after the European Parliament was directly elected by universal suffrage for the second time), it is worth examining what the European Communities have actually achieved (and the many opportunities missed) along the path followed to date.

Our aim therefore was to find a way of assessing one of the most controversial areas where the Treaty establishing the EEC requires the formulation of common policies, namely the common transport policy. In so doing, we were conscious of the fact that, because transport is such a vast subject if all the various modes are included, we would then gain a clear idea of the major themes of European economic integration.

Benefiting from the experience gained at the Commission of the European Communities and by the Court of Auditors of the European Communities, we have attempted to analyse what has been achieved in the sphere of European transport policy and to use this to gain an insight into the Community's institutional and procedural problems, which in many cases are deliberately perpetuated by national governments for all too obvious reasons since this is a grey area safely removed from the glare of European public opinion.

In this way it is to be hoped that the student of transport economics will find in this book sufficiently up-to-date information on the whole history of transport policy within the Community and on the problems facing the various modes of transport in the Member States as reflected at Community level. In addition, young people wanting to know more about certain aspects of Europe will also find illumination. Whether this is merely a glimmer or whether a flood of bright light, it will still show him the way along the long road of good intentions which he is destined to follow, perhaps without being aware of it, treading in the footsteps of those who, in various ways, have worked towards a Europe which has managed to shake off some of the old and self-satisfied national egoism. We have dedicated this book to two such people who both pledged their whole lives to building a new community of Europeans specifically in the field of transport, namely Bruno Minoletti and Lambert Schaus, to whom we are tremendously indebted. Here we would like to link their names with that of one of the great architects of European thought, past and present, Hendrijk Brugmans.

Dyver, Bruges, College of Europe

PART ONE

General considerations

1. The need for a common transport policy and difficulties in setting it up

1.1 Some preliminary definitions

As soon as one begins to investigate the transport provisions of the Treaty establishing the European Economic Community, one is immediately struck by the limited scope of the articles devoted to the subject and of the aims to be achieved under the Treaty.

In fact, the provisions of the Treaty of Rome which relate to transport are rather like a jigsaw puzzle consisting of pieces whose shape can be changed to fit the circumstances. Some pieces definitely fit while others are missing or doubtful; in other words, according to Santoro,[1] some matters are the explicit responsibility of the Community, others are mentioned but no responsibilities are defined and others do not seem to be the Community's responsibility at all.

But however one evaluates the rules laid down by the Treaty on the subject of transport, one thing is certain: neither the Treaty establishing the EEC, nor the Treaties establishing the ECSC and Euratom contain a single definition of the term 'transport'. What is actually covered by the term has to be decided on the basis of its general meaning as defined by law, learned opinion and jurisprudence in the Member States.

In law and economics, of course, the term 'transport' refers to all activities undertaken with the purpose of moving people and goods from one place to another. Transport economics is a field of study concerned particularly with how economic laws apply specifically to activities undertaken with the purpose of moving people and goods from one place to another and how all these sectors relate to the rest of the economic system.

'Transport' thus includes transport operations for hire or reward, transport operations conducted by undertakings on their own account and using their own means, and transport operations by private individuals (and in particular the carriage of persons in private cars). 'Transport policy' on the other hand means all the legislation, regulations and administrative provisions enacted by the public authorities which relate to activities undertaken with the purpose of moving people and goods from one place to another and all the different kinds of technical infrastructure required to achieve this purpose. This definition obviously implies that public bodies should make a consistent effort to tackle

---

[1] F. Santoro, *La politica dei trasporti della Comunità Economica Europea*, UTET, Turin, 1974, p. 3.

all transport problems together rather than taking *ad hoc* economic policy measures whenever the need arises.

Similarly, 'common transport policy' in the sense of the Community transport policy referred to in the EEC Treaty should consist of a set of measures applied to transport by the Member States. Under the Treaty, these measures should take the form, as we shall see in greater detail later, of common rules which in accordance with Community law - Article 189 of the Treaty - may be regulations, which are generally applicable legal acts binding in their entirety and directly applicable in all Member States, directives, which are binding as to the result to be achieved upon each Member State to which they are addressed but allow the national authorities to choose the ways and means of achieving these results, or decisions, which are binding in their entirety upon those to whom they are addressed. Thus, the measures to be implemented by the Member States must be based on a set of common rules and principles which will obviously be defined jointly according to the degree of convergence of national positions. In fact, the common policy is a much broader concept than the coordination mentioned in Articles 6 and 105 of the Treaty with reference to the economic policies of the Member States. As we shall see, a common policy implies not only organizing national legal arrangements in the same way (approximation of legislation) but also joint action in the form of systematic legislation at Community level, which is thus directly applicable in the Member States, together with sectoral policies for each different mode of transport and a staunch commitment by the Member States to defending the transport interests of the Community *vis-à-vis* non-Member States.[1] The common transport policy thus consists of a set of measures which from time to time will be translated into various objectives in the form of coordination, harmonization or standardization and which thus also constitute one aspect of the Community's overall economic policy. This in turn consists of two separate sets of measures which are both complementary: general measures which relate to economic systems in their entirety and specific measures which relate to the individual major economic sectors rather than to economic systems as a whole.

In the Treaty establishing the European Economic Community, Title IV - 'Transport' - which includes Articles 74 to 84 is in Part Two of the Treaty - 'Foundations of the Community'. Whereas Part One sets out the principles on which the Treaty is based and Part Three, entitled 'Policy of the Community', consists of four titles which basically contain provisions designed to bring about the integration of the various economic sectors through general action by the Community in these sectors which will lead to the achievement of genuine economic union within the Community, Part Two of the Treaty contains all the provisions which lay down the principles on which the Community is to be founded. Since the ultimate objective of the Community is the establishment of an economic union, these principles are summed up in the four basic freedoms

---

[1] Cfr. N. Bellieni, 'Commento agli artt. 74-84' in *Commentario al Trattato Istitutivo della Comunità Economica Europea,* Vol. 1, Giuffré, Milan, 1965; idem, 'Titre IV - Transports', in *Droit des affaires - Marché Commun,* Ed. Jupiter, Brussels, 1973.

of movement of goods, people, services and capital. Thus since transport corresponds to the objective of free movement of services it is dealt with in Title IV of Part Two which, as is the case with agriculture too, covered by Title II, includes provisions on transport in as far as it is the subject of specific integration measures taken by the Community institutions.

1.2 The reason for an EEC transport policy

Whether transport is regarded as a self-contained economic sector or as an instrument of general or regional economic policy, there is no denying that it is an important component of the economy. For this reason, individual states or, on a wider level, states associated in an economic union, must adopt an overall conception of transport policy. And just as each nation state already has a transport policy - irrespective of whether it takes a *laissez-faire* or an interventionist approach - in the same way when two or more Member States decide to set up an economic union or some other form of economic community they obviously cannot ignore the transport sector. The degree of precision with which transport policy is defined within the framework of the union which is to be set up will then depend on the extent to which the participating States intend to integrate. Accordingly, since the Treaty of Paris signed on 18 April 1951 to establish the European Coal and Steel Community was designed solely to bring about partial integration in these two basic sectors, transport is included (Article 70 in Chapter IX of Title Three 'Economic and social provisions') purely to ensure the application of such rates and conditions for the carriage of coal and steel as will afford comparable price conditions to comparably placed consumers. Commercial transport policy, on the other hand, and in particular the fixing and altering of rates and conditions of carriage, the making of rates on a basis calculated to secure for the transport undertakings concerned a properly balanced financial position and measures relating to coordination or competition between different modes of transport, continues to be governed by the individual Member States.

The position of transport in the Treaty establishing the European Economic Community is very different. This is because the Treaty's objectives are much grander, namely the establishment, in the short term, of a customs union and, in the longer term, of a genuine economic union intended ultimately to become a political union too.[1] These objectives would be achieved by establishing a common market with all the features of an internal market and as such enjoying free movement of goods, people, services and capital. The consequence of all this is that the various sectors of the economy would have to be comprehensively integrated by introducing a whole range of common policies. This being the case, the Treaty could not then avoid stating as an objective the adoption of a common policy in the sphere of transport too (Article 3(e)).

---

[1] In fact, the first words of the preamble of the Treaty, after listing the Heads of State of the six Member States are: 'Determined to lay the foundations of an ever closer union among the peoples of Europe'.

1.3 How the Member States approach transport policy

The Member States have rather different and often divergent approaches to transport policy. These are conditioned to a large extent by considerations of geography and population and by economic policy.

As a result, in the run-up to the signing of the Treaty of Rome, and ever since in fact, discussions did not concentrate only on the theoretical question of whether transport could be classed as a totally self-contained sector of the economy like all the other economic sectors and as such should not be subject to public service obligations or eligible for concessions (*laissez-faire* approach) or whether it should be used as an instrument for achieving other general or sectoral economic policy goals and as such would be subject to intervention by the public authorities. Discussions also focused upon the economic geography of the individual Member States and the consequent importance of the railways in each of them.[1] In view of all these factors, the different approaches of the six Member States ranged from a *laissez-faire* approach (the Netherlands in particular, but also Belgium and Luxembourg) to a decidedly interventionist approach (Federal Republic of Germany). France, on the other hand, was theoretically interventionist but less rigid in practice and Italy's traditional *laissez-faire* approach to transport was in opposition to its actual policy decisions on transport which clearly pointed in the opposite direction. This range of different attitudes is not surprising in view of the fact that the Netherlands and Belgium have a very high density of population distributed over a relatively small area, most of which is flat, and have extremely concentrated rail, road and waterway networks. Considering its size, the Netherlands plays an extremely important role in Europe because of the ideal position of the port of Rotterdam in Northern Europe and the excellent way in which its transport undertakings are managed.

France is well known for its rigid centralization. Everything revolves around Paris, which means that traffic between regions is severely constricted. At long last attempts have been made over the last few years to remedy the situation by improving the entire road and rail network.

Since Germany was split following the Second World War, most of the road and rail traffic in the Federal Republic of Germany travels along the north-south axis.[2] Finally, the Grand Duchy of Luxembourg has its own special problems because its country is so small (only 2 586 km²). In addition, more so than in any other Member State, Luxembourg's road, rail and river (Moselle) networks are virtually Community thoroughfares and carry a large proportion

---

[1] Of interest in this connection is the careful study made by N. Bellieni, 'Titre IV - Transports', op. cit. pp. 11-12.

[2] An important disadvantage of this is that the major German ports on the North Sea are deprived of their natural hinterland. See A. Vallega, *L'organizzazione delle regioni portuali nella CEE,* Fratelli Bozzi, Genoa, 1970, pp. 33-44.

of the transit traffic to and from France, Belgium and Germany since the country is an enclave, wedged in between the Ardennes and the Moselle.

The inland waterways also play an important part in the transport systems of some Member States like the Netherlands, Belgium, Germany and, to some extent, France. Again, apart from the land-locked Grand Duchy, all the Member States are maritime countries, which means that their road transport policies are conditioned to a greater or lesser degree by decisions taken on shipping policy and ports. The accession of the three new Member States, and more recently of Greece, has done nothing to help the obvious confusion surrounding the Community's approach to transport. Denmark, Ireland, the United Kingdom and Greece are all maritime States and their attitude to transport policy is basically one of *laissez-faire*.

It is generally true to say that, as far as inland transport is concerned, the geographically peripheral Member States of the Community are more dependent on road transport than the central Member States, which tend to rely more heavily on the railways. As a result the former tend to favour deregulation of road transport whereas the latter attach more priority to uniform conditions of competition.

1.4 Distinctive features

There are a number of 'distinctive' features which make the transport market different from other sectors of the economy and which closely relate to the question of whether transport is an economic policy instrument or a self-contained sector of the economy. Because of these distinctive features it can be argued that transport should be treated differently from other sectors of the economy, particularly as regards the application of rules on competition.

During negotiations on the EEC Treaty, in fact, the delegations from five of the six countries (i.e. all except the Netherlands) argued that these distinctive features should be maintained and that transport should be given special treatment. Thus Article 75 - in Title IV of the Treaty which constitutes a veritable *lex specialis* on transport - explicitly refers to 'the distinctive features of transport' for the purpose of implementing Article 74 which, as we shall see, refers to a common transport policy to be pursued by the Member States. Clearly therefore recognition of these distinctive features and their importance is bound to have a considerable effect on the formulation of a common transport policy.

It is thus important to make clear from the outset what these distinctive features are and how they will affect the formulation of a common transport policy.

1.4.1 *Infrastructure and the public authorities*

Decisions on investment in transport infrastructure are generally taken by the public authorities (i.e. the government and regional or local authorities) and in the case of roads and inland waterways they generally finance the infrastructure themselves. They also have various supervisory powers over investment in railway infrastructure although the railway undertakings have free and exclusive use of this infrastructure. Moreover, so that free competition within the transport sector is affected as little as possible, the cost of using infrastructure has to be charged equally to those who use it. In fact it is widely argued that infrastructure charging, in other words, the equitable allocation of the cost of using infrastructure between the various users, is of fundamental importance in setting up a sound transport policy; in fact the Commission of the European Communities in Brussels has been working on this problem for many years.

1.4.2 *Special features of supply and demand in the transport sector*

Clearly the transport market, with all the various modes, presents special features which are a direct result of differences in structures between the transport sector and other sectors of production.

The first thing to remember is that, as Isard pointed out,[1] transport services are consumed at the same moment as they are provided and as such cannot be 'stored' and placed on the market after they have been produced.

The fact that transport services are ephemeral clearly means that fixed costs (i.e. costs which do not depend on tonnes-km or passengers-km but are nevertheless incurred even if the service is not paid for) cannot be recovered, even in part. In other words, the fact that many of the costs of providing the transport service are a function of the productive capacity of the means of transport - which means that scheduled services can be treated as production at combined costs[2] - means that on occasions there may be an imbalance in the use of means of transport which may upset the price formation mechanism of that service. If it becomes necessary or desirable to remedy this situation, it is possible to impose various restrictions either on the supply of transport services or in the form of tariffs.

From the point of view of supply of transport services, it is striking how much variation there is in the types and sizes of undertakings operating the various modes of transport. As far as rail transport is concerned, the fact that the

---

[1] See W. Isard, *Localizzazione e spazio economico,* Italian edition by A. Riva, Istituto Ed. Cisalpino, Milan-Varese, 1962.

[2] For further information on problems regarding the production of transport services see in particular U. Marchese, *Aspetti economici e territoriali del sistema dei trasporti,* ECIG, Genoa, 1980, pp. 53-157.

railways can provide both passenger and goods transport services and the fact that there is usually only one railway undertaking means that the railways enjoy an advantage over rival modes of transport, namely road transport and inland waterway transport, although the latter have the advantage of being more flexible to manage. Again, in many cases the road transport and inland waterway transport sectors comprise not only small firms with a handful of employees, but also larger companies or even groups of companies. It is clear therefore that each mode of transport enjoys its own natural advantages. To the extent that the three modes of transport expressly mentioned in the *lex specialis* constituted by Title IV of the Treaty establishing the EEC (i.e. rail, road and inland waterway) are placed on an equal footing, it should be possible to apply the rules on competition as fully as possible to transport, with due consideration for the distinctive features of transport mentioned in Article 75 of the Treaty. This should have the effect of optimizing use of the different modes of transport by transport users so that customers would decide which mode of transport to use for which purpose according to its relative convenience, and would thus enjoy the full benefits of competition between different carriers and different modes of transport.

Lastly, there are a number of different factors which clearly affect the development of transport, notably economic considerations, geography and population. Different regions have different geographical features, their relative population densities vary and so does the location of their economic activities. The way in which road and inland waterway transport services are managed thus depends to a large extent on basically natural and seasonal factors. As a result, it is probably necessary to allow transport operators a certain amount of freedom as regards setting tariffs in order to make it easier for them to manage their businesses.

1.4.3 *Public service obligations*

The concept of 'public service' is found in French public law (*service public*) and in German public law (*öffentlicher Dienst*).[1] However, it in no way corresponds to the notion of *Gemeinwirtschaftliche Leistung* used by German economists, and even less to that used by Dutch economists: witness the fact that in the Dutch version of Article 77 of the Treaty the term is given quotation marks. The obligation to provide a public service is totally unconnected with the commercial interests of the undertaking concerned but can be described as an activity carried out in the public interest, either directly by the authorities or by private sector undertakings under the control or supervision of the public authorities.

These public service obligations, which include the obligation 'to operate' a transport service, the obligation 'to carry' and 'tariff obligations',[2] apply in

---

[1] The transport obligations which the German Basic Law (*Grundgesetz*) imposes on *Deutsche Lufthansa* and on the German railways (*Bundesbahn*) on behalf of the Federal Post Office (*Bundespost*).
[2] See Regulation (EEC) No 1191/69 of the Council of 26 June 1969 (OJ L 156, 28.6.1969, p. 1).

particular to the railways. There are two considerations here, however. Firstly, it is impossible, as Sontoro rightly points out,[1] to establish clearly the distinction made by the regulation in question between the various obligations which constitute the overall public service obligation when transport services are being considered from the point of view of their economic characteristics. Secondly, it should be pointed out that whereas it may be in the public interest to impose certain public service obligations on certain transport operators, tariff obligations for example, and whereas these may benefit specific types of user, specific sectors of the economy or specific regions, the carriers themselves should not have to bear the burden of providing these services. In other words, specific national or regional economic policy decisions should not have the effect of placing an additional burden on transport operators.

To conclude therefore, since, as we shall see when we examine the articles of the Treaty which contain provisions on transport, most of the delegations at the inter-governmental conference responsible for drafting the Treaty establishing the EEC were aware of the distinctive features of transport, specific reference was in fact made to these distinctive features in Article 75(1) of the Treaty. On the subject of the 'obligations inherent in the concept of a public service' mentioned in Article 77, the Community has published a special regulation, already referred to, which lays down specific rules to be observed by the Member States, since this is undoubtedly an important aspect of the transport sector in general.[2] Even so, criticisms have rightly been levelled against the way in which the regulation is formulated,[3] and there is a clear relationship between this regulation and the two subsequent regulations on normalization of the accounts of railway undertakings[4] and aids.[5]

---

[1] F. Santoro, op. cit. p. 232.
[2] Regulation (EEC) No 1191/69 - already mentioned in footnote 2 on the previous page - of the Council of 26 June 1969 'on action by Member States concerning obligations inherent in the concept of a public service' (OJ L 156, 28.6.1969, p.1).
[3] F. Santoro, op. cit. p. 231 *et seq.*
[4] Regulation (EEC) No 1192/69 of the Council of 26 June 1969 on common rules for the normalization of the accounts of railway undertakings (OJ L 156, 28.6.1969).
[5] Regulation (EEC) No 1107/70 of the Council of 4 June 1970 (OJ L 130, 15.6.1970).

2. Working out the framework, guidelines and content for a European transport policy

The organization of transport in Europe has been a problem ever since the end of the Second World War when trade links within Europe were restored and intensified. Various institutions were set up to cope with this problem and they still exist alongside the Community institutions responsible for transport in Europe. It is worth taking a brief look at these institutions.

2.1 International institutions responsible for transport in Europe which do not come under the EEC

2.1.1 *Central Commission for the Navigation of the Rhine (CCR)*

The Central Commission for the Navigation of the Rhine (CCR) is the oldest of the European institutions responsible for transport. It was first set up under the Mannheim Convention of 17 October 1868, which was amended on 20 November 1963. This Commission supervises the Rhine navigation system and has powers to issue regulations and to police these regulations. The current Contracting States to the Convention are Belgium, France, the Federal Republic of Germany, the Netherlands, Switzerland and the United Kingdom. Because Rhine navigation is subject to the provisions of this Convention and because the CCR includes one state (Switzerland) which is not a member of the Community, there have been, and still are, a number of awkward problems which affect the establishment of a common transport policy by the Community.

Following an exchange of letters between the President of the EEC Commission and the President of the CCR on 6 June 1961, links were established between the two institutions that same year on the basis of the powers conferred upon the executive arm of the Community by the second paragraph of Article 229 of the Treaty which states that 'the Commission shall ... maintain such relations as are appropriate with all international organizations'. The Commission of the European Communities also sends observers to CCR meetings.

2.1.2 *International Convention on the Canalization of the Moselle*

The Convention on the Canalization of the Moselle was signed on 27 October 1956 by representatives of the three countries through which the Moselle flows: France, the Federal Republic of Germany and the Grand Duchy of Luxembourg. It guarantees freedom of navigation on the Moselle between Metz and Koblenz. The navigation system is exactly the same as on the Rhine and is controlled by the Moselle Commission.

2.1.3 *Economic Commission for Europe (ECE)*

The Economic Commission for Europe (ECE) is a United Nations body based in Geneva. It includes all the European member States of the United Nations together with the USA and Switzerland.

The activities of the ECE are carried out by various committees of which the Inland Transport Committee is by far the most important as regards the establishment of a common transport policy.

Through the work of this Committee, a number of technical international agreements have been concluded to facilitate international transport within Europe. Of particular importance as regards speeding up customs formalities at frontiers are the two agreements on rail transit, which introduced the TIT form, and the agreement on the international carriage of goods by road which set up the TIR system.

The ECE has also been working with some success to standardize the different highway codes. In the social field, the European Agreement concerning the work of crews of vehicles engaged in international road transport (AETR) was signed under the aegis of the ECE in 1970.

However, although the international agreements concluded under the ECE or as a result of its efforts are undoubtedly extremely useful, as an organ of inter-governmental cooperation the ECE is not in a position to take an overall approach to the problems facing transport in Europe.

Since 1958 the Commission of the European Communities has established links with the ECE, again based on Article 229 of the Treaty, the first paragraph of which states that 'it shall be for the Commission to ensure the maintenance of all appropriate relations with the organs of the United Nations, of its specialized agencies and of the General Agreement on Tariffs and Trade'.

The EEC Commission also sends observers to attend meetings of the ECE Inland Transport Committee and of its various subcommittees.

2.1.4 *European Conference of Ministers for Transport (ECMT)*

Shortly after the Treaty of Paris establishing the ECSC came into force, the European Conference of Ministers for Transport (ECMT) was set up in Brussels on 17 October 1953. The ECMT emerged from the OEEC (which is now the OECD, an organization which brings together not only European countries but also Canada, Japan and the USA)[1] and includes the seventeen member States of that organization on a basis of institutionalized inter-governmental cooperation. The protocol to the agreement establishing the ECMT laid down two main objectives for the organization, namely:

(a) to take all appropriate steps to secure the best utilization and most rational development of European inland transport of international importance, generally and regionally;

(b) to coordinate and encourage the work of international organizations concerned with internal European transport, bearing in mind the activities of supra-national authorities in this field.

In fact, the emergence of the ECMT gave rise to some controversy. Some saw the creation of this inter-governmental conference as a reaction by national authorities to the establishment of the ECSC High Authority to which the Treaty of Paris assigned extensive supra-national powers that could also be extended to transport.[2]

One thing is certain however. The existence of the ECMT does not seem to have done anything to facilitate the introduction of a common transport policy by the EEC since the very fact that the ECMT already existed makes it an institution which to some extent ranks higher than the Council of Transport Ministers of the EEC, although the ECMT, being an inter-governmental body, obviously does not have the power to take decisions which bind the participating States.

Nevertheless, the achievements of the ECMT should not be under-estimated. The studies and reports it has produced are of an extremely high quality and its annual reports on infrastructure investment are particularly interesting. The ECMT has also made some very important technical recommendations which in many cases have seen the light of day, like the scheme for creating the Europa pool of rail wagons and the establishment of the Eurofima company for the international financing of railway rolling stock.

Thus although the ECMT has neither the institutional authority nor the political will to bring about its own genuine European transport policy, it nevertheless has undoubted technical influence, and also promotes bilateral agreements and

---

[1] For further information on the institutional functions of the OECD, see L. Cartou, *Organisations Européennes,* Dalloz, Paris, 1967, pp. 41-49.

[2] See in this connection the remarks made in the 'Faller report' published on behalf of the Transport Committee of the European Parliament as Doc. PE 75 of 18 October 1962.

multilateral agreements and conventions. Links were established between the EEC Commission and the ECMT in 1958 based on the second paragraph of Article 229 of the EEC Treaty referred to above.

In order to establish more formal and permanent ties it was agreed in 1975 that the Community would be invited to send representatives to meetings of the ECMT Council of Ministers and Committee of Deputies, although they would not have voting rights. The EEC Council of Ministers has adopted a formula whereby it now sends to these meetings a representative of the Member State holding the Presidency of the Council and a representative of the Commission.

2.1.5 *European Coal and Steel Community (ECSC)*

From an institutional point of view, the aim of the Treaty of Paris of 18 April 1951 which established the ECSC was to create joint decision-making bodies.[1] From an economic point of view, however, the aim of the ECSC was of course to establish a common market for coal and steel based on the principles of free trade, non-discrimination, equality of treatment and competition. Since the Treaty of Paris was based on the idea of pooling these two basic resources, it could not ignore those transport problems which particularly affected the two sectors concerned. Thus, as we have already seen, Article 70 of the Treaty of Paris and Article 10 of the Convention on the Transitional Provisions contain special provisions relating to the transport of coal and steel by rail, road and inland waterway. The main objective of the ECSC Treaty as far as transport is concerned is to ensure that the carriage of coal and steel is conducted in such a way as to 'afford comparable price conditions to comparably placed consumers'. However, since the ECSC serves merely to bring about the functional integration of certain sectors, and, what is more, only two sectors - albeit extremely important ones - of the economy at that, it was not in a position to come up with an overall transport policy. Moreover, the fifth paragraph of Article 70 expressly left commercial transport policy up to the individual Member States.

Thus the ECSC Treaty confers upon the High Authority the powers typical of only partial integration, even though these powers are very substantial if related to transfers of power within a national context. As a result, although rapid progress was made in eliminating the most flagrant cases of discrimination in transport operations between Member States, other much more serious cases of discrimination relating to failure to publish transport tariffs as required by the third paragraph of Article 70 or to harmonization of rates and conditions as provided for in the first paragraph of Article 70 have still not been eliminated. This is because under the Treaty the ECSC institutions were not able to bring

---

[1] See H. Brugmans, *L'idée européenne, 1918-1965*, De Tempel, Bruges, 1965, p. 133, 'L'heure était venue d'une proposition qui aurait les États-Unis d'Europe comme but, la réconciliation franco-allemande comme charnière et la supranationalité fonctionnelle comme méthode'.

any influence to bear on the formulation of national tariff policies. It was totally inconceivable, therefore, that it would ever actually be possible to harmonize transport rates and conditions within the Coal and Steel Community if national tariff policies were subject to no constraints at Community level. In fact, point 2 of the third paragraph of Article 10 of the Convention on the Transitional Provisions annexed to the Treaty provides that a Committee of Experts shall 'establish through international tariffs' for carriage within the Community, whereas no mention is made of the national tariffs in force in individual Member States.

2.2 Attempts to set up a transport authority in Europe

The idea put forward by Jean Monnet and Robert Schuman of setting up a supranational body, independent of national governments, to manage certain sectors of the economy for the purposes of vertical integration was taken up again at the beginning of the 1950s by both the Council of Europe and the ECSC in connection with transport.

2.2.1 *Action taken on transport by the Council of Europe*

The Treaty establishing the Council of Europe was signed in London on 5 May 1949. The objective was to establish an 'inter-State body to form a general framework' in the service of all areas of European policy' and, specifically, to 'bring about a closer union between the Member States'.[1] On 5 May 1951 the French delegate, Edouard Bonnefous, put to the Parliamentary Assembly of the Council of Europe a plan to coordinate transport in Europe which provided for the establishment of a High Authority for transport along the lines of the ECSC. Although the plan was approved by the Parliamentary Assembly, it was never discussed by the Committee of Ministers, the deliberative body of the Council of Europe, which, although legally it has no decision-making powers,[2] could according to the statutes at least have made a recommendation to the Member States in this connection.

At about the same time, other plans for European transport were submitted to the Council of Europe. It is worth mentioning the plan devised by Count Carlo Sforza, the Italian Minister for Foreign Affairs, appointed by Italy as plenipotentiary in the negotiations on the establishment of the Coal and Steel Community. The plan contains a number of interesting proposals: the establishment of a consortium of European airlines in order to improve the economic

---

[1] L. Cartou, op. cit. Dalloz, Paris, 1967, p. 5.
[2] It is often said of the Council of Europe that it is an international institution which can discuss anything but decide nothing. This is perfectly true if one looks at the structure of its two political bodies, namely the Parliamentary Assembly and the Committee of Ministers.

management and efficiency of air transport in Europe, the introduction of a genuine 'European air navigation union' and the setting up of a supranational authority to manage air transport within Europe in the context of a single European air space.

Another important proposal was put forward by the Dutch delegate, Van de Klieft, for the establishment of a European transport office to be specifically responsible for organizing transport throughout continental Europe.

Lastly, the French delegate, Lemaire, suggested a plan to set up a European council for inland transport which would be responsible solely for settling a number of problems of particular importance like tariffs, standardization of equipment, investment and setting up a rolling stock pool. All these proposals suffered the same fate as the Bonnefous plan.

2.2.2 *Action taken on transport by the ECSC*

Problems relating to transport were considered and discussed by the institutions of the ECSC (High Authority, Common Assembly and Special Council of Ministers) with considerable interest. Various attempts were made to go beyond the limited scope of the provisions on transport set out in Article 70 of the Treaty establishing the ECSC, in order to bring about a genuine European transport policy.

In particular, in May 1955, the three Benelux countries submitted a memorandum proposing the establishment within the ECSC of a common body to study the major transport issues. Although this proposal was given a very cool reception it was forwarded to the Intergovernmental Committee set up by the Messina Conference the following June. The conclusions reached by the Committee are set out in the report published by the Heads of Delegation on 21 April 1956 and sent to the Ministers for Foreign Affairs of the six Member States. This was the so-called Spaak Report and its conclusions are significant: 'The problems concerning transport do not warrant the establishment of a separate institution'.

In the Common Assembly of the ECSC, which was a consultative and supervisory body, a number of delegates also expressed considerable interest in transport issues. Particular mention should be made of the Dutch delegate, P.J. Kapteyn, who worked hard to promote a European transport policy within the Assembly. In 1957, as a result of his efforts, a Commitee of Experts submitted to the Assembly a draft report on coordination of transport in Europe which is the most comprehensive document ever produced by that body on the subject of transport and is referred to as the 'Kapteyn report'.[1] Although

---

[1] Kapteyn was also the author of a comprehensive report submitted to the European Parliament in Luxembourg after the establishment of the EEC. See P.J. Kapteyn, *Rapport sur les problèmes concernant la politique commune des transports dans le cadre de la CEE,* Eur. Parl. 1961.

scientifically sound, the report did not correspond sufficiently with the requirements of the EEC Treaty which was on the point of being introduced. In particular, it took no account of the important change made to the Community decision-making process established in the ECSC Treaty. The new EEC Treaty in fact transferred all decision-making powers to the Council of Ministers of the Member States, acting unanimously as a rule, in the first stage at least, and did not reiterate the powers assigned to the High Authority in Article 14 of the ECSC Treaty to take legal acts of a binding nature.[1]

It is worth noting that later on Kapteyn again proposed the establishment of a special transport commission within the European Economic Community inspired in particular by the example of the Interstate Commerce Commission (ICC) in the USA. This proposal was not followed up.

The fact was that during these very early stages of the establishment of an economic union the Member States of the EEC were not inclined to adopt within the Community the principles, typical of a federal state, which inspired the ICC in the context of a common transport policy. Moreover, the institutional framework provided by the Treaty of Rome did not allow for the establishment of a commission which would not only be relatively independent administratively but would also have considerable legislative powers.[2]

2.3 Transport within the framework of the EEC

2.3.1 *The negotiating stage*

On 1 and 2 June 1955 the Foreign Ministers of the six Member States of the ECSC met in Conference in Messina in the Parliamentary constituency of Gaetano Martino (who supported revival of the European idea after the failure of the European Defence Community (EDC), the serious effects of which, in Community terms, are now very apparent). Since this meeting decided to establish a common market which set itself the ambitious aim of bringing about a genuine economic union, and not merely sectoral integration which was the aim of the ECSC, it was obvious that transport too would have to be integrated within the general framework provided by the new European Economic Community. It was reasonable to assume, therefore, that the Treaty which would establish this Community would have to contain specific rules on the introduction of a proper common transport policy.

---

[1] For further information see N. Catalano, *Manuale di Diritto delle Comunità Europee,* Giuffré, Milan, 1965, pp. 58-68.

[2] It would nevertheless be very instructive to examine the ICC approach to USA transport policy if ever the clear political will emerged in the Community for the formulation of an effective common transport policy. See in this connection J.P.B. Tissot van Patot and T.E. Rueb, *De navolging van de amerikaanse vervoerspolitiek en van de Interstate Commerce Commission in de Europese gemeenschappen,* Verkeerswetenschappelijk Centrum, Rotterdam, 1961, p. 250 *et sqq.;* H. Gosse, 'Die Nachfolge der amerikanischen Verkehrspolitik und der Interstate Commerce Commission in den Europäischen Gemeinschaften', in *Europaverkehr,* Darmstadt, 1963, n. 1, pp. 5-7.

At Messina, the six Foreign Ministers felt that before actually commencing negotiations prior to the formulation of the Treaty establishing the Community, they should sound out the opinions of the various governments in order to determine the measure of agreement on the various problems on the table, and on possible solutions, so that negotiations could then be conducted with some likelihood of a favourable outcome.

An Intergovernmental Committee of experts was set up for this purpose under the chairmanship of Paul-Henri Spaak, the Belgian Foreign Minister. This Committee first met in Brussels on 9 July 1955 and concluded its work on 21 April 1956 with the 'Report from the Heads of Delegations to the Ministers for Foreign Affairs' which served as a basis for the Conference of Foreign Ministers held in Venice the following May.

The report, which is commonly referred to as the 'Spaak report' includes a Title II on 'Common market policy', Chapter 3 of which deals with 'Transport tariffs and policy'.[1]

It mentions three points in particular: adjusting the system of rates and conditions in international transport, as far as is necessary for the operation of the common market, the formulation of a common transport policy and the development and financing of infrastructure investment.

Tariff problems are dealt with in the report principally from the point of view of international trade and in the context of the operation of the common market. On investment, it is interesting to note that particular importance is given to an accurate assessment of the social costs and benefits of the different modes of transport, the aim being to determine the total social cost of each mode of transport so that they can all operate under comparable conditions. With regard to transport policy in general, the report merely lists a number of general principles which show that the authors consider transport basically as a means of establishing and operating the common market rather than as an independent sector of the economy. In fact, they are reluctant to tackle the complicated range of problems facing the various modes of transport. However, it is worth noting that the report calls for urgent action in certain fields, particularly air transport and aircraft manufacturing, on the principle that the establishment of a common market should gradually liberalize air transport and that aircraft manufacturing is the kind of industry which requires an extensive market.
Nevertheless, the authors of the report seemed to be opposed in principle to establishing a separate institution for transport within the new Community. Instead they preferred to make the new Community executive responsible for working out a common transport policy.

The Spaak report was adopted by the Conference of Foreign Ministers in Venice as a basis for discussion and subsequent negotiation. The process was continued

---

[1] L. Schaus, 'Fragen der Auslegung und Anwendung des Vertrages zur Gründung der Europäischen Wirtschaftsgemeinschaft auf dem Gebiete des Verkehrs', in *Deutscher Industrie- und Handelstag*, Bonn, 27 October 1960.

by an Intergovernmental Conference for the Common Market and Euratom which met in Brussels in the verdant setting of the Château de Val Duchesse. As well as the Conference, there were meetings of Foreign Ministers - in Paris in October 1956 and in Brussels in February 1957 - and of Heads of Government - in Paris in 1957. This long preparatory stage finally ended on 25 March 1957 with the signature at Campidoglio of the two Treaties establishing the European Economic Community (EEC) and the European Atomic Energy Community (EAEC or Euratom).

2.3.2 *Negotiating methods and the dramatis personae*

During the long negotiations which led up to the signing of the Treaties of Rome, it was at head of delegation level, under the chairmanship of Paul-Henri Spaak, that the major problems were discussed and the main policy decisions made. Other technical and scientific problems - including transport - were tackled by groups of high-level government experts whose findings then had to be approved by the Committee of Heads of Delegations. In most cases government experts on transport were senior officials from national transport Ministries already accustomed to meeting in various international forums and thus already well acquainted. However, as stalwart bureaucrats brought up and moulded in the national framework of their respective countries, they were naturally inclined to defend, blindly at times, the points of view of their governments. Moreover, since in all the negotiating countries except the Netherlands, the railways were to some extent controlled by the government, the interests of the railways were generally staunchly defended during the negotiations, whereas road and inland waterway transport, which tend to be managed by the private sector, did not have spokesmen who ranked high enough to be members of the various delegations.

2.3.3 *Stumbling blocks*

It has already been pointed out that in some respects the interests of the six countries differed considerably. Similarly, the interests of the three inland modes of transport under discussion also conflicted in many respects, or at least did not correspond. For example, although the various countries were facing basically similar problems with regard to the management of the railways, it was not possible during the negotiations to lay down common rules for solving them. Moreover, even the introduction and application of international through rail tariffs under the ECSC Treaty caused considerable difficulties for all concerned. In particular, the general issue of publishing freight rates was regarded as scandalous, especially by the Dutch delegation. With regard to the inland waterways, on the other hand, it was the Rhine navigation system which gave rise to some not inconsiderable problems. Lastly, as far as road transport was concerned, the economic interests of the larger countries, and in particular

France and the Federal Republic of Germany, lay less with international transport than with national transport whereas Italy was specifically in favour of widespread deregulation of international road transport. Again the Benelux countries, within their Union which had been set up on 3 February 1958, had liberalized road transport throughout the Union and wished to see the same thing done for international traffic throughout the Community, the Dutch seeing themselves, to some extent, as the future road hauliers of Europe. Ultimately, however, the basic obstacle was the different views taken by the different Member States on the role of transport in the economy. As we have seen, during negotiations, the Netherlands were most in favour of a *laissez-faire* approach whereas the Federal Republic of Germany tended to prefer intervention, and in this was usually supported by France. In fact, there was severe opposition between these two camps. The *laissez-faire* camp saw transport as a completely independent sector of the economy and thus subject to the normal rules on competition whereas to the interventionists transport was just one more instrument for achieving general or sectoral economic policy goals and as such was subject to obligations and intervention, and also eligible for aids and subsidies. The other delegations, notably the Italian delegation, tended to have a more pragmatic and less doctrinaire approach.

2.3.4 *Achievements*

Even though all the political negotiations were now practically concluded, the working parties of transport experts still had a long way to go. Thus, once the general negotiations had finished, the Intergovernmental Conference was faced with a choice: it could either delay the signing of the Treaty, which in view of the political climate at the time was extremely inadvisable, or it could exclude transport from the field of application of the Treaty establishing the EEC. From a political point of view both choices were unacceptable.

It was decided in the end, therefore, to include in the Treaty merely a few principles and a few special rules of limited scope and to specify a procedure which would enable the EEC institutions to establish a common transport policy. Those articles of the Treaty which relate to transport were thus drafted in a hurry and deliberately left rather vague, since it was not possible to obtain agreement on a more precise formulation. Regretfully, therefore, it has to be concluded that the negotiators of the Treaty establishing the EEC, for a number of different reasons, were not able to arrive at a sufficiently clear definition of the common transport policy, the introduction of which is a requirement of the Treaty. It is to a large extent because of the Treaty's lack of precision that the EEC is still a long way from achieving a common transport policy. Moreover, more than a quarter of a century after the establishment of the EEC, it is now clear that only those Community policies which are specifically required by the Treaty establishing the EEC have in fact been implemented. Conversely, wherever the Treaty left it up to institutional procedures to find ways of defining and implementing policies, the progress made has almost always been minimal.[1] This is not surprising considering the structural weaknesses of the institutional framework set up by the Treaties of Rome since the only body with any real decision-making powers (apart from certain budgetary powers vested in the Parliament) is the Council of Ministers, which is a mouthpiece for government interests and has been hamstrung since 1966 by the Gaullist 'empty chair' policy and the disastrous practice of taking decisions unanimously.

What made matters worse was that there was still clear opposition on transport policy between the various partners which could be traced back to the linkage between major economic policy decisions and specific interests in the transport sector. These interests relate both to the central role played in the Community transport network by the small countries, particularly the Netherlands, because they are so small and because of the geographical location of the major port of Rotterdam, and the relatively greater importance of the railways in the larger Member States, which were accustomed to assigning general economic policy responsibilities to the railways. These countries were therefore reluctant to accept a common transport policy which did not provide the means for intervention. And this in spite of the fact that during the negotiations the representatives of the railways had been largely in favour of a *laissez-faire* approach provided that the railways were treated in exactly the same way as the other modes of transport by being allowed full commercial and financial independence and by being freed of any burdens or constraints not imposed on other modes of transport.

2.3.5 *Provisions of the EEC Treaty relating to transport*

We have already explained the reasons for including the *lex specialis* on transport in Title IV of Part Two of the Treaty on 'Foundations of the Community'. Apart from the articles in the Title specifically on transport (Articles 74 to 84), which we shall examine shortly, there are also provisions relating to transport in Articles 3 and 61.

Article 3 is in Part One which sets out the principles on which the Treaty is based. In point (e) it states that the activities of the Community shall include, as provided in the Treaty and in accordance with the timetable set out therein, 'the adoption of a common policy in the sphere of transport'. This Article outlines in very broad terms the general programme of activities of the Community, merely establishing principles but not committing the Community to any specific action. The provision on transport in this Article can thus be described as general. Article 61 of the Treaty is in Chapter 3 of Title III on 'Free movement of persons, services and capital' in Part Two of the Treaty.

---

[1] It is interesting to note the difference between what has been achieved at Community level with regard to indirect taxation, which Article 99 of the Treaty specifically requires the Member States to harmonize, and what has not been achieved with regard to direct taxation, for which there is no such requirement.

The first paragraph of Article 61 states that 'freedom to provide services in the field of transport shall be governed by the provisions of the Title relating to transport', i.e. by Title IV and thus not by the general provisions on services. The Article is thus part of the *lex specialis* on transport constituted by Title IV so that it is Article 61 and Articles 74 to 84 of the Treaty which contain the specific body of rules on transport.

There are two reasons why the EEC Treaty had to include special provisions on transport: firstly, it was impossible to exclude transport from the scope of the common market; secondly, it was impossible to liberalize it in accordance with the rules applicable to the provision of services in general. In fact, although it was impossible for the Treaty to ignore transport because of the risk of tariff barriers being set up by Member States to replace the customs barriers which were to be abolished, it was also impossible to liberalize transport in accordance with the common rules contained in Articles 59 to 66, since in actual fact the Treaty could only liberalize those activities which already enjoyed a measure of freedom in Member States, unlike transport which in many cases was placed under the strict control of the public authorities.[1] The *lex specialis* constituted by Title IV actually makes two different types of provision on transport: provisions designed to lay the foundations for the common organization of transport and provisions designed to prevent Member States from using rates and conditions to distort competition and influence trade within the Community.

Article 74 states that 'the objectives of this Treaty shall, in matters governed by this Title, be pursued by Member States within the framework of a common transport policy'. As has rightly been pointed out,[2] the wording of this Article clearly constrasts with the wording of Article 3(e) mentioned above.

It is one thing to state that the activities of the Community shall include the adoption of a common policy in the sphere of transport and another to relate this policy to the objectives of the Treaty pursued by the Member States. In other words, there is a clear contradiction between Article 3 which lists the common transport policy as an objective of the Community and Article 74 which sees transport policy as a way of helping to achieve the objectives (other than the common transport policy) which prompted the Member States to establish the European Economic Community. This contradiction should not be overemphasized - although it has certainly caused problems for lawyers trying to reconcile the two articles - since it is merely the result of the hurry and panic to include special provisions on transport in the EEC Treaty.

The following Article 75 contains what are indisputably the most important provisions on transport in the whole of Title IV. It explains the procedure to be followed for achieving the aim of the previous article, in other words the implementation of a common transport policy, and also gives guidelines on the minimum content of this policy. Paragraph 1 states that: 'For the purpose of

---

[1] See L. Cartou, op. cit., p. 225.
[2] See F. Santoro, op. cit. p. 12-13.

implementing Article 74, and taking into account the distinctive features of transport, the Council shall, acting unanimously until the end of the second stage and by a qualified majority thereafter, lay down, on a proposal from the Commission and after consulting the Economic and Social Committee and the Assembly:

(a) common rules applicable to international transport to or from the territory of a Member State or passing across the territory of one or more Member States;

(b) the conditions under which non-resident carriers may operate transport services within a Member State;

(c) any other appropriate provisions.'

The guidelines referred to above are provisions (a) and (b) and will ultimately mean in particular the abolition of import and export tariffs between Member States, the specification of transit tariffs and the prohibition of 'support' tariffs. Their scope is thus relatively limited and they tackle transport essentially from the point of view of the common market and the freedom to provide services. In what could be criticized as confused drafting, since procedural aspects and matters of substance are lumped together,[1] (c) of the same article contains a provision which, in contrast to the limited scope of the two previous points, empowers the Community bodies to adopt any provision they consider appropriate for the establishment of a common transport policy. It is quite clear that because they could not agree on a common approach regarding the main features of a European transport policy, the authors of the Treaty preferred to solve the problem by leaving the Community institutions the task (which in actual fact was now rather difficult precisely because of the institutional framework!) of defining the objectives, principles and procedures for establishing a Community policy. As it happened, it was actually on paragraph 1(c) of Article 75 that the Commission based its proposals for regulations or directives on common transport policy matters since, for the reasons given above, the Treaty provided no other legal basis.

Another point worth noting is that paragraph 3 of the same Article contains an important derogation from the procedural provisions of its paragraph 1. The actual wording is: 'By way of derogation from the procedure provided for in paragraph 1, where the application of provisions concerning the principles of the regulatory system for transport would be liable to have a serious effect on the standard of living and on employment in certain areas and on the operation of transport facilities, they shall be laid down by the Council acting unanimously. In so doing, the Council shall take into account the need for adaptation to the economic development which will result from establishing the common market'. In requiring the Council to take decisions unanimously, even after the end of the second stage, on matters which are defined extremely vaguely and thus allow considerable scope, this provision shows how much care was taken by the Member States to make fundamental decisions on transport the exclusive

---

[1] See N. Bellieni, op. cit., 'Comments on Article 75', No 1, Jupiter, Brussels, 1973.

responsibility of governments acting unanimously. Evidence for this view is that the formula was proposed by the German delegation, supported by the Dutch delegation, and swiftly accepted by all the other delegations.

Less important, however, is the reference in paragraph 1 of the same Article to the 'distinctive features' of transport. Although as we pointed out at the beginning this reference constitutes an obligation, it cannot by its very nature have binding force since the actual wording of the text requires only that the Community institutions take these distinctive features 'into account' and does not even define them. Thus, although the Community institutions are required to examine and assess each one of them, they are nevertheless absolutely free to reach their own conclusions.

Of even less importance are the following articles which make up the *lex specialis* which refer to objectives which are more specific but relatively limited in scope.

Thus, Article 76 imposes upon the Member States a 'standstill' clause similar to Article 12 of the Treaty on customs duties and charges having equivalent effect, in that it prohibits Member States from changing the *status quo* which existed when the Treaty entered into force by making provisions which have a 'less favourable' effect on carriers of other Member States as compared with national carriers, without the unanimous approval of the Council.

Article 77 states that aids shall be compatible with the Treaty if they meet the needs of coordination of transport or if they represent reimbursement for the discharge of certain obligations inherent in the concept of a public service. This is in opposition to the Treaty's general rules on competition, which, in Article 92(1), state that any aid granted by a Member State or through state resources in any form whatsoever which distorts or threatens to distort competition by favouring certain undertakings or the production of certain goods shall, in so far as it affects trade between Member States, be incompatible with the common market.

The Article reflects the situation which often occurs whereby, in the public interest, Member States impose obligations upon transport undertakings, the financial burdens of which can be met only through various kinds of subsidy.

Article 78 imposes a restriction which acts as a kind of safeguard clause for carriers. It states: 'Any measures taken within the framework of this Treaty in respect of transport rates and conditions shall take account of the economic circumstances of carriers.' In other words, the Article expresses the generally accepted opinion that transport services must be operated on a sound economic basis. This means that the transport undertakings which make up a transport network set up to meet the transport needs of the general public may not have constraints imposed upon them regarding transport rates and conditions which might undermine their ability to compete.

The purpose of Article 79 is to eliminate various forms of discrimination based on the nationality of the goods transported. It thus applies to transport the principle laid down in Article 7 of the Treaty which prohibits any discrimination on grounds of nationality.

In some exceptional cases, however, the forms of discrimination referred to in paragraph 1 (charging different rates and imposing different conditions for the carriage of the same goods over the same transport links on grounds of the country of origin or of destination of the goods in question) are part of common commercial practice. Accordingly, paragraph 2 of the same Article states that the above-mentioned paragraph shall not prevent the Council from adopting other measures in pursuance of Article 75(1)(c).

Since transport rates and conditions may be used by Member States for their own economic policy purposes, Article 80 states the principle that the imposition by a Member State of rates and conditions 'involving any element of support or protection in the interest of one or more particular undertakings or industries' shall be prohibited. In prohibiting support or protection tariffs, this Article echoes Articles 92 and 93, which prohibit aids granted by Member States which distort or threaten to distort competition.

In compliance with the provisions of Article 80(1), such measures were prohibited for the six original Member States as of 1 January 1962, for the three new Member States as of 1 January 1973 and for Greece as of 1 January 1981.

However, the Commission may authorize rates and conditions which to some extent support and protect undertakings in accordance with a Community procedure provided for in paragraph 2 of the same Article. This takes particular account of the requirements of an appropriate regional economic policy, the needs of under-developed areas and the problems of areas seriously affected by 'political circumstances' on the one hand, and of the effects of such rates and conditions on competition between the different modes of transport on the other.

Finally, paragraph 3 of Article 80 states that the prohibition provided for in paragraph 1 shall not apply to tariffs fixed to meet competition. This refers to tariffs set below normal tariff levels which a transport undertaking offers to users to eliminate competition from other undertakings of the same type or operating a different mode of transport.

The scope of Article 81 is relatively limited. It states merely that charges or dues in respect of the crossing of frontiers which are charged by a carrier in addition to the transport rates shall not exceed a reasonable level after taking the costs actually incurred thereby into account. However, the Article also states that the Member States themselves are responsible for reducing these costs progressively and that the Commission may only make recommendations to Member States in this connection.

Article 82 relates specifically to Germany and the fact that the country was divided after the Second World War. This is also taken into account in other articles of the Treaty and in particular in the Protocol on German Internal Trade and connected problems annexed to the Treaty. Thus the Federal Republic of Germany is authorized to make transport provisions which may contravene the Treaty provided that such measures are required in order to compensate for the economic disadvantages caused by the division of Germany to the economy of certain areas of the Federal Republic affected by that division. These are the 'Zonenrandgebiete' which include in particular the Länder of Berlin, Hamburg and Lower Saxony.

Article 83 provides for the setting up of an Advisory Committee on transport consisting of experts designated by the Governments of Member States. The Committee is completely independent of the Economic and Social Committee and can be consulted by the Commission whenever it considers it desirable. In fact, the responsibilities of this Advisory Committee are somewhat different to the powers of the transport section of the Economic and Social Committee since it is consulted by the Commission during the preparation of regulations, directives and decisions but not afterwards. Once the Commission has drafted proposals, they are submitted to the Economic and Social Committee in accordance with the provisions of the Treaty.

Finally, Article 84 is recognized to be of particular importance in that it defines the scope of the *lex specialis*. Logically, from a legal point of view, its provisions should have been restructured to constitute two separate articles. As with other articles in Title IV, however, it is the result of a drafting compromise arrived at during the preparatory stage. Paragraph 1 states: 'The provisions of this Title shall apply to transport by rail, road and inland waterway'. Article 2 states: 'The Council may, acting unanimously, decide whether, to what extent and by what procedure appropriate provisions may be laid down for sea and air transport'.[1] Although all the delegations did agree to include provisions to prevent the use of transport as a means of discrimination or of distorting competition in the context of the priority objective of establishing a customs union between the Member States, which was the basis for Articles 79 to 81 of the Treaty, they could not, as we have seen, reach any form of agreement on whether transport, like other economic sectors, should be the object of genuine economic integration. Therefore, since at that time it was difficult to imagine that sea and air transport might give rise to discrimination or distortion of competition which might have an impact within the Community, the experts on these two modes of transport were not involved in the negotiations.

Their absence was felt when, at the request of the Dutch delegation, it was finally accepted that transport too should be the object of gradual economic integration, since, because of the major difficulties which had already arisen during attempts to find a compromise formula for inland transport, it seemed

---

[1] This is surprising considering that in the institutional system established by the Treaty there are very few cases where, after the transitional period, the Council is required to act unanimously. What is even more surprising is that the Article does not require the Commission necessarily to submit a proposal, thus confirming the absolute sovereignty of the Member States in this field.

Programme
of the Commission
for 1987

Transport

Extract from

Bulletin
of the European Communities

Supplement 1/87

Europe at the crossroads

A year after the accession of Spain and Portugal the Single Act is due to enter into force. The Community is thus experiencing in rapid succession two of the most important changes that it has known since its inception 30 years ago.

The timing is no accident. If a larger Community was not to be a weaker one, the level of its ambitions had to be raised and its institutional system renovated. This is the purpose of the Single Act. It represents a long overdue strengthening of the institutions rendered imperative by enlargements. But, more significantly, it sets new objectives for the Community, including completion of the internal market and the achievement of economic and social cohesion. Completion of the internal market is vital for progress in other areas and for the economic future of Europe. Greater cohesion is a political necessity following enlargement of the Community to include less-favoured countries in southern Europe. But it is an economic necessity too if the Community is to find a coherent response to the challenges facing it.

The importance of this period in the Community's history did not escape the governments of the Member States and led to a number of major decisions — at Fontainebleau in 1984 on financial resources and in Luxembourg in 1985 on the structural Funds in the context of greater cohesion. A decision has also been taken to press ahead with the change of direction given to management of the common agricultural policy two years ago. Recent debates in Parliament indicate that it too is keen to see early decisiions being taken in these three areas.

Technically these three areas form a single whole. The same is true politically because the Member States' response to the Commission's proposals in these three areas will shape the new Community of Twelve in the years to come.

Without prejudice to any new initiatives regarding foreign policy or joint security, it is the pace of economic integration that will determine the outcome of Europe's fight for survival. This pace has still to be set: the Community must choose between a common market embellished with a few financial transfers between Member States with differing standards of living, and the construction of a common economic area in which national and common policies combine to promote stronger growth and more jobs thanks to greater concentration in fields where the Community can achieve more than the Member States acting individually. Examples are R&D and the environment — both specifically mentioned in the Single Act — and the establishment of the basic transport and telecommunications infrastructure that is essential for the smooth functioning of the internal market.

The Commission's proposals are, then, more than mere technical adjustments. Discussions in the European Council, and the experience of recent years, have shown just how politically sensitive these three areas are and how easily disagreements about them can paralyse the Community. In all three areas — the common agricultural policy, the structural Funds and the budget — the Commission's main conclusion is the same: if the Community is to continue to progress, the Member States must make a fresh effort and the institutions must accept stricter discipline.

Transport

The Community's transport policy, aimed at a liberalized system, is a component of the large internal market. Progress will therefore need to be made in a number of significant respects in 1987. The Commission will pursue its efforts to secure gradual application of the principle of freedom to provide services and to eliminate distortions of competition in a sector which has a direct economic impact on trade and industry.

The *Nouvelles Frontières* judgment was a milestone on the road to achieving the goals set in the 1984 Memorandum on air transport. The impetus it provided was strengthened by the conclusions of the European Council in The Hague in June 1986. At the end of 1986 the discussions within the Council allowed some progress to be made. The Council and the Commission will continue their efforts to achieve rapidly the degree of competition and deregulation required by the Treaty. The Commission's efforts will also be aimed at achieving easier access to the interregional market, along the lines set out in the communication submitted last September.

As far as shipping is concerned, the regulations aimed at ensuring healthier competition both within and outside the Community (ocean trades, competition, tariffs, freedom to provide services) have been adopted at last. Approval of these four components of the shipping package means that the Commission can move on to a new stage of the programme for implementing the Community's shipping policy, under which freedom to provide services would be backed by measures to approximate social legislation, technical aspects and State aid. Proposals may also be made for recourse to a Community flag as a means of combating the crisis being experienced by the Community fleet.

As far as inland transport is concerned, the Commission will concentrate on the transition to the new organization of the road haulage market from 1992 and freedom to provide freight and passenger transport services. The Commission's main objective on rail transport will continue to be the financial reorganization of the railways. A similar objective will be pursued in relation to inland waterway transport (scrapping).

Completion of the internal market in 1992 will imply a new approach to relations with non-member countries which are of vital importance in the transport sector. The top priority in the immediate future will be inland freight transport. The Commission will submit a communication with proposals on the problem of goods transiting through non-member countries.

There is also a need for a Community dimension in the matter of transport infrastructure, which has considerable implications for completion of the internal market and increased economic and social cohesion within the Community. Under the medium-term programme of transport infrastructure of European interest which the Commission proposed last year, 1987 should see effective recognition of the major importance and specific nature of action by the Community to develop this powerful factor for integration which will create new outlets and guarantee the competitiveness of industry.

The Commission has now clarified the catalytic role the Community can play in the promotion of major projects in this area which is full of potential. It is important that, in addition to existing instruments, financial engineering techniques should be used from 1987 onwards to create conditions favourable to the planning and realization of major projects and to mobilize the market for new forms of Community funding (budget guarantees and project financing).

Initiatives of this kind will provide concrete examples of what the Community can do to supplement its cooperative growth strategy for more employment.

Transcript

Road transport

☐ Proposal to amend Regulations 117/66, 516/72 and 517/72 (common rules on international passenger transport)

☐ Proposal concerning the conditions under which non-resident carriers can carry out national passenger transport operations

☐ Proposal for a directive designed to tighten up the conditions relating to access to the occupation of freight transport operator and passenger transport operator

☐ Communication and proposals concerning inland transport of goods through non-member countries

☐ Proposals on negotiations with Yugoslavia for a limited agreement on occasional international road passenger services and the conclusion of an agreement on combined transport with various non-member countries

Air transport

☐ Continuation of the determined effort made in 1986 to achieve greater flexibility in the organization of air transport (fares, capacity, competition) in line with the objectives set out in Memorandum No 2 in 1984

☐ Proposals on easier access to the air transport market, the principles underlying airport charges, consultations between airports and users

Shipping

☐ Next phase of a Community shipping policy (approximation of legislation, technical aspects, State aid)

☐ Proposals on the use of a Community flag, and studies on the possibility of introducing a ship-scrapping scheme

Follow-up to Road Safety Year

☐ Proposals on safety, the environment and social matters (safety belts, technical characteristics of tyres, transport of dangerous goods, mutual recognition of licences and certificates etc.)

preferable at that point to exclude these two modes of transport from the *lex specialis* in Title IV.

However, the somewhat ambiguous wording of paragraph 2 has, as we know, resulted in clear differences of interpretation between the Commission and most of the governments of the Member States. In fact, since paragraph 1 does not mention that the provisions of Title IV may be applied to modes of transport other than those listed, there has been much conjecture as to whether Treaty provisions other than those in Title IV, in other words the general provisions of the Treaty, should be applied to the modes of transport mentioned in paragraph 2. As might be expected, in most cases the Commission has tended to hold different views to those of the Member States, the latter generally favouring the more restrictive interpretation.

2.3.6 *Application of the general provisions of the Treaty to transport*

Another problem of interpretation which is much more general than the one we have just mentioned and which for a long time was a vexed question is the extent to which the general provisions of the Treaty, in other words provisions outside Title IV, apply to transport. In fact, there has been much conjecture as to whether, within the system established by the EEC Treaty, transport is governed solely by the provisions of Title IV or whether Articles 74 to 84 constituted merely a set of rules specifically on transport and that the general provisions of the Treaty apply to transport as to any other sector of the economy.

The Commission has always argued that the Treaty is of universal application[1] and that the general provisions of the Treaty apply to all sectors of the economy except where the Treaty expressly states to the contrary. Certain governments of the Member States, on the other hand, in their own underlying national economic interests, had always argued in favour of a different approach, namely that transport is governed solely by the provisions contained in Title IV and not by the other provisions of the Treaty.

It became particularly urgent to solve this controversy when the provisions of Articles 85 and 86 of the Treaty on the competition rules applying to undertakings took effect in accordance with the procedure outlined in Article 87. Under pressure from the economic interests concerned, the governments which had come down in favour of the most restrictive interpretations, were forced - whether they liked it or not - to recognize that the general provisions of the

---

[1] Cf. L. Schaus, op. cit. in *Deutscher Industrie- und Handelstag*, Bonn, 1960, and N. Bellieni, op. cit., 'Comment on Article 74', pp. 11-13, Brussels, 1973.

Treaty did apply to transport, although they expressed a specific reservation on the question of law.[1]

Of decisive importance in this connection was the Judgment handed down by the Court of Justice of the European Communities on Case 167/73 on 4 April 1974. Asked for a ruling on the application of Article 48 (free movement of workers within the Community) and Article 84(2) (sea and air transport), the Court expressly stated the following principles:[2]

'When Article 74 refers to the objectives of the Treaty, it means the provisions of Articles 2 and 3, the attainment of which the fundamental provisions applicable to the whole complex of economic activities seek to ensure. Far from involving a departure from these fundamental rules, the object of the rules relating to the common transport policy is to implement and complement them by means of common action. *Consequently the said general rules must be applied insofar as they can achieve these objectives.*'

Thus the Court of Justice supported the Commission's argument that the Treaty is universally applicable. This meant not only that sea and air transport which were not covered by the special provisions of Title IV, were nevertheless subject to the general rules of the EEC Treaty, but also that these general rules applied to transport as a whole, since the special rules on transport contained in Title IV and in Article 61 do not state otherwise.

2.3.7 *How the provisions of the EEC Treaty relate to the Treaty establishing the ECSC*

The States which signed the EEC Treaty are of course the same States which signed the Treaty establishing the ECSC. The States which have joined the European Communities in more recent years acceded to the three Communities established by the Treaties of Paris and Rome, ECSC, EEC and EAEC, together.

With regard in particular to how the provisions of Title IV of the EEC Treaty apply to transport of products covered by the ECSC Treaty, Article 232(1) of the Treaty establishing the EEC expressly states that 'the provisions of this Treaty shall not affect the provisions of the Treaty establishing the European Coal and Steel Community, in particular as regards the rights and obligations of Member States, the powers of the institutions of that Community and the rules laid down by that Treaty for the functioning of the common

---

[1] On the applicability to transport of rules on competition before the Court ruled on Case 167/73, see N. Catalano, op. cit., Milan, 1965, p. 545 and Regulation (EEC) No 1017/68 of the Council of 19 July 1968 applying rules of competition to transport by rail, road and inland waterway (OJ L 175, 23.7.1968, p. 1).

[2] Court of Justice of the European Communities, Case 167/73 *Commission of the European Communities v French Republic* [1974] ECR 359.

market in coal and steel'. This affirms the principle that *lex posterior generalis non derogat priori speciali*. The provision is included to avoid possible conflict with regard to the jurisdiction of the two Treaties over transport. The inter-relationship between the provisions of the two Treaties can be summarized as follows:

(i) the provisions of the EEC Treaty apply to transport of coal, steel and other products covered by the ECSC Treaty provided that the ECSC Treaty or other Community acts adopted by virtue of it do not already contain regulations on the subject;

(ii) consequently, irrespective of regulations which can be adopted on transport within the framework of the EEC Treaty, transport of ECSC products remains subject to ECSC provisions on the application of rates and conditions (first paragraph of Article 70), the publication of scales and rates (third paragraph of Article 70) and the different agreements concluded within the framework of the ECSC Treaty on through international tariffs, freight rates on the Rhine and various other matters;

(iii) as far as discrimination in rates and conditions is concerned, transport of ECSC products is governed by the provisions of the second paragraph of Article 70 of the ECSC Treaty and not those of Article 79 of the EEC Treaty;

(iv) on the subject of support tariffs, transport of ECSC products is governed by the fourth paragraph of Article 70 of the ECSC Treaty and not by Article 80 of the EEC Treaty;

(v) lastly, the Council may apply to transport of ECSC products all measures adopted by it in accordance with the procedure laid down in Article 75(1)(c) of the EEC Treaty.

It is clear, therefore, that the common transport policy which is an objective of the EEC Treaty also covers undertakings manufacturing the products governed by the Treaty establishing the ECSC and the carriage of these products in those cases where the ECSC Treaty or acts adopted pursuant to it lay down no specific rules for the functioning of the common market in coal and steel as referred to in Article 232 of the EEC Treaty. This is not surprising in view of the limited objectives of the kind of sectoral agreement envisaged by the ECSC Treaty - which makes no mention of transfers of powers from national level with regard to commercial policy - as compared with the ambitious objective set by the EEC Treaty, namely the adoption of a genuine common policy in the sphere of transport, based in particular on integration of the transport market and all the other economic activities of the Member States.

3. The main features of Community action on transport

3.1 The role of EEC institutions and other Community bodies in establishing a common transport policy

As we have already seen, the specific rules on transport contained in Title IV are rather limited in scope, apart from the provisions of Article 75(1)(c). However, the other general provisions of the Treaty outside Title IV also apply to transport where no derogation exists in the *lex specialis*. On this legal basis, the Treaty requires that the EEC institutions and other Community bodies establish a common transport policy as a means of pursuing the Treaty's objectives in the sphere of transport (under the combined provisions of Articles 3 and 74).

3.1.1 *The role of the institutions*

3.1.1.1 The Commission

The basic powers assigned to the Commission by the Treaty are well known. Apart from being the motive force behind the Community, the Commission is also the promotor because of its responsibility for making proposals. Moreover, it acts as guardian of the Treaty[1] since it monitors the application of the provisions of the Treaty and of the provisions adopted by the institutions under the Treaty and exercises the decision-making powers which are conferred upon it by the Treaty or by the Council.

In most cases - and this includes those provided for in Article 75(1) - the Council may only act on a proposal from the Commission. Proof of the enormous importance of this power of initiative within the system laid down by the Treaty is that in cases where the Council is required to act by a qualified majority - in other words, in most cases after the end of the transitional period - the Treaty states that acts which are required to be adopted on a proposal from the

---

[1] Although not in a legal sense, since, as we shall see, this function is exercised by the Court of Justice.

Commission may still be adopted even if there are not at least six Member States voting in favour as required in all other cases (Article 148).[1]

The Commission therefore has considerable responsibilities as regards establishing a common transport policy.

It is basically true to say that the Commission has so far done a good job as 'guardian' of the implementation of the provisions of the Treaty. With staunch support from the European Parliament, it has not hesitated to intervene whenever it has had grounds for thinking that there may have been a violation of the Treaty or of provisions adopted under it. In the most serious cases, it has resorted to the infringement procedure provided for in Article 169 and has even brought matters before the Court of Justice.

The Commission has taken the 'necessary decisions' in areas for which it is responsible, in particular with regard to the implementation of Article 77 (on aids), Article 79 (on discrimination) and Article 80 (on support tariffs). In its basic task of preparing legislative proposals (for regulations, directives or decisions) to be put to the Council of Ministers, it has had the assistance of the Advisory Committee set up under Article 83 of the Treaty. As has already been explained, the responsibilities of this committee of government experts should not be confused with those of the Transport Section of the Economic and Social Committee. As a rule, the Commission asks the Committee to prepare studies or give opinions when preparing proposals for the Council of Ministers.

In addition, the Commission has established direct links with economic operators concerned with the transport sector and consultations have proved valuable. The Commission has also set up joint advisory committees on the most important transport areas and has been engaged in cooperation with the numerous international organizations, those with general responsibilities (ECE and OECD) and those concerned purely with European matters (ECMT and CCR), with the aim of coordinating all their various activities and avoiding unnecessary duplication.

To conclude, therefore, on the basis of the Commission's record to date, it would seem unfair to accuse it of conspicuous failure to establish a common transport policy. If blame can be attributed, it should be levelled against the general institutional framework of the Communities. We shall now examine this in greater detail.

---

[1] As far as the day-to-day running of the Community is concerned, this provision has unfortunately remained a dead letter because of the so-called 'Luxembourg compromise' obtained by the Gaullist government in February 1966. Since then all Council decisions have had to be taken unanimously, a practice which goes even more against the spirit than against the letter of the Treaty of Rome and has been disastrous for the real progress of the Community.

3.1.1.2 **The Assembly**

Often referred to as the 'European Parliament', and sometimes wrongly by journalists as the 'Strasbourg Parliament',[1] the Assembly, which was established by Articles 137-144 of the Treaty, is an important institution.

There is no doubt - and Parliament's recent action against the Council for failure to act is confirmation of this - that Parliament has always played a very important role as the driving force behind attempts to establish a common transport policy.

The Parliament is essentially a consultative body and has always prepared extremely pertinent and well-argued opinions on all proposals concerning transport matters compulsorily submitted to it by virtue of the provisions of the Treaty. In addition, on its own initiative, its Transport Committee has drafted some extremely valuable reports, often highly technical or political, on specific problems relating to the common transport policy.

Nor has Parliament been sparing in its harsh criticism of the action taken by the Commission on transport, with regard both to its general policies and to the specific solutions it has proposed for particular problems. It has to be remembered that, under the system set up by the Treaty, it is the Commission more than the Council which is the Assembly's regular and special interlocutor. The Assembly thus addresses its criticisms to the Commission, whereas frequently it is indirectly taking the Council to task for its virtually constant reluctance and failure to do anything to bring about the common transport policy. If one had to make a brief assessment of Parliament's overall record on transport policy, one would have to admit that it is extremely good. Although some of the opinions expressed by Parliament tend to be rather theoretical this is more the fault of the unsatisfactory institutional framework within which Parliament acts solely as an advisory body with real powers only in respect of

---

[1] It would be more correct to call it the Luxembourg Parliament since the Secretariat of the European Parliament is in Luxembourg. Like Luxembourg and Brussels, Strasbourg is just one of the places where Parliament meets, and in fact normally holds its plenary sessions, whereas Brussels is where most of the Parliament's committees meet. The Parliament tends to be associated with Strasbourg because that is where the first plenary session of the first European Parliament directly elected by universal suffrage in 1979 was held, in the chamber which used to house the Consultative Assembly of the Council of Europe. The municipal authorities of Strasbourg and the French Government have conducted a vigorous campaign in the media, which has so far been unsuccessful, to have the Parliament's Secretariat transferred from Luxembourg to Strasbourg. Now, however, it is looking increasingly likely that Brussels will be chosen because it already has the other two institutions involved in the Community decision-making process, namely the Commission and the Council of Ministers.

the budget.[1] Since it has no real decision-making powers,[2] Parliament is sometimes in danger of missing the point of practical problems of management and producing opinions or conclusions which, while unexceptional in theory may not take sufficient account of all the factors which contribute to the complexities of the transport sector at Community and national level. But it is also perhaps worth pointing out that excessive concern about the logistics of transport may have the converse effect of making operational problems seem more insurmountable than they actually are and encouraging the adoption of the restricted political view of the 'step by step' approach . Clear proof of this would seem to be the attitude of certain national authorities to transport policy.

3.1.1.3 The Council of Ministers

According to the provisions of the Treaty, the Council of Ministers would seem to be the most important institution of the Community, the only one which has any basic decision-making powers - apart from a few limited powers which the Treaty assigns to the Commission through Council decisions. The Council is a collegiate body consisting of representatives of the governments of the Member States and as such directly expresses national interests. Article 145 of the Treaty states that, to ensure that the objectives set out in the Treaty are attained, the Council shall ensure coordination of the general economic policies of the Member States and have power to take decisions. Although the Council is the legislative body of the Community *par excellence*, the extensive powers given to the Council by the Treaty are nevertheless moderated by the obligation to exercise them in close cooperation with a body of a somewhat different nature, namely the Commission, which has the basic task of making proposals and which, because of its responsibilities and composition, tends to be much more independent of national governments. Moreover, this independence of its members is confirmed by Article 157 and by the staff recruitment provisions of the Staff Regulations applicable to officials of the European Communities. The aim is to ensure that the Commission is a supranational body which defends the interests of the Community, which are to some extent supranational, and promotes the construction of Europe.

---

[1] These are the exclusive power to give a discharge to the Commission in respect of the implementation of the budget in accordance with Article 206(2) of the Treaty and the power, under Article 203(9), which covers the complex procedure for adoption of the budget, to have the last word on non-compulsory expenditure, i.e. 'expenditure other than that necessarily resulting from the Treaty or from acts adopted in accordance therewith'. For further information see D. Strasser, *Les finances de l'Europe*, PUF, Paris, 1975, pp. 63-64, 85-86, 138 et seq. (the revised version of which is available in English in the 'European Perspectives' series of the European Communities).

[2] This being the case, we can only welcome Spinelli's attempts to draw up plans for a European Union and to set up within the Community the two-chamber system commonly used in the Member States' national parliaments. The European Parliament would thus be given the powers and duties of a lower house while the Council of Ministers which at the moment is virtually the sole decision-making body, would act as an upper house.

On transport policy, however, one reluctantly has to admit that the Council of Ministers has so far shown very little readiness to use its institutional powers to set up the common transport policy which is one of the Treaty objectives.

Some of the Transport Ministers of the Member States, who make up the Council of Ministers on transport matters, have appeared to be very doubtful about the need to establish a common transport policy at Community level and have shown very little political will to achieve it. The Council's basic neglect of transport problems in the Community - proof of which is the fact that it meets very infrequently each year - has gradually shown itself to be genuine failure to act. On these grounds the European Parliament on 22 January 1983 vociferously denounced the Council and brought an action before the Court of Justice on the basis of Article 175. In so doing the Parliament argued that the Council had infringed the EEC Treaty 'by failing to introduce a common policy for transport and in particular to lay down the framework for such policy in a binding manner'.[1]

Parliament cited at least sixteen Commission proposals on which the Council had failed to reach a decision. If the Court of Justice finds that the Council has failed to act, the Council, under Article 176, shall be 'required to take the necessary measures to comply with the judgment of the Court of Justice', which means that it will be required to take decisions on these Commission proposals.

Clearly the Parliament's action is of such consequence that it could mark the beginning of a new, and certainly delicate, stage of the common transport policy. It will be especially interesting to hear the arguments the Council uses to justify its 'failure to act' - which in any case will be a useful source of information for all those inside and outside the Community interested in developing a common transport policy. Whatever happens, under the Treaty, the Council will be forced to break its silence on the common transport policy.

Within the Council of Ministers has been set up a Permanent Representatives Committee - commonly referred to by its French acronym 'Coreper' - which has the important technical function of preparing the work of the Council (it is to this Committee that Commission proposals for the Council are first submitted) and carrying out the tasks assigned to it by the Council.

Coreper was set up on the basis of the Treaty although the Treaty does not specify its tasks or its responsibilities. It is made up of diplomats or government officials working in the Permanent Representatives' Offices and accredited to the European Communities. Coreper ultimately evolved its own *raison d'être* and responsibilities, carving out a niche for itself and making itself indispensable to the Council as an effective aid, helping it in particular with the preliminary examination of legislative proposals sent by the Commission for its approval.

---

[1] OJ C 49, 19.2.1983, pp. 9-11.

Article 4 of the Merger Treaty of 8 April 1965 made the Committee official by confirming that 'a committee consisting of the Permanent Representatives of the Member States shall be responsible for preparing the work of the Council and for carrying out the tasks assigned to it by the Council'.

Coreper has played an important part within the institutional system of the Community, and has done some useful work on transport. As the Council of Transport Ministers began meeting less and less frequently, Coreper eventually became the only forum in the Council which could devote regular attention to transport problems. However, Coreper consists solely of national officials, ranging from the accredited Permanent Representative at ambassadorial level to his special advisers, who can act only upon the specific instructions of their Ministers. Although we shall be considering precisely how the existence and composition of Coreper affected progress on Community transport policy in more detail later on, it is true to say that one of the immediate effects of the inertia of governments has been the extent to which Coreper officials, albeit with the best of intentions, have been prepared to take initiative on the common transport policy.

3.1.1.4 The Court of Justice

Article 164 of the Treaty assigns the Court of Justice the important task of ensuring that the law is observed in the interpretation and application of the Treaty. Referred to as the legal guardian of the Treaty,[1] the Court has certainly played an especially important role with regard to transport and in some cases has made a decisive contribution towards defining a common policy. By means of some particularly significant judgments it has established the basic principles for interpreting the provisions of the Treaty and for defining the scope of the common policy.

In view of the Council's continual failure to act, particularly on matters of transport which has given rise to the recent action taken by Parliament under Article 175 mentioned above, and in view of the Council's failure to take decisions in certain other areas, the Court's role is becoming increasingly important - although not all its actions are beyond reproach - in the complex process of building Europe. Moreover, the judges of the Court frequently find themselves in the position of creating new laws and thus determining the development of Community law in a variety of fields.

In those areas governed by the ECSC Treaty, the Court has tended to favour 'true' rates and conditions for transport. The Court has therefore tried to ensure that rates and conditions are transparent, partly by requiring Member States to publish tariff rules in accordance with the provisions of Article 70 of the ECSC Treaty. It has also established the principle that special tariffs, support

---

[1] See G.L. Weil, *Handbook on the EEC,* College of Europe, Bruges, 1956.

tariffs and tariff discrimination in general must not be such as to distort competition.

These principles laid down by the Court with reference to the Treaty establishing the ECSC also apply *mutatis mutandis* to the application of the provisions of the EEC Treaty. In those areas governed by the EEC Treaty, the Court has in particular solved the controversy regarding the contractual responsibility of the Community in international transport in connection with the AETR and the vexed question of whether the general provisions of the Treaty outside Title IV apply to transport.

Lastly, it has ruled on matters as diverse as the taxation of transport, the problem of the public service obligations imposed upon the railways and non-discrimination in the employment of crews of merchant vessels.On many occasions, when deciding on particular cases brought before it, the Court has established basic general principles like the particularly important ones expressed in its judgment of 4 April 1974 in Case 167/73 regarding the application of the general provisions of the Treaty outside Title IV to transport as a whole.

In conclusion, it is true to say that the Court's rulings on transport have been uniformly constructive, thus helping to define the scope of the common policy in the very best interests of the Community. Possibly, the fact that the Court of Justice is a Court of first and last instance, has resulted in some cases in the pronouncement of judgments which, because of the conflict of interests, would perhaps have merited a second opinion. However, as we know, the Treaty does not make provision for appeal to a court of second instance against the judgments of the Court.

3.1.2 *The role of other Community bodies*

3.1.2.1 Economic and Social Committee (ESC)

The Economic and Social Committee is an advisory body set up under Article 193 of the Treaty and consisting of representatives of various categories of economic and social activity. It is consulted after the Commission has prepared its proposals for legislation. In fact, both the Council and the Commission are required to consult the Committee where the Treaty so provides and they may also consult the Committee whenever they consider it appropriate.

Commission proposals on transport or on matters relating to transport are examined by the Committee's Transport Section provided for in Article 197. The Section prepares draft opinions which are put to the Committee meeting in plenary session for its approval. This means that any opinion finally adopted reflects all the views of the representatives of the various categories of economic and social activity. The opinion of the Committee and that of the Section, together with a record of the proceedings, are then forwarded to the Council and to the Commission.

On matters relating to transport, the Treaty requires that the ESC be consulted on most proposals made by the Commission, and in particular those based on Article 75(1)(c). However, as we have seen, the Committee may be consulted by the Commission (and by the Council too, although the Council has made relatively little use of this facility) in all cases which it considers appropriate before making final proposals.

It is worth pointing out that frequently on matters relating to transport the Committee has judiciously recommended introducing measures on an experimental basis initially, partly with the idea of making them acceptable to the Council.

3.1.2.2 European Investment Bank (EIB)

The European Investment Bank is a Community body subject to the provisions of Articles 129 and 130 of the Treaty. Article 130 defines its task as being to contribute 'to the balanced and steady development of the common market in the interest of the Community'. However, this rather broad remit is restricted somewhat when the same Article goes on to state that the Bank may grant loans and give guarantees to finance only those projects which fall into at least one of these three categories:

(a) projects for developing less developed regions;

(b) projects for modernizing or converting undertakings or for developing fresh activities called for by the progressive establishment of the common market;

(c) projects of common interest to several Member States which are of such a size or nature that they cannot be entirely financed by the various means available in the individual Member States.

These aims are specified in more detail in the Statute of the European Investment Bank and in the general guidelines laid down by the Board of Governors of the Bank. On this basis the EIB finances:

(a) according to certain priority criteria, investment projects in the production sector, in infrastructure and in the energy sector which help to develop regions in difficulties, i.e. investment of regional interest;

(b) investment projects on energy saving or other energy-related investment which will help to reduce the Community's dependence on oil;

(c) infrastructure projects of benefit to the Community or to a region of the Community which will help towards European economic integration or towards the achievement of Community objectives like protection of the environment;

(d) investment in modernizing or converting undertakings in connection with action made necessary by structural difficulties, specific investment projects which will help to develop sectors with high innovation potential or will introduce advanced technologies, and certain types of investment project which result from close technical and economic cooperation between undertakings in different countries.

The Bank has also taken action to help the reconstruction of areas of Italy and Greece affected by earthquakes.[1]

Moreover, because of its institutional responsibilities, the Bank now operates not only in the Community but also in non-Community countries (Turkey and other Mediterranean countries and the ACP countries) in accordance with the Community's economic and financial cooperation policy. Clearly, therefore, the Bank also has an important role to play in transport, since economic progress within the Community and the drawing together of its regions will depend primarily upon faster and easier links between Member States and on making the peripheral regions of the Community less isolated. For all these reasons, the EIB has always devoted a considerable proportion of its resources to improving communications. The EIB does of course have its own resources: its own capital of 14 400 million ECU subscribed by the 10 Member States, funds raised by loans issued on capital markets, operational surpluses and special resources granted by the Communities or by the Member States and managed 'off balance-sheet' in a Special Section which can be regarded as a revenue and expenditure account of trustee funds. This Section includes in particular loans granted under the New Community Instrument (also called the 'Ortoli facility') set up in 1978 and loans granted by the Community to help the development of the Mediterranean countries and of the ACP countries, the signatories of the Lomé Convention.[2,3]

Between the date of its establishment and 31 December 1982 the EIB granted a total of 4 687.6 million ECU[4] (equivalent to 20.84% of all its financing operations within the Community, totalling 22 487.9 million ECU) in assistance to the transport sector. This amount can be broken down as follows (in million ECU):[5]

Railways:	474.0	(2.1%)
Roads and infrastructure:	1 659.7	(7.4%)
Sea and inland waterway transport:	341.7	(1.5%)
Air transport:	227.2	(1.0%)
Power lines:	600.5	(2.7%)
Oil and gas pipelines:	1 379.6	(6.1%)
Other projects:	4.9	(0.02%)
	4 687.6	

Thus the Bank's contribution to the transport sector is far from negligible.

---

[1] EIB, *Annual Report 1982*, Luxembourg, 1983.
[2] See D. Strasser, op. cit., Paris, 1975 and EIB, *Annual Report 1982*, 1983.
[3] The Second ACP-EEC Convention was signed at Lomé on 31 October 1979 (OJ L 347, 22.12.1980).
[4] On 30 December 1982 1 ECU = £ 0.598269 (On 31 January 1986 1 ECU = £ 0.641957)
[5] EIB, *25 years - 1958-83*, Luxembourg, 1983, p. 49.

3.2 Establishing and implementing a common transport policy

We have already pointed out that the reason why the regulations which go to make up the *lex specialis* on transport, Title IV of the Treaty, are so vague is the differences of opinion and the conflicts of interest which divided the six original Member States of the EEC when the Treaty was signed. In fact, there was a whole range of contentious points: the division of responsibilities between public authorities and private business, deciding whether as a general principle users should be free to choose their mode of transport, the problems deriving from the adjustments required to make the conditions affecting the various modes of transport comparable and the problem of whether to adopt a *laissez-faire* or interventionist approach to commercial policy on the various modes of transport.[1]

Nevertheless, the Member States also had a number of basic features in common as far as transport was concerned, consisting chiefly, with a few exceptions, of clear traditions of national intervention in this sector of the economy, close links between the State and the railways and the fact that the road and inland waterway transport sectors consisted of a large number of often very small firms.

Furthermore, as we have already seen, attitudes on the extent to which the State should intervene in the transport sector differed considerably - from the interventionist tendencies of the Federal Republic of Germany and France to the *laissez-faire* attitude of the Netherlands, which was reluctant to agree to any form of market organization which would tend to undermine the principles of competition it held so dear, particularly with regard to transport on the Rhine and on the roads. There were also clear differences of interest between the various modes of transport. The widely dispersed road and inland waterway transport firms looked somewhat askance at tariff deregulation which did not go hand in hand with measures to improve the financial management of the railway monoliths. Lastly, there were some conflicts of interest between these three modes of transport and the general public, which obviously preferred to be able to take advantage of a certain surplus in the supply of services in order to attempt to influence rates and conditions to their own benefit.

Ultimately it was the failure to specify clear rules on the content of the common transport policy that resulted from these political and economic differences in attitude and interests which helps to explain why the common transport policy

---

[1] See F. Santoro, op. cit., p. 17.

has developed the way it has. Throughout its history, the main features of the common transport policy have been:

(a) the considerable emphasis placed on the institutional process, i.e. the Commission's proposal-making role and the Council's decision-making role, in preparing the body of legislation required to supplement the Treaty's inadequacies;

(b) the disadvantages inherent in this law-making process in that the Commission often finds itself obliged, in order to reconcile the divergent opinions of the Member States, to devise compromise proposals which can be adopted by the Member States in principle but generally give rise to discussion when it comes to putting them into practice.

Basically, during the first fifteen-year period from 1959 to 1973 when the Community was enlarged to include Denmark, Ireland and the United Kingdom, there were two distinct stages in the process of establishing and implementing a common transport policy. The first stage, from 1959 to 1964, consisted primarily of attempts by Community institutions to decide on their actual policy on transport. The second stage, which started in 1965 and continued until the enlargement of the Community in 1973, saw the first decisions taken in accordance with the policies adopted.

Enlargement in 1973 heralded the beginning of a second period during which the Community's approach to transport changed, while 22 January 1983, the date on which the President of the European Parliament, Mr Dankert, brought the action against the Council of Ministers for failure to act with the Court of Justice, marks the beginning of a third period which, it is to be hoped, will, if nothing else, at least bring a change in the relationships between the European Parliament, the Commission and the Council of Ministers in their efforts to establish and implement a common transport policy.

3.2.1 *Attempts to establish a policy and define its content during the first period (1959-72): the integrated transport market*

Under the institutional system established by the Treaty and because there were no rules defining the content of a common transport policy, it was up to the Commission - since it was basically responsible for making proposals - to establish the principles which were to form the basis for the policy and to work out in general terms how the policy would be implemented. Accordingly, on 10 April 1961, after two years of study and reflection, the Commission came up with a remarkably comprehensive transport policy plan. This 'Memorandum on the general lines of a common transport policy' set out the basic principles and content of the policy and the means of implementing it and was followed on 23 May 1962 by the 'Action programme on a common transport policy'.

The purpose of these two important documents was to suggest to the Council a policy approach, a programme and a strict timetable of measures to be taken, there being three basic options which we shall examine in a moment. It should first be emphasized that the Commission's conception of a common transport policy expressed in these documents was accepted in principle by both Parliament and the Economic and Social Committee. The Council of Ministers too, although it never discussed the Memorandum in detail, never objected to either its content or its approach.

There were three basic policy options, as we have said: to base transport policy on the principles of competition, to accept a certain degree of organization of the transport market or gradually to establish a Community market in transport.

On the first of these options, the competitive approach, the idea was to achieve the best possible distribution of traffic between the various modes of transport through the play of market forces rather than by attempts to coordinate tariffs and the like as in some Member States.

The second option was to attempt to 'organize' the transport market by adopting measures:

(i)   to put the various modes of transport and the transport undertakings operating each of the various modes of transport on an equal footing by harmonizing conditions of competition and by allocating infrastructure costs fairly;

(ii) to correct the irregularities which could arise through the play of competition, like the abuse of dominant positions on the market and cut-throat competition, by taking suitable steps to control capacity;

(iii) to help to achieve regional and social policy objectives where they cannot be achieved through the normal play of competition.

Lastly, according to the third option outlined in the Memorandum, a Community transport market would be established based on competition. This process would be gradual because of the considerable differences between the national policies of the Member States, which made it preferable not to push parallelism between the various sectors to extremes but to make progress in one sector depend on similar progress in another sector, so as to avoid rapidly reaching a situation of deadlock where nothing would be achieved.

3.2.1.1 The principles of the common transport policy

The principles of the common transport policy which inevitably derive from the options set out by the Commission in its Memorandum are equal treatment for transport users and transport operators, the financial independence of transport undertakings and their freedom of action and competition, free choice for users and coordination of infrastructure investment.

Equal treatment for transport users and transport operators

Equality of treatment is necessary to guarantee healthy competition. Users should be free to choose their carriers, and this means specific measures to abolish discrimination, to authorize support tariffs under exceptional circumstances, to legitimize competitive tariffs and to guarantee the necessary transparency of rates and conditions of transport, which implies publishing this information.

Equal treatment of undertakings operating the three modes means, in particular, prohibiting subsidies, supervising agreements, cartels and monopolies and abolishing all forms of discrimination - fiscal, regulatory or administrative - between the three modes of transport.

Financial independence of undertakings

Financial independence of undertakings covers a number of factors which include responsibility for financial management, operation of undertakings to make them profitable, fixing rates on the basis of actual costs and fair allocation between undertakings of the infrastructure costs borne by the taxpayer.

Freedom of action and competition between undertakings

Freedom of action and competition between undertakings is the basic option adopted by the Commission in its Memorandum and involves the application of a number of principles, which can be summarized as follows:

(i)   public and private transport undertakings must be left free to manage themselves;

(ii)   enforcement of the principle of fair competition;

(iii)   competitive rates to be permitted;

(iv)   government intervention only where strictly necessary, principally to coordinate transport services, with proper compensation for transport operators where such intervention affects transport rates;

(v)   free access to the transport market, but perhaps with certain restrictions for road and inland waterway transport.

Free choice for users

Leaving users free to choose between different transport services means that they are free to choose the means of transport best suited to their requirements, i.e. the mode of transport and the transport undertaking. Freedom to provide transport services on own account is based on this very principle, which is obviously in opposition to the setting up or maintenance of any type of monopoly.

Coordination of infrastructure investment

Although to begin with, the principle of coordinating investment outlined in the Memorandum can be achieved by harmonizing national decisions on investment projects of Community interest, the ultimate aim would be to coordinate all transport investment throughout the Community. Both this principle and the matter of infrastructure charging are embodied in the system proposed by the Commission for transport infrastructure and projects adopted under it.

3.2.1.2 The content of the common transport policy

According to the definition given in the Commission's Memorandum and Action Programme, the common transport policy covers four main areas.

Controlling the supply of transport services

It is considered essential to prepare common rules on admission to the occupation of road transport operator, access to the market and control of transport capacity. Although the Commission considers that any artificial restrictions on capacity should be lifted, it nevertheless feels that capacity should be adjusted to actual transport demand. Thus the adoption of proper supervisory and control measures should ensure that there are no supply surpluses or shortages. These measures apply chiefly to road and inland waterway transport and not to rail transport where the situation is different.

Organization of the transport market

In an attempt to align tariffs which differ from one mode of transport to another or from one country to another, the Commission, in its Memorandum, proposed setting up a system of bracket tariffs, in other words requiring that rates be kept within specific upper and lower limits. The upper limit would be designed to prevent exploitation of dominant positions and the lower limit to prevent cut-throat competition. Within these limits prices could be set freely in line with changes of supply and demand on the market. The 1962 action programme allows one important derogation from these bracket tariffs, namely special contracts, whereby undertakings would be allowed to sign contracts for rates outside these limits in cases where specific tonnages are being handled or transport operations are sufficiently regular or profitable.

Harmonization of conditions of competition

Since to begin with the conditions of the various modes of transport within the Member States and the transport operators belonging to the various Member States were somewhat different from the point of view of social and tax regulations and the public service obligations imposed on undertakings subject to the control of the public authorities, the Commission felt that it was necessary to align these positions before it could set up a transport market regulated by pricing mechanisms designed to guarantee free choice for the user and to ensure conditions of fair competition.

Transport infrastructure

The Memorandum distinguishes two aspects relating to transport infrastructure: infrastructure charging, the aim of which should be to allocate the cost of using infrastructure fairly between those who use it, and the problem of coordinating investment, the aim of which should be to achieve an economically sound allocation of resources for the maintenance and construction of transport infrastructure.

3.2.1.3 Decisions taken on the implementation of the common transport policy

The first period was devoted principally to working out the principles and content of a transport policy. During this period several points set out in the Commission's 1961 Memorandum and the 1962 Action Programme were actually implemented in the form of four proposals submitted by the Commission to the Council in May 1963.

Before taking a closer look at what was in these proposals, it is worth mentioning that the Council never managed to reach a consensus on the content of the Memorandum submitted to it on 10 April 1961, a document which incidentally marked the culmination of two years of painstaking study and consultation in all sectors of the economy concerned with the intricate problems relating to the definition of a Community policy on the three inland modes of transport. Subsequently, on 23 May 1962, in answer to a request from the Council itself, the Commission came up with the Action Programme which contained a whole series of measures to be taken and a timetable for their adoption. Once again, the Council examined the document but, even after four long meetings, could not reach a single decision on it.

The lack of response from the Council prompted the Commission to take it upon itself to come up with some practical proposals, since it was clear that the Council would not be able, in the short term, to reach unanimous agreement on a general approach to transport policy or on a general programme for its implementation.

In May 1963 the Commission forwarded to the Council four proposals, three of them relating to all three modes of inland transport:

    (i)   the introduction of a system of compulsory bracket tariffs;
    (ii) the organization of a survey on infrastructure costs;

(iii) the harmonization of certain provisions relating to competition (taxation, social legislation and State intervention);

and one to road transport in particular:

(iv) the introduction of a 'Community quota' of authorizations for transport operations between Member States.

Although the period from 1959 to 1963 was marked principally by the Community's attempts to decide on an approach to the common transport policy, the period did nevertheless see the adoption of a number of measures by the Community, some more important than others.

Perhaps the most important was the Council Decision of 21 March 1962 instituting a procedure for prior examination and consultation in respect of certain laws, regulations and administrative provisions concerning transport proposed in Member States[1] 'liable to interfere substantially with the implementation of the common transport policy'. The Decision was later amended on 22 November 1973 by a Decision which extended the period within which the Commission must submit its observations. In order to make the multilateral consultation process more effective, the Commission was authorized to examine all proposals having a significant effect on the implementation of the common transport policy either at the request of a Member State or on its own initiative. After the Member State concerned has submitted its own observations and after consulting all the other Member States, the Commission formulates an opinion or a recommendation. However, the Member State concerned is still legally free to take its own decisions. Thus, until a full definition of the common transport policy is arrived at and even though it has no further powers in this area, apart from the 'standstill' requirement in Article 76, the Commission does have a useful instrument for verifying that national policies do not diverge too much, although it does not have the legal powers to stop them if they do.

As a result of this Decision, which at the time was fully complied with by the Member States, the Commission formulated a total of 53 opinions basically endorsing measures adopted at national level and 12 recommendations suggesting that Member States make minor - or significant - changes to their plans. Undoubtedly, therefore, the Decision did help to bring national measures on transport into line with Community objectives. It is thanks to this Council Decision, for example, that it was possible considerably to attenuate the more restrictive aspects of the 'Leber plan' adopted by the Federal Republic of Germany, which we shall examine later.

It is also worth mentioning Council Regulation No 11 concerning the abolition of discrimination in transport rates and conditions in implementation of Article 79 (1) of the EEC Treaty which is designed to abolish discrimination on grounds of the country of origin or of destination of the goods carried.

---

[1] OJ 23, 3.4.1962, p. 720.

As a result of this Regulation, some 200 cases of tariff discrimination were abolished, plus another 250 cases of tariff differentiation which were not directly covered by Article 79 in that the tariffs related to traffic within a specific Member State or to the export or transit traffic of that Member State. These were in fact the subject of 'common action' undertaken by the Member States in 1964 at the Commission's initiative. There was also the First Council Directive of 23 July 1962, which exempted certain types of international carriage of goods by road from 'any quota or authorization system'. This Directive applied in particular to frontier traffic and to the carriage of goods in motor vehicles, the laden weight of which did not exceed six tonnes.

Lastly, from 1 January 1962 onwards, the Commission consistently applied Article 80 of the Treaty which prohibits rates and conditions involving any element of support or protection but gives the Commission the power to authorize them in the cases referred to in paragraph 2 of that Article, which mentions in particular the requirements of regional economic policy and the needs of under-developed areas.

3.2.2 Initial progress on the common transport policy during the first period (1965-72)

3.2.2.1 The false start in 1965

The Council meeting of 13 May 1965 marked the beginning of the first stage in the implementation of a common transport policy in accordance with the basic principles and content set out in the 1961 Memorandum and the 1962 Action Programme. In particular, the meeting adopted the Council Decision of 13 May 1965 on the harmonization of certain provisions affecting competition in transport by rail, road and inland waterway.[1] This was a far-reaching Decision designed to harmonize the differences between Member States in terms of social legislation, taxation and State intervention. On the basis of the Decision the Council was later to take the important step of improving management of the railways and adopt a first Regulation on the harmonization of existing social legislation on road transport.

At the same meeting, the Council also decided to organize a survey on infrastructure costs in order to determine how to charge for the use of infrastructure.[2] The time seemed right, therefore, for the submission of a document setting out a final policy on a number of controversial points which could act as a starting point for the implementation of a common transport policy.

---

[1] OJ 88, 24.5.1965, p. 1500/65

[2] An important document in this connection is the study prepared at the request of the EEC Commission by R. Malcor, *Problems arising in the practical application of charges for the use of road infrastructure,* Commission of the European Communities, Studies Collection, Transport series, No 2, Brussels, 1970.

In fact this was, to all appearances, the perfectly balanced set of proposals which the Commission submitted to the Council on 23 May 1965.

Altogether, the proposals covered integration of transport, organization of the transport market and harmonization of certain measures affecting competition and seemed perfectly attuned to the policy of gradual and parallel progress towards establishing a transport policy proposed by the Council. However, it immediately became clear that this package of measures would never meet with the Council's approval. The Dutch Government objected immediately to the proposal for a system of bracket tariffs to apply to the three modes of transport which it felt to contravene the rules on Rhine navigation. The consequent rejection by the Council of the series of measures proposed by the Commission was to constitute a serious obstacle to the future development of the common transport policy and ultimately led to the first serious Community transport crisis.

The Commission and the Council tried to find some way out of the impasse through the Council agreement of 22 June 1965 on organization of the transport market which basically set out to dissociate national transport from international transport. Since the Commission proposal of May 1965 to introduce compulsory bracket tariffs for the three modes of transport had been firmly opposed by the Netherlands, because it affected the system of total freedom set up by the Mannheim Convention, the agreement of 22 June attempted to circumvent this obstacle by introducing an important innovation, namely that, alongside the compulsory tariff system, there would also be a system of reference tariffs whereby operators would be free to fix rates but would have to publish any rates set outside the brackets specified for the various types of transport service.

Under the terms of the agreement, for a first period of three years international transport operations by rail and road would be subject to compulsory bracket tariffs, while, as a concession to the Netherlands' objection to restrictions, inland waterway transport would be subject only to the reference tariff system. For a second period, the reference tariff system would be extended to apply to certain national transport operations, still to be determined, which, in the first period, would be totally exempt from any tariff rules adopted at Community level. Thus, and this was always the Commission's aim, this agreement maintained a certain parallelism between measures on access to the market and measures to harmonize the conditions of competition. It was to be hoped, therefore, that the agreement would serve to re-invigorate the common transport policy. Unfortunately, the success of the Community's efforts was undermined shortly afterwards, on 30 June 1965, when the first serious institutional crisis broke. This was France's doing, the idea being to speed up the implementation of the common agricultural policy, which was of vital interest to France. It thus introduced its 'empty chair' policy whereby French delegations stopped attending all meetings of the Council of Ministers. This immediately caused all Community activities to grind to a halt and they only really started up again after the 'Luxembourg compromise' arrived at after a marathon session in February 1966.

This was a real 'agreement on disagreement' which for a long time would adversely affect the Community decision-making process.

Discussion of the Commission proposal which translated the June agreement into a Regulation at the meeting of the Council of Ministers held on 27 October 1965 clearly highlighted the differences in interpretation of the agreement between the Member States. It was not until 19 and 20 October 1966 that the Council of Transport Ministers was able to meet again, and it was only at the meeting in December 1967 that the Community policy was relaunched.

3.2.2.2 1967: Ready to try again

After finally abandoning the idea of organizing the transport market by first of all solving tariff problems, the Council decided instead to tackle problems of capacity, admission to transport occupations and harmonization of rules on competition.

To this extent the resolution adopted by the Council at that first meeting after the Luxembourg compromise marks a new departure which was finally re-affirmed in the communication on the common transport policy which the Commission prepared on the basis of this resolution and presented to the Council on 10 February 1967. The communication contained a work programme which gave rise to lengthy debate crystallizing into the important Decision taken by the Council of Transport Ministers on 14 December 1967 on certain measures of common transport policy.[1] In this document it committed itself to carrying out a series of measures according to a precise timetable in three different stages. These measures were:

(a) first stage:

    (i)   to harmonize working conditions in road transport;

    (ii)   to apply competition rules to the transport sector;

    (iii) to make rules on aids for transport;

    (iv) to abolish double taxation of vehicles used for international transport;

    (v)   to standardize provisions regarding the duty-free admission of fuel contained in the fuel tanks of commercial motor vehicles;

    (vi) to establish a Community quota for the carriage of goods by road between Member States;

---

[1] OJ 322, 30.12.1967.

(vii) to introduce a bracket tariff system for the carriage of goods by road between Member States;

(b) second stage:

    (i) action by the Member States concerning the obligations inherent in the concept of public service as applicable to rail transport;

    (ii) normalization of railway accounts;

(c) third stage:

    (i) harmonization of the taxation structure in respect of commercial motor vehicles;

    (ii) the introduction of a permanent standard system of accounting for expenditure relating to the infrastructure of each mode of transport.[1]

The Decision also provided for the setting up of specialist committees to work on each of these measures. Thus 1967 is clearly the year when the common transport policy took off again. To some extent this was probably due to concern that national laws were being drafted (e.g. the 'Leber plan' in the Federal Republic of Germany) which showed that certain countries were determined to solve at national level those problems which the Community had so far failed to solve. Since it was then in favour of relaunching the common transport policy, it was the Italian Government that submitted a Memorandum on 21 September 1967 which suggested putting together a package of the less controversial measures on the table so that final solutions could be found at Community level.

This whole set of proposed measures was adopted according to the timetable laid down in the above-mentioned Council resolution at a series of meetings on 18 July 1968, 17 and 18 March 1969, 26 and 27 January 1970 and 4 June 1970, with the exception of the measures on the elimination of double taxation and the harmonization of taxation on commercial motor vehicles.

3.2.2.3 The common transport policy after 1968

In 1968 the Council took a number of important decisions, although of rather limited scope, on the basis of proposals submitted by the Commission, some more recent than others. In particular, on 19 July 1968 the Council adopted Regulation No 1017/68 applying rules of competition to transport by rail, road

---

[1] A more detailed study of the measures contained in the Decision of 14 December 1967 and of negotiations behind the scenes is contained in *La politique commune des transports de la CEE de janvier 1967 à fin mars 1968* published by the Studiecentrum voor de Expansie van Antwerpen, Antwerp, 1968, pp. 31-39.

and inland waterway,[1] Regulation No 1018/68 introducing a Community quota for the carriage of goods by road between Member States,[2] and the Directive on the standardization of provisions regarding the duty-free admission of fuel contained in the fuel tanks of commercial motor vehicles.[3] On 30 July 1968 the Council adopted Regulation No 1174/68 on the introduction of a system of bracket tariffs for the carriage of goods by road between Member States.[4]

On 19 July 1968 the Council had agreed in principle on a proposal for a Regulation on the harmonization of certain social legislation relating to road transport without finally adopting it. The Regulation[5] did not come into force until 25 March 1969, after certain difficulties caused by the provisions of the AETR to be adopted in the framework of the ECE had been ironed out. The Council had also decided that the Community road haulage quota would not be applied until after a full solution had been found to the whole tariff problem, since Regulation No 1174/68 of 30 July 1968 had only very limited scope of a temporary and experimental nature. As we have already mentioned, the Council's failure to establish a general and coherent transport policy at Community level made some governments consider themselves justified in adopting measures which were purely national in scope on matters of importance to their transport sectors. This was a dangerous trend and the only way the Commission could counter it was by invoking the Decision of 1962 instituting a procedure for prior examination and consultation, although it was of course at liberty to bring to bear the procedure for failure to fulfil an obligation under the Treaty laid down in Article 169.

A good example in this connection is the 'Transport policy programme for 1968-72', better known as the 'Leber plan', which the German Minister for Transport, Georg Leber, put forward in September 1967 and which was adopted by the Federal German Government on 8 November 1967.[6] One of the basic aims of the plan was to transfer certain types of traffic from the roads to the railways by introducing a 'coordination' tax (*Leberpfennig*). Since it was clear that, even though it did not contravene the provisions of the Treaty, this measure, like similar national measures, would certainly not facilitate the

---

[1] OJ L 175, 23.7.1968, p. 1. In view of the distinctive features of transport, this Regulation allowed some important exceptions in the application of rules on competition to the transport sector. As a result some argued that it would be more correct to describe it as a Regulation 'guarding against abuses of agreements' rather than a Regulation prohibiting agreements. Nowadays of course these disputes are merely of historic interest since the judgment handed down by the Court of Justice on 4 April 1974, which legally recognized that the general provisions of the Treaty, including those on competition, should be applied to the transport sector, has now passed into law.

[2] OJ L 175, 23.7.1968, p. 13.

[3] *Idem,* p. 15.

[4] OJ L 194, 6.8.1968, p. 1.

[5] See Regulation (EEC) No 543/69 of the Council of 25 March 1969 on the harmonization of certain social legislation relating to road transport (OJ L 77, 29.3.1969, p. 49).

[6] For a detailed study of the Leber plan see *La politique commune des transports de la CEE de janvier 1967 à fin mars 1968* published by the Studiecentrum voor de Expansie van Antwerpen, Antwerp, April 1968, pp. 21-30.

introduction of a common policy by the Community, the Commission countered it by using the consultation procedure.[1]

A number of important measures were adopted by the Council in 1969:

   (i) Regulation No 543/69 of 25 March 1969 on the harmonization of certain social legislation relating to road transport (which covers in particular driving periods and control procedures);[2]

  (ii) Regulation No 1191/69 of 26 June 1969 on action by Member States concerning the obligations inherent in the concept of a public service in transport by rail, road and inland waterway;[3]

 (iii) Regulation No 1192/69 of 26 June 1969 on common rules for the normalization of the accounts of railway undertakings;[4]

  (iv) Council Directive 69/467/EEC of 8 December 1969 on returns, to be made on the basis of regional statistics, in respect of international carriage of goods by road.[5]

3.2.2.4 The end of the transitional period

The end of 1969 marked the end of the transitional period provided for in Article 8 of the EEC Treaty.

According to Article 75(2) common rules applicable to international transport to or from the territory of a Member State or passing across the territory of one or more Member States, and the conditions under which non-resident carriers may operate transport services within a Member State should have been laid down during the transitional period. In actual fact, the measures adopted by the Council in these two spheres were totally inadequate to meet the Treaty objectives. An important judgment handed down by the Court of Justice[6] established the principle that Article 52 of the Treaty regarding abolition of restrictions on the freedom of establishment of nationals of a Member State in the territory of another Member State is directly applicable in the Member States and allows individuals rights which the national courts are bound to safeguard after the end of the transitional period. Whether or not the Council, in accordance with the provisions of Article 54(2) or Article 57(1) of the Treaty, had adopted directives to implement the general programme on the abolition of restrictions on freedom of establishment provided for in Article 54(1) and finalized on 18 December 1961 thus became relevant. This general principle of freedom of establishment within the Community, which was recognized by the Court, also applies to the transport sector.

---

[1] See the Commission's recommendation to the Government of the Federal Republic of Germany of 31 January 1968 (OJ L 35, 8.2.1968).
[2] OJ L 77, 29.3.1969, p. 49.
[3] OJ L 156, 28.6.1969, p. 1.
[4] OJ L 156, 28.6.1969, p. 8.
[5] OJ L 323, 24.12.1969.
[6] Case: 2/74 *Reyners* v *Belgian State* [1974] ECR 631.

As far as the provisions of the articles constituting the *lex specialis* in Title IV are concerned, it is worth mentioning that the 'standstill' provisions of Article 76 were in fact applied. Likewise the provisions of Articles 77, 78, 81, 82 and 83 were directly applicable from the date of entry into force of the Treaty. As has already been mentioned, support tariffs (Article 80) have been prohibited since the second stage of the transitional period (31 December 1965).

It has to be admitted, however, that, in general terms, apart from those measures of rather limited scope covered by the above-mentioned articles, relatively little had been achieved by the end of the transitional period towards implementating the common transport policy as provided for in Articles 3 and 74 of the Treaty, apart from some progress in the area where action was felt to be most urgent, namely road transport, and, to a lesser extent, in rail transport.

In its General Report[1] the Commission was forced to admit that by the end of 1970 very little real progress had been made towards organizing the transport market.

In fact, even 1970, 1971 and 1972, the years immediately following the end of the transitional period, were lean years for transport in general, in spite of the vigorous efforts made by the Commission to regenerate a constructive attitude in the Council. Two documents in particular, forwarded to the Council on 14 September 1971, testify to the Commission's attempts to give new direction to the common transport policy.

The first, on organization of the transport market, expresses the hope that the Council will adopt and consolidate the various proposals already put forward by the Commission on admission to the occupation of road transport operator, and further that it will introduce Community control of international road haulage capacity and will take pains to introduce the scheme for laying up vessels already suggested by the Commission as a means of controlling the capacity of inland waterway goods transport. Lastly, on 8 November 1971, the Commission sent the Council a communication on the development of the common transport policy which contained a five-year programme of priority measures on harmonization (of social regulations, taxation, etc.), on organization of the market (integration and liberalization) and on development of the common policy (road safety improvements, infrastructure charging, coordination of investment and research on future means of transport).

However, since the Council was reluctant to take any fundamental decisions so close to the accession of the new Member States and since it felt that it had already concluded the partial programme on transport with its Decision of 14 December 1967, it contented itself solely with selecting from this timetable only the 1972 programme, which dealt with problems relating to the harmonization of weights and dimensions of commercial vehicles, harmonization of the taxation structure in respect of these vehicles, autonomy for the railways and a

---

[1] Fourth General Report, point 279.

scheme for temporarily laying up inland waterway vessels. The Council nevertheless failed to reach any decision on these matters during the course of 1972.

At its meeting on 18 December 1972, the Council got no further than taking a number of decisions on relatively trivial matters, even though it had been called upon to take decisions on the technical standardization of the weights and dimensions of commercial vehicles. On this particular matter the Council of the six Member States, at its previous meeting on 17 and 18 May 1972, had finally decided unanimously on a straightforward maximum weight of 11 tonnes per axle and a total fully laden weight of 40 tonnes.

3.2.3 Development of the common transport policy following the enlargement of the Community. Second period (1973-82): the Community transport system

The Community transport policy came to a standstill during the first year after the Six became Nine, principally because of the continuing disagreement between the original Six and the new Three over the weights and dimensions of commercial vehicles. In fact, at the Council meeting on 22 November 1973, the Transport Ministers of the enlarged Community could not reach agreement on this problem or on the related problem of adjusting the Community quota for the carriage of goods by road between Member States to take the three new Member States into account. The only decision to come out of the meeting was the adoption of a Commission proposal to extend the scope of the First Council Directive of 23 July 1962 which exempted carriage of goods by road for hire or reward from any quota or authorization system.

In the field of international relations, however, important negotiations began with Switzerland on 22 February 1973 on the subject of Rhine navigation.

Of significance too is the Commission's communication on the development of the common transport policy which was prepared on the basis of the decisions taken at the Paris Summit in October 1972 and was forwarded to the Council on 24 October 1973. This represents a new departure as far as the common transport policy is concerned.[1]

The communication is a fairly comprehensive document and sets out the reasons why the content and scope of the common transport policy should be extended. The document concentrates on the objectives established at the Paris Summit (establishment of an economic and monetary union by setting up proper regional, social, environmental and economic policies covering such areas as

---

[1] Communication of the Commission to the Council on the development of the common transport policy, Doc. COM(73) 1725 final of 24 October 1973.

land-use planning, social progress, improving the quality of life, protecting the environment and safeguarding of material and non-material assets). It also argues in favour of closer links between transport policy and other policies (regional, structural, social, fiscal, industrial and energy policies).

However, the starting point for this new approach to transport policy is concentration on more strictly economic considerations. In the past the common transport policy had been based primarily on consideration of the economic interests of undertakings so that its main aim was the organization of a common market in transport operating freely in accordance with market economy principles. In order to achieve this, however, it was necessary to harmonize conditions of competition between the various modes of transport and within each mode, a process which had hitherto been undertaken piecemeal by the Member States.

The Commission therefore felt that although the objective of liberalization continued to be valid, a new dimension should be added. It was becoming clear that the transport sector was costing society more and more, not only in terms of expensive infrastructure but also in terms of the social costs incurred by using land and energy, and more generally the diseconomies inherent in transport operations. As these costs could not be reduced simply by allowing market forces free play, the Commission proposed that the market be not only organized but also integrated. This would constitute a new approach, since all modes of transport - including sea and air transport, transport by pipeline and all the most recent methods of transport - would together form one integrated network.

In other words, the ideas in the 1973 communication were not totally divorced from the objectives set out in the 1961 Memorandum. Valid common policy aims were still freedom to provide services, harmonization of conditions of competition within and between modes of transport and the development of a common transport market based on the free play of market forces with intervention only in exceptional circumstances. These measures nevertheless had to be combined with structural measures, a priority being to combine national transport systems into a Community system. Community help would be necessary in planning and financing this integrated network and in organizing the transport market so that resources could be put to the best possible use. Measures would also need to take account of the interdependence between transport policy and other Community policies designed to improve living and working conditions and to recognize the role played by the public authorities in the transport sector.

Thus the public authorities were being asked to choose between the various transport options and to bring everything together in an intermodal network in which the different modes of transport would play complementary roles.

In order to direct their choice to achieve the most efficient distribution of resources, the Commission saw its proposals on infrastructure charging to be still as important as ever. It hoped to see improvements in the consultation procedure on coordination of investment instituted by its Decision of 28 February 1966 and, more generally, considered that in order to achieve the wide-ranging objectives set for the common transport policy there would, in the future, have to be more intervention by the public authorities, particularly on infrastructure. In spite of all this, however, transport undertakings and their economic interests were still of priority concern since they had been the main target of the common transport policy and had hitherto been promised the most liberal conditions of competition possible.

According to the proposed timetable, this new Community system was to be implemented over the next ten years in conjunction with and alongside the proposed European Economic and Monetary Union.

The Commission also undertook to prepare a number of practical proposals designed to bring about this new programme since the proposals it had already submitted did not fully meet these objectives.

The action programme which accompanied the communication[1] stressed the urgent need to tackle certain problems:

(i)   realization of a transport network in accordance with the previously agreed plan, which would include a formula for solving problems relating to the planning and financing of Community infrastructure;

(ii) charging for the use of transport infrastructure;

(iii) defining the role of the railways in the transport system of the future and solving their financial problems;

(iv) planning the development of the inland transport markets.

The Commission had prepared a special communication containing a coherent set of proposals on the organization of the transport market in 1975.[2]

As we go on to examine the main areas of action, it will become apparent how, yet again, the Council paid very little attention to this second programme designed to establish a common transport policy.

3.2.3.1 The common transport policy and the Tindemans report on European Union

For a whole variety of reasons, a long series of difficulties has been affecting the process of European integration in the Community for many years. Although to some extent these were the result of the complex economic problems facing a

---

[1] Together with the various updated versions: Community programmes 1978-80, Doc. COM(77) 596 final of 23 November 1977 and 1981-82, Doc. COM(80) 582 of 21 October 1980.

[2] Doc. COM(75) 490 final of 1 October 1975.

Europe which in some respects had not really managed to live up to its never-to-be-repeated past, there is no doubt that they were basically ineluctable.[1]

At their Summit Conference in October 1972, the Heads of State and of Government made it a basic objective to transform all relations between Member States into a European Union before the end of the decade and in full observance of the Treaties. They therefore asked the Community institutions to prepare a report for submission to another Summit Conference before the end of 1975. The basic objective to set up a European Union was later confirmed at the Summits held in Copenhagen in December 1973 and Paris in December 1974. At the Paris Summit, the Heads of State and of Government asked Leo Tindemans, the Belgian Prime Minister, to prepare a summary report based on reports prepared by the Community institutions and on consultations with governments and public opinion leaders in the Community. These reports were completed and forwarded to the Heads of State or Government of the Nine and to European public opinion leaders on schedule.

A number of conclusions can be drawn from these reports regarding the common transport policy.

First of all, the general remarks on common rules and common policies which are expressed in different ways in the various reports also apply to transport. Thus although the Court of Justice does not actually mention transport in its 'Suggestions' it would seem to be covered by the general opinions expressed. Much less easy to explain, on the other hand, is why the European Parliament, which has always paid considerable attention to the common transport policy, should have failed to mention transport in its Resolution of 10 July 1975 as one of the policies whose implementation it feels is of particular importance.

Lastly, the opinion of the Economic and Social Committee specifically mentions the common transport policy as one of the areas where it feels delays would seriously undermine the building of the Community.

In his report,[2] Leo Tindemans mentions as an aim of the European Union 'improved transport and communication, if necessary by harmonizing rules and by abolishing tariffs which discriminate between national transport and telecommunications and those taking place within the Union'.

These are the features of a common transport policy which were felt to be necessary.

---

[1] And we cannot do better here than recall the words of Hendrijk Brugmans, that great European federalist: 'Will Christians renounce their traditional conservatism and nationalism? Will the Jews abandon their isolation as the chosen people? (Chosen to do what?) Will the humanists who have no particular beliefs concentrate their minds? Will any of them have enough energy? There is no intellectual or political answer to these questions. The only answer is an act - an act of faith.' H. Brugmans, *L'Europe vécue*, Casterman, Tournai, 1979.

[2] L. Tindemans, *Report on European Union,* Brussels, 1975, Chap. IV.

3.2.3.2 **Achievements in the second half of the 1970s**

Unfortunately, as things turned out, no positive action followed this attempt to launch new proposals in 1975. In fact, it is true to say that at the beginning of the 1980s, in other words five years after the Tindemans report on European Union and seven years after the Commission's communication to the Council of 24 October 1973 on the development of the common transport policy, which as we have seen was a new departure in this area, very few of the objectives set in this communication have been achieved.

Very little has been done to liberalize markets. Though the three new Member States endorsed the Commission's view on the introduction of a system of reference tariffs for the carriage of goods by road between the Member States, the original Six generally prefer the system of compulsory tariffs, although they are tending, France in particular, to reduce the number of obstacles.

It seems, in fact, that the idea of general freedom to establish tariffs is very gradually beginning to take hold.

The quotas which share out traffic under the Community quota system between the different Member States according to their respective importance with regard to the international carriage of goods by road have been extended each year and by 1980 reached a total of 3 751 authorizations. Nevertheless, this figure still represents only a small proportion (5%) of all road haulage traffic within the Community. On the subject of bilateral quotas, an important Council decision of 20 December 1979[1] specified a number of Community criteria for adjusting quotas to developments in the trade concerned by means of intergovernmental agreements. Again, Member States should have taken account in this connection of information obtained from market studies conducted by the Commission on an experimental basis in accordance with the declaration arrived at during the Council meeting of June 1978.

Thus a sector which hitherto had been the sole responsibility of Member States was made subject to Community authorizations.

Lastly, at the same meeting in December 1979, the nine Member States adopted, and included in the above-mentioned Decision, a measure which in practice frees some 85% of road transport on own account between Member States from any form of quota or transport authorization. This applied to all transport previously subject to such systems except for vehicles which were rented or purchased under leasing arrangements.

However, as long as the system of bilateral quotas continues to exist, applying to more than 90% of road traffic between Member States, it is difficult to talk in terms of real integration of the road transport market - not to mention a number of restrictions on freedom which are beginning to emerge on some

---

[1] Council Decision 80/48/EEC of 20 December 1979 (OJ L 18, 24.1.1980).

inland waterway routes within the Community nor the difficulties in implementing certain provisions like those on driving periods and rest periods in road transport. Perhaps the market observation system introduced by the Commission in 1979 in conjunction with the social and economic organizations concerned will to some extent prevent governments, and particularly the Government of the Federal Republic of Germany, from trotting out the old excuse - insufficient harmonization of technical, fiscal or social conditions of competition - which they often use to prevent the further opening up of transport markets. Some progress has been made in coordinating national infrastructure policies and in setting up a network of communication links of Community interest, stated as objectives in the Commission communication to the Council of October 1973. This progress is due in part to the Council Decision[1] of February 1978 instituting a consultation procedure and setting up a special committee, even though the Commission's additional proposal to grant financial support for projects of Community interest has still not been adopted. On the other hand, the end of the 1970s did see a major new development: the consideration at Community level of air and sea transport problems, the importance of which was mentioned in a Commission communication as long ago as October 1973.

Various factors helped to expand Community interest in these two basic modes of transport and we shall look at these in greater detail later on. A key factor was certainly the judgment handed down by the Court of Justice on 4 April 1974, but contributory factors were also the concern of some Member States, like the Federal Republic of Germany, the United Kingdom and the Netherlands, about the 'abnormal' and rather uncommercial practices of some merchant fleets belonging to the eastern bloc state-trading countries and the spate of oil-spills (notably the environmental disaster caused in Brittany by the *Amoco Cadiz*), which finally convinced the EEC governments of the need for concerted action to protect these threatened sectors.

In 1979, therefore, the Council adopted a number of measures as a first step towards combating competition from certain non-Community countries, particularly State-trading countries (the USSR in particular). These entailed collecting information first of all, but also included measures on the safety of shipping and protection against pollution of the sea. In the Commission's opinion these measures were inadequate.

Equally important, as far as its consequences were concerned, was the Regulation adopted by the Council on 8 May 1979 concerning ratification by Member States of the United Nations Convention on a Code of Conduct for Liner Conferences.

On air transport, a Decision was adopted in December 1979 initiating a Community consultation procedure concerning international action in the field of air transport along the lines of the procedure already set up for shipping in

---

[1] Council Decision of 20 February 1978 instituting a consultation procedure and setting up a committee in the field of transport infrastructure, OJ L 54, 25.2.1978.

September 1977. This was the instrument which would enable the Nine to act on the Commission's Memorandum of July 1979 to encourage the development of air transport services within the Community.

3.2.4 *Recent developments and the beginning of the third period (1983)*

There was a conspicuous lack of measures adopted by the Council on transport in 1980 and 1981.[1] There was absolutely no progress on harmonizing conditions of competition and with regard to access to the market, the Council merely adapted existing measures to take account of the accession of Greece on 1 January 1981 and authorized only a very small increase in the quota of Community authorizations for the carriage of goods by road between Member States and the liberalization of a few new special transport categories. For the rest, apart from completion of the first stage of the procedure to introduce Community driving licence, the Council had come to a virtual standstill.

All the same, in an attempt to arouse the Council from its lethargy, the Commission, on 24 October 1980, forwarded to it a list of priorities and a timetable of decisions to be taken before the end of 1983. The list corresponded with the approach to the common transport policy adopted by the Commission in its communication of 24 October 1973 and took into account the points of view already expressed by Parliament, the Council and the Economic and Social Committee. The main items on the list were:

(i)   priority for the establishment of a transport infrastructure network to meet the Community's needs;

(ii) making transport services within the Community more flexible, more profitable and better suited to requirements at the lowest possible total cost;

(iii) improving the financial situation of the railways and encouraging cooperation between the various railway undertakings on a Community level;

(iv) keeping shipping profitable in a world context;

(v)   creating the conditions to help airlines become more productive;

(vi) devoting proper attention to all forms of transport and their use in the broader context of international relations;

(vii) rational use of energy;

(viii) social considerations.

---

[1] See pages 1 to 4 of *La politique commune des transports dans la CEE - bilan de 1980-1981*, published by the Studiecentrum voor de Expansie van Antwerpen, Antwerp, 1982.

In actual fact the Commission's proposal was a compendium of all those matters which had to be settled urgently by the Council, according to the new approach to the common transport policy set out in the communication of 24 October 1973. The document included a draft Council Resolution with, in annex, a list of 35 points on which the Council was asked for decisions, according to a three-stage timetable: i.e. from October 1980 to the end of 1981, during 1982 and during 1983.

However, at its meeting on 26 March 1981, the Council did no more than adopt a resolution approving only a very limited number of these topics, 12 of the 35 proposed. Not only did these not include some of the subjects which had most prompted the Commission to make the proposal but even this short list did not contain one decision with any binding force. The Council merely declared itself ready to discuss these matters before 1983.[1] The deep disappointment at the Council's attitude felt by the European Parliament and the Economic and Social Committee prompted the Committee's Transport Section to hold its first joint meeting with the Transport Committee of the European Parliament on 23 April 1981. They discussed the integration of European transport policy and some strident criticism was levelled against the Council's inactivity.

Later, during its 29-30 April 1981 session, the ESC solemnly reaffirmed the need to end this period of stagnation and to get the European transport policy moving again, particularly as the economic and energy situations were continuing to worsen.

In its turn, the European Parliament's Transport Committee instructed its Vice-President, Angelo Carossino, to summarize the criticisms made of the Council at the joint meeting of 23 April 1981 in a special report. Carossino presented this report on the common transport policy[2] on behalf of the Transport Committee on 15 February 1982. In view of its importance, it is worth dwelling on for a moment, although a more detailed analysis will be made in the conclusions.

The report was adopted by the Parliament's Transport Committee on 8 March 1982. It emphasizes a number of important points.

Both the Commission and the Council of Ministers come in for some detailed criticism. A number of suggestions are also made for breaking out of the impasse in which the European transport policy has been for so long.

---

[1] One of these priorities in fact was the facilitation of frontier crossings, on the basis of which, on 1 December 1983, the Council adopted Directive 83/643/EEC on the facilitation of physical inspections and administrative formalities in respect of the carriage of goods between Member States (OJ L 359, 22.12.1983, pages 8-11). If this had already been applied by the Member States, it would certainly have helped to avoid the serious disruptions of motorway traffic at the Brenner frontier.
[2] European Parliament *Working Documents 1981-82, Doc. 1-996/81* of 15 February 1982.

The Commission is criticized for contenting itself with a 'step-by-step' approach[1] and submitting to the Council only those proposals which it has previously ascertained will have some chance of success. This approach has the disadvantage of not making the Council face up to its full responsibilities and at the same time of weakening the supervisory powers which the European Parliament has over the activities of the Council. Specifically, in a proposal for a resolution, it asks the Commission to extend the programme of priorities it put before the Council on 24 October 1980 until the year 1984 as a means of implementing a common transport policy.

Turning to the Council, the report contains a special annex which lists the 49 proposals on which the Commission is waiting for a decision from the Council. These proposals cover seven main policy areas: infrastructure; operation of the markets; tax problems, State aids, social progress, safety, reform, modernization and cooperation; shipping; air transport; external relations; weights, dimensions and other technical specifications of vehicles. The report asks the Council without further delay to specify the framework for a common transport policy referred to in Article 74 of the Treaty and the regulatory system for transport referred to in Article 75(3) and to take decisions on the 49 Commission proposals on which Parliament has already expressed its opinion. To this end, the report - and this is an extremely significant point - suggests that the Council refrain from systematically taking decisions unanimously,[2] except in those cases expressly provided for by the Treaty (Article 75(3)), and asks the Council that when, under exceptional circumstances, it does intend to resort to this procedure, it should first justify its use when requesting an opinion from the Parliament. Lastly, the proposal for a resolution does consider initiating the procedure for failure to act referred to in Article 175 of the EEC Treaty by bringing an action against the Council for failing to adopt a common policy in the sphere of transport.

The Carossino report was followed by the Seefeld report on the institution of proceedings against the Council of the European Communities for failure to act in the field of transport policy. The report[3] was dated 1 July 1982 and contained a motion for a resolution, based in particular on an opinion by the Legal Affairs Committee that the President of the European Parliament should be instructed to bring before the Court of Justice of the European Communities

---

[1] The *Kleine Schritte* policy particularly preferred by the German delegation, as confirmed by C. Wölker and H.S. Seidenfus in their reports to the 'Seminar of advanced studies on transport organization in European economic integration, 24th international course', at the University of Trieste from 1 to 10 September 1983.

[2] As has been pointed out, the practice of unanimous voting (which has a disastrous effect on the Community decision-making process) was imposed by the French Government at the time of the Luxembourg compromise in February 1966 as a condition for its discontinuation of its 'empty chair' policy. Since that time, after the first Community crisis concerning the operation of the common agricultural policy had been solved, the practice has continued, in disdain of the provisions of the Treaty which require that after the transitional period the Council should take decisions by qualified majority in virtually all cases. As far as transport is concerned, this is based on an erroneous interpretation of Article 75(3) of the Treaty.

[3] European Parliament *Working Documents 1982-83,* Doc. 1-420/82 of 1 July 1982.

an action against the Council based on Article 175 of the EEC Treaty. First, however, a letter would be sent to the Council calling upon it to act and giving it two months to send an opinion for detailed examination.[1]

This action against the Council of Ministers was brought before the Court of Justice on 22 January 1983 by Piet Dankert, President of the European Parliament. It accused the Council of violating Articles 3 and 74 of the Treaty by failing to adopt a common policy in the sphere of transport and in particular by not establishing a binding framework for this policy. Following the procedure set out in Article 175, Parliament, after calling upon the Council to act within two months, and after waiting a further period of two months, asked the Court to rule that the Council had not taken decisions on a series of Commission proposals which should have formed the basis for the implementation of the common transport policy. Parliament based its action on 16 Commission proposals (out of the 49 listed in the Carossino report) on which the Council had failed to take a decision. If the Court rules that the Council has failed to act, the Council, under Article 176 of the Treaty, 'shall be required to take the necessary measures to comply with the judgment of the Court of Justice' or, in other words, to take decisions on the Commission's proposals. The 16 proposals mentioned in the Parliament's submission are, under the various headings:

Social legislation

(1) Proposal for a Council Regulation on the harmonization of certain social provisions relating to goods transport by inland waterway (OJ C 259 of 1975 as amended by OJ C 206 of 1979, opinion of the European Parliament (EP), OJ C 57 of 1977, opinion of the Economic and Social Committee (ESC), OJ C 61 of 1977).

Tax harmonization

(2) Proposal for a First Council Directive concerning the adjustment of national systems of commercial vehicle taxation (OJ C 95 of 1968, EP opinion, OJ C 63 of 1969, ESC opinion, OJ C 48 of 1969).

(3) Proposal for a Council Directive amending Directive 68/297/EEC on the duty-free admission of fuel (OJ C 104 of 1974, EP opinion, OJ C 155 of 1974, ESC opinion, OJ C 142 of 1974).

---

[1] See footnote 3, previous page.

Technical harmonization

(4) Proposal for a Council Directive concerning the weights and dimensions of commercial road vehicles and certain additional technical requirements concerning such vehicles (OJ C 90 of 1971 as amended by OJ C 16 of 1979 and COM(81) 510 of 11.9.1981, EP opinion OJ C 124 of 1971 and resolution of 7.5.1981, OJ C 144 of 1981).

Harmonization of action by Member States

(5) Proposals for Council Regulations supplementing and amending Regulation (EEC) 1191 of 1969 on action by Member States concerning the obligations inherent in the concept of a public service in transport by rail, road and inland waterway (Doc. COM(72)1516 of 7.12.1972 and OJ C 268 of 1981, EP opinion OJ C 37 of 1972 and OJ C 260 of 1981).

(6) Proposal for a Council Regulation amending Regulation (EEC) No 1192/69 on common rules for the normalization of the accounts of railway undertakings (OJ C 307 of 1977, EP opinion OJ C 163 of 1978).

Operation of the market

(7) Proposal for a Regulation on the adjustment of capacity for the carriage of goods by road for hire or reward between Member States (OJ C 247 of 1978, EP opinion OJ C 67 of 1979, ESC opinion OJ C 133 of 1979).

(8) Proposal for a Council Directive on own-account carriage of goods between Member States (OJ C 41 of 1979, EP opinion OJ C 127 of 1979, ESC opinion OJ C 113 of 1980).

(9) Proposal for a Council Directive amending the First Directive on the establishment of common rules for certain types of carriage of goods by road between Member States and Council Directive 65/269/EEC (OJ C 253 of 1980, EP opinion OJ C 327 of 1980, ESC opinion OJ C 138 of 1981).

(10) Proposal for a Council Directive amending Directive 65/269/EEC on the standardization of certain rules relating to authorizations for the carriage of goods between Member States (OJ C 350 of 1980, EP opinion OJ C 144 of 1981, ESC opinion OJ C 138 of 1981).

(11) Proposal for a Council Regulation amending Regulation (EEC) No 3164/76 on the Community quota for the carriage of goods by road between Member States (OJ C 350 of 1980, EP opinion OJ C 144 of 1981, ESC opinion OJ C 138 of 1981).

(12) Proposal for a Council Regulation relating to access to the inland waterway freight market (OJ C 95 of 1968 as amended by Doc. COM(69)311 of 25.4.1969, EP opinion OJ C 108 of 1968, ESC opinion OJ C 100 of 1968).

Observation of markets

(13) Proposal for a Council Regulation concerning a system for observing the markets for the carriage of goods by rail, road and inland waterway between the Member States (OJ C 1 of 1976, as amended by Doc. COM(80)785 of 5.12.1980, OJ C 351 of 1980, EP opinion OJ C 293 of 1976, ESC opinion OJ C 281 of 1976).

(14) Proposal for a Council Decision on the collection of information concerning the activities of road hauliers participating in the carriage of goods to and from certain non-member countries (opinion of 9 July 1982).

Infrastructure

(15) Proposal for a Council Regulation on support for projects of Community interest in transport infrastructure (OJ C 207 of 1976, as amended by OJ C 249 of 1977 and OJ C 89 of 1980, EP opinion OJ C 293 of 1976, OJ C 183 of 1977 and OJ C 197 of 1980, ESC opinion OJ C 56 of 1977 and OJ C 300 of 1980).

Air transport

(16) Proposal for a Council Regulation concerning the authorization of scheduled interregional air services for passengers, mail and cargo between Member States (Doc. COM(80)624 of 19.10.1980, as amended by Doc. COM(81)771 of 10.12.1981, EP opinion OJ C 287 of 1981).[1]

For the moment, the Commission is waiting to see the outcome of the case against the Council of Ministers brought before the Court of Justice by the European Parliament and has still not expressed a final opinion. It is likely that the Commission will decide on conciliation if the Council agrees to go along with the new action programme set out at the beginning of 1983 in a document which was submitted to the Council by the Commission and covers 1983, 1984 and 1985. The document,[2] part of which is annexed to this chapter, not only restates the main features of the common transport policy but also includes a work programme broken down into half-yearly sections (thus corresponding to the length of the Presidency of the Council of Ministers which is held in turn by each Member State). It covers the three modes of inland transport and places particular emphasis on infrastructure and international transport policy as well (and explicitly refers to the liberalization of intermodal transport).

Of the three modes of inland transport, the railways are given particular attention in the document since they are considered to be the crucial sector. The

[1] Later converted into and adopted as Council Directive 83/416/EEC of 25 July 1983 (OJ L 237, 26.8.1983, p. 19).
[2] Communication from the Commission to the Council of 11 February 1983 on 'Progress towards a common transport policy - Inland transport', OJ C 154, 13.6.1983.

Commission argues that in order to help solve the problem of competition between the various modes of transport, which lies at the heart of any attempt to make progress on a common transport policy, it is essential first of all to take action to reduce the financial burdens on the railway undertakings. This should be done, not by penalizing competing modes of transport, but by helping to improve the efficiency of the railways and to make their services more attractive. To this end the Commission proposes:

(a) to support the programme to improve cooperation between railways, concentrating its own efforts on overcoming the various material, legal and commercial obstacles which prevent the railways from taking advantage of the longer routes and the extended range of activities open to them in the Community market. The Commission also undertakes to put forward other measures to encourage the development of combined transport (and in particular road-rail transport, or 'piggyback transport' as it is sometimes called);

(b) to attempt to overcome distortions in respect of infrastructure charging by proposing that infrastructure costs should be borne specifically by Member States and that the railways, like the other modes, should pay compensation for the cost of using the infrastructure.

With road transport, the aim remains to improve and, ultimately, eliminate the system of capacity controls. The immediate objective is to increase the proportion of traffic moving under Community authorizations and to introduce a method for calculating long-term increases in the Community quota. These measures would be combined with the development of a compensation system for transit countries. Other measures include proposals for a new, permanent pricing system for international road haulage to replace the present interim arrangements and a series of measures to improve the efficiency of the road haulage industry. The Commission also expresses its intention to pursue its proposal for a first directive on the adjustment of national taxation systems for commercial vehicles.

The main problem facing the inland waterways is structural over-capacity. The Commission proposes to harmonize and improve national scrapping schemes and to take steps to encourage the implementation by the Community of the Supplementary Protocol to the Mannheim Convention defining the access conditions to the Rhine Basin for non-EEC, non-riparian operators.

On infrastructure, the Commission will submit further proposals for the creation of a Community system for allocating the costs of using infrastructure and will maintain its objective of helping to finance projects of Community interest.

With international transport policy the Commission will concentrate on extending its policies to neighbouring countries and on the role it can play in the ECE, the ECMT and the CCR.

The Commission also proposes to the Council a resolution on the implementation of this programme in stages whereby the Council would agree in principle to take decisions on a series of measures based on the policies set out in the programme. At the same time the Commission would undertake to present similar programmes for the sea and air transport sectors. While awaiting the outcome of the case before the Court, the Commission emphasizes that this new programme is not at odds with the action brought by Parliament for the Council's failure to act, but rather that the two moves are in fact complementary.

It recognizes that no proper common transport policy has been implemented and holds the Council primarily responsible, although it does admit that some tangible progress has been made as a result of the adoption of 170 Community measures in the transport sector. With regard to the Council's conduct, the Commission states in its document: 'The objective of a Community transport policy and market to be achieved within the deadline provided for in Article 75(2) of the Treaty, or at least before the end of the transitional period was not met and regrettably has not even been achieved to date. The Commission repeatedly invited the Community institutions to discuss its ideas and proposals for the formulation and implementation of a coherent Community transport policy. But ... no substantial dialogue was held with the Council, while the European Parliament and the Economic and Social Committee discussed and basically supported the Commission's transport policy concept.'[1]

Subsequently, the Commission published two detailed and important political documents on progress towards the development of a common transport policy which we shall examine in detail in Chapter 7. One was on air transport[2] and the other on maritime transport[3] and they are designed to supplement the document of February 1983 on inland transport. Taken together, these three documents fulfil Parliament's wish to see a global approach taken towards the common transport policy.

So much for the positions of the various institutions. It is now up to the judges of the Court of Justice to make a final ruling on the conduct of the Council of Ministers with regard to the common transport policy.

The future development of the common transport policy depends to a large extent on the judgment handed down by the Court and, of course, on the outcome of the 'European Union' proposal for institutional reform put forward in September 1983 by Altiero Spinelli. If this is adopted, it will introduce at

---

[1] Commission Communication of 11 February 1983, op. cit., p. 3 *et seq.*
[2] Communication and proposals by the Commission to the Council - Civil Aviation Memorandum No 2 - 'Progress towards the development of a Community air transport policy' (Doc. COM(84) 72 final of 15 March 1984).
[3] Communication and proposals by the Commission to the Council - 'Progress towards a common transport policy '- Maritime transport (Doc. COM(85) 90 final of 14 March 1985).

Community level the bicameral system usual in the Member States of the European Communities thus breaking the virtual monopoly on decision-making now held by the Council which, to make matters worse, is hamstrung by the ridiculous rule that its members - once six, then nine, now 10 and soon to be 12 - have to vote unanimously on matters concerning subjects like transport where there are often severely conflicting national interests.

Communication from the Commission to the Council of 11 February 1983

A. DRAFT PROGRAMME OF PROPOSALS TO BE PRESENTED IN THE FIELD OF INLAND TRANSPORT

NEW INITIATIVES

In 1983

More than one mode of transport

New approach to infrastructure costs for the three modes of inland transport (communication). Rational use of energy in transport; common measures enabling transport operations to be carried out between Member States in the event of oil rationing (in the context of the general programme relating to energy)

Combined transport.

Containers

(a) Examination of rates and tariff conditions

(b) Setting up of an international information centre

Promotion, with a view to the setting up of a piggyback company

Promotion (third stage), covering:

— Weights and dimensions

— Own account

— Charging system

— Sea and air

Investment

— System of rail links

— Transfer centres

Extension of action concerning facilitation relating to obstacles at frontiers with certain third countries (only if the Council adopts the proposal relating to obstacles at internal frontiers).

Railways

Financial balance of railway undertakings, State responsibility for rail infrastructure, and infrastructure charges to be paid by the railways.

Calculation of the marginal costs of using rail infrastructure.

Cooperation between the railways

(a) Removal of legal obstacles - the railways' status

(b) Removal of frontier obstacles arising from operating difficulties

(c) Rail infrastructure

Marshalling operations

High-speed international network

(d) Passengers

Joint marketing services

Harmonization of commercial tariff measures

Implementation of a charging system (TEV)

Package trips (Travel agencies)

Setting-up of a joint body for the coordination of activities

(e) Freight

Pool

Increase in speed

(f) Freight
Development of inter-network trains
Increase in the speed with which consignments are forwarded
(g) Freight
Intensification and diversification of whole-trainload services
Monitoring of trains
(h) Freight
Joint marketing services
Better information
International tariffs with common scales; delegation of powers
Revenue pools
Setting-up of a joint body for the coordination of activities
Harmonization of reduced fares for certain categories of passengers ('social tariffs')
Cooperation between the railways; determination by the Governments of the roles and tasks of the railways:
Split between commercial tasks and public service tasks
Concentration on profitable services
Sectoral responsibilities, etc.

Roads

Community quota; new method
Creation of Community authorizations for specific types of transport
Methods of compensation for transit transport by road
Better application of Regulations (EEC) No 543/69 and (EEC) No 1463/70
Admission of duty-free fuel
Admission of hired vehicles
Amendment of Regulation (EEC) No 543/69 (extension of working hours and spreadover)

Inland waterways

Transposition of the CCR Resolution into Community law and extension of the 'genuine link' system to inland waterway transport not covered by the Mannheim Convention
Calculation of the marginal costs of using inland waterway infrastructure
Access to the occupation of inland waterway carrier (professional competence)
Mutual recognition of diplomas, certificates and other evidence of formal qualifications for access to the occupation of inland waterway carrier
Harmonization of the Member States' programmes relating to the breaking-up of inland waterway vessels
Modernization in relation to north/south traffic
Freighting conditions in relation to north/south traffic (communication)
Amendment of the proposal concerning the harmonization of social conditions in the inland waterway sector

In the first half of 1984

More than one mode of transport

Accession to the ECMT
Summertime
Withdrawal and replacement of the proposal concerning public service obligations (Regulation (EEC) No 1191/69)
Revision of the Regulation on aids (EEC) No 1107/70 - restructuring aids)

Railways

Second programme of cooperation between the railways; joint purchasing and research

Roads

Driving licence (second stage - harmonization of classes/standards)
Technical amendment of the tachograph
Roadworthiness testing of private cars

Infrastructure

Financing of transport infrastructure projects

In the second half of 1984

More than one mode of transport

Transparency of infrastructure costs for the three modes of inland transport
Rational use of energy; other measures relating to energy-saving in each mode of transport
Standardization of the technical specifications for swap bodies

Roads

Creation of a multilingual form authorizing the transport of abnormal indivisible loads
Operating rules relating to passenger transport by road

Inland waterways

Accession to the Mannheim Convention (CCR)
Inland waterway infrastructure charges

Infrastructure

Financing of transport infrastructure projects
Master plan for infrastructure links of Community interest

B. DRAFT WORK PROGRAMME FOR THE PERIOD 1983 TO 1985[1]

First half of 1983

Programme of priorities for the period 1983 to 1985
Financial support
Cooperation between the railways
Passengers; commercial management, including pricing
Weights and dimensions
First Tax Directive
Duty-free fuel
Implementation of Additional Protocol No 2 to the Mannheim Convention ('genuine link')

Facilitation of formalities and inspections in respect of the carriage of goods between Member States

Infrastructure programme (on the basis of the Council's request of 10 June 1982)

Trial projects of Community interest (on the basis of the Council's request of 10 December 1981)

The conditions under which non-resident inland waterway carriers may operate transport services within a Member State

First half of 1984

Community quota (new method)

Creation of Community authorizations for specific types of transport

Methods of compensating for transit transport by road

Better application of Regulations (EEC) No 543/69 and (EEC) No 1463/70

Calculation of the marginal costs of using rail infrastructure

Financial balance of the railway undertakings, State responsibility for rail infrastructure, and infrastructure charges to be paid by the railways

Cooperation between the railways (points a-h of the proposals to be submitted in the first half of 1983)

Common action under Article 116 concerning the harmonization of social conditions in the inland waterway sector

Transposition of the CCR Resolution into Community law and extension of the 'genuine link' system to inland waterway transport operations not covered by the Mannheim Convention

Second half of 1984

Market observation

Extension of action concerning facilitation relating to obstacles at frontiers with certain third countries

Combined transport:
— promotion (third stage)
— containers
— investment

Access to the occupation of inland waterway carrier (professional competence)

Mutual recognition of diplomas, certificates and other evidence of formal qualifications for access to the occupation of inland waterway carrier

Harmonization of the Member States' programmes relating to the breaking-up of inland waterway vessels

Modernization in relation to north/south traffic

Freighting conditions in relation to north/south traffic

Amendment of the proposal concerning the harmonization of social conditions in the inland waterway sector (Regulation)

First half of 1985

Public service obligations (Regulation (EEC) No 1191/69); withdrawal and replacement of proposal

Accession to the ECMT

Summertime

Second programme of cooperation between the railways; joint purchasing and research

Driving licence (second stage - harmonization of classes/standards)

Amendment of Regulation (EEC) No 543/69 (extension of working hours and spreadover)

Second half of 1985

Creation of a multilingual form authorizing the transport of abnormal indivisible loads
Inland waterway infrastructure charges
Accession to the Mannheim Convention (CCR)
Transparency of infrastructure costs for the three modes of inland transport
Master plan for infrastructure links of Community interest

PART TWO

Organization and integration of the transport market

1. Transport rates and conditions

1.1 General principles

A necessary precondition for the adoption of a transport policy as provided for in Articles 3(e) and 74 of the Treaty establishing the EEC is the organization and integration of the transport market. By this is meant solving all problems connected with setting rates and determining conditions for transport services and with access to the market.

We have already seen how, apart from the specific provisions of Articles 79 and 80 of the Treaty, which relate respectively to discrimination and support tariffs, Article 75(1)(c) gives the Community institutions general powers to adopt any provisions they consider appropriate for the establishment of a common transport policy. The institutions are thus empowered to adopt provisions on the organization of the transport market in accordance with the procedures laid down in the Treaty.

Community action must therefore be confined to those measures which are necessary to achieve the objectives of the Treaty in this sphere, in other words measures relating to integration of the transport market and the safeguarding of competition within the Community transport market. These measures will obviously have to take account of the objectives the Community is also following with regard to social, regional and environmental policy. Neither should measures taken by Member States at national level be allowed to undermine achievement of the objectives set by the Treaty.

Measures taken at Community level may relate to international transport between Member States, national traffic within each Member State or international transport between Member States and non-Member States. Obviously, international transport is given priority over national traffic, the aim being ultimately to eliminate differences between the rules governing national transport and the rules governing transport within the Community. Naturally the adoption of any Community measure in this sector must correspond with the Treaty objectives.

With regard to transport rates and conditions, Article 78 of the Treaty makes a provision which constitutes a kind of safeguard clause for carriers. Although somewhat vague, the Article states the principle that account should be taken 'of the economic circumstances of carriers', thus circumscribing the powers of the authorities with regard to the adoption of measures affecting transport rates and conditions. This rule applies both to Member States and to Community institutions even though transport undertakings as such would not seem to be authorized to appeal to the Court of Justice against general measures which may affect their economic circumstances. Individual undertakings do, however, have the right provided for in the second paragraph of Article 173 of the Treaty to institute proceedings against the decisions referred to in Article 189 which apply to them and against measures which, although in the form of regulations or decisions which apply to other persons, will directly and individually affect them. The most logical and effective way of introducing a climate of healthy competition into the transport sector is to harmonize the rules and regulations which affect competition, although this alone will not be enough to bring about the organization and integration of the transport market. Thus, at least to begin with, these measures will have to be combined with intervention by the public authorities.

1.2 Action on transport rates and conditions

Action taken on transport rates and conditions in the context of the adoption of a common transport policy is designed essentially to prevent, on the one hand, the abuse of dominant positions on the market or in a substantial part of it, as referred to in Article 86 of the Treaty, and, on the other, the development of cut-throat competition, which can have a particularly disastrous effect on the smaller transport undertakings.

Action is directed at transport rates, i.e. the price paid by the user to the transport operator for a specific transport service. Unit price means, of course, the price per unit of goods carried and per distance. Rates are systematically established by the carrier beforehand and these rates together constitute a tariff.

Conditions of transport means all legal or contractual clauses which, in addition to the price, bind the transport operator or user. These can be prescribed by the authorities or can be agreed as part of normal commercial practice or may be specified by the transport operator.

It is obviously necessary to publish transport rates and conditions to some extent in order to guarantee transparency on the market, which is one of the basic means of providing the user with free choice and helping to maintain a climate of healthy competition.

There are two aspects to the problem of harmonizing tariffs within the Community: the structure of tariff systems and the level of actual prices.

1.2.1 *Action on tariffs within the framework of the ECSC*

We have already examined the special provisions of the Treaty establishing the ECSC concerning the carriage of coal and steel on overland routes, the limitation being that integration within the ECSC is restricted solely to coal and steel resources. We also briefly mentioned the efforts made by the High Authority towards achieving the objectives set out in Article 70 of the Treaty and in paragraph 10 of the Convention on the Transitional Provisions annexed to the

Treaty. In fact, by 1953 the High Authority had managed to eliminate the most flagrant cases of discrimination with regard to transport rates and conditions based on the country of origin or destination of products. It then went on to align the tariffs applicable to international transport on those applicable to transport within the Member States.

The ideal solution would have been to establish a single tariff throughout the Community so that all differentials would be standardized, but in practice this would have been unworkable because of the widely differing starting positions. This solution having been rejected, an inter-governmental agreement of 29 March 1955 established a system of through international tariffs for the carriage by rail of coal and steel and other ECSC products, which at least had a standard price structure in that rates decreased as a function of total distance.[1]

This had the effect of eliminating the need for the split tariffs which had been in force previously whereby each national network insisted on working out a new set of rates all over again at its own frontier. No longer having to pay split tariffs was obviously more of an advantage for the users of rail services than for the railway undertakings. These tariffs were later adjusted and, following agreements with Switzerland and Austria, extended to include transit traffic passing through these two countries. They were subsequently extended to include the new Member States. As regards the application of special internal rates and conditions in the interests of one or more coal- or steel-producing undertakings, the fourth paragraph of Article 70 of the ECSC Treaty states that this shall require the prior agreement of the High Authority, which may only authorize their application if they are designed to overcome temporary or exceptional difficulties. In any case, so far the High Authority has made very circumspect use of this facility. After the cases brought before the Court of Justice, it is now possible to rely on the Court's judgments in order to determine the lawfulness of special rates and conditions under the Treaty, i.e. only if the protective rates 'enable the undertakings in whose favour they are made to overcome exceptional temporary difficulties resulting from unforeseeable circumstances which are likely to result in a situation in which the composition of production costs no longer corresponds to their (i.e. the undertakings') natural (operating) conditions'.[2]

As for freight rates on inland waterways, one major obstacle to action by the High Authority on tariffs has always been the Rhine navigation system set up by the Mannheim Convention, to which we have already referred. In actual fact, on 9 June 1957, the High Authority did persuade the Member States to agree to sign the Petersberg Agreement, which was designed to eliminate existing tariff disparities under the Rhine system. The aim of the Agreement was actually

---

[1] For fuller information on the problem of harmonizing transport rates within the ECSC, which we deal with here only briefly, reference should be made to F. Santoro, op. cit., pp. 93-107 and 127-144.

[2] Cases 3/58 to 18/58, Case 25/58 and Case 26/58 *Barbara-Erzbergbau AG and 17 other applicants* v *High Authority*; Case 19/58 *Federal Republic of Germany* v *High Authority;* Case 27/58, 28/58 and 29/58 *Givors* v *High Authority* [1960] ECR 369, 469 and 503.

to provide a compromise solution taking into account the provisions governing Rhine navigation. The idea was to bring about cooperation between the authorities in the Member States and the High Authority to make it possible first of all to take a fuller and more accurate view of the whole situation regarding freight rates in Rhine navigation. The next stage was for the High Authority, in cooperation with the professional organizations concerned, to specify the freight rates which would apply to international traffic between Member States. As it turned out, because of specific national objections, this Agreement never came into force and the transport undertakings operating on the Rhine never actually informed the High Authority of the tariffs they were applying.

More generally, with regard to the harmonization of tariffs referred to in point 3 of the third paragraph of Article 10 of the Convention on the Transitional Provisions, the measures taken by the High Authority ran up against serious obstacles relating primarily to the publication of transport rates required to guarantee the necessary market transparency. Although Article 60 states that coal and steel products must be sold under conditions of fair competition by making public the price lists and conditions of sale applied by undertakings within the common market, the third paragraph of Article 70 states that, in addition, the scales, rates and all other tariff rules of every kind applied to the carriage of coal and steel within each Member State and between Member States shall be published or brought to the knowledge of the High Authority. However, for the purposes of safeguarding conditions of healthy competition, the problem of publishing transport rates would not be too important if ECSC products were sold 'free at place of origin'. But often in line with standard commercial practice, sales prices are set 'free at place of destination' so that it is essential to know the transport cost in order to establish equivalent prices for products delivered to the various destinations. In fact it would be easy to get round the provisions of Article 60, which are specifically designed to guarantee proper transparency on the coal and steel market, by 'manipulating' freight rates and this would obviously have important repercussions in the case of products for which transport costs represent as much as 35% of the final price. Hence the need to publish tariffs.

One particular requirement with regard to the publication of transport rates is that they should be governed solely by economic criteria. The Court of Justice has established basic principles in this connection and has ruled that the High Authority has specific rights with regard to the publication of transport rates and conditions, although these rights are limited and may be exercised only in the form of a recommendation.[1] In practice, however, the High Authority has always reacted against any refusal by Member States or the economic interests concerned to agree to the proper publication of transport rates and conditions in respect of products covered by the ECSC Treaty.

---

[1] Case 20/59 *Italian Republic* v *High Authority* [1960] ECR 669 and Case 9/61 *Netherlands* v *High Authority* [1962] ECR 419.

1.2.2 *Action on tariffs within the framework of the EEC*

1.2.2.1 **Abolishing discrimination in respect of transport rates**

Article 79 of the EEC Treaty applies to the transport sector the general principle set out in Article 7 prohibiting any discrimination on grounds of nationality. Article 79 is particularly concerned with discrimination on grounds of the country of origin or of destination of the goods in question, in other words their 'nationality'. The Article prohibits such discrimination 'in the case of transport within the Community' and thus applies both to transport within the Member States and to transport within the Community. The types of discrimination with which Article 79 is concerned may be the most obvious but they are certainly not the most important in terms of standard commercial practice. However, in accordance with the provisions of the first and third paragraphs of Article 79, the Council adopted, within the specified deadline, on 27 June 1960, the above-mentioned Regulation No 11/60 on the abolition of discrimination in transport rates and conditions.[1]

Even though, for the reasons we have already explained, the scope of this Regulation was bound to be somewhat limited since it concerned the abolition (by the end of the second stage of the transitional period) of forms of discrimination which were not particularly widespread, it was nevertheless interesting to see that the Commission was granted specific powers of supervision and enforcement. Regulation No 11/60 is not logically applicable to transport on own account, although it does cover the activities of forwarding agents and other intermediaries since discrimination of the kind covered by the Regulation may result from their actions.

To begin with, the Regulation was not applied to Rhine navigation by those Member States which belonged both to the EEC and to the Central Commission for the Navigation of the Rhine. The Netherlands was the first country to adopt this approach, to be followed by Belgium, France and the Federal Republic of Germany.

It was only after the Commission in 1969 commenced the procedure for infringement provided for in Article 169 of the Treaty against the above-mentioned States that first Belgium and then the other Member States declared in 1970 that they would apply Regulation No 11/60 to Rhine navigation. In fact, implementation of this Regulation led to the abolition of some 200 cases of tariff discrimination.

However, in view of the limited occurrence in practice of the discrimination on grounds of the nationality of the goods transported referred to in Article 79(1)

---

[1] OJ 52, 16.8.1960, p. 1121.

which Regulation 11/60 was designed to eliminate, paragraph 2 of the same Article rightly states that the Council may adopt other measures in pursuance of Article 75(1)(c) for the purposes of establishing a common transport policy, thus assigning general powers to the Community institutions.

Instead of putting forward a proposal for a regulation to abolish the other major cases of discrimination, the Commission preferred to introduce in 1964 'common action' with Member States, investigating some 650 tariffs to decide whether they were discriminatory. On their own initiative, the Member States and transport undertakings then amended or abolished some 250 discriminatory tariffs which had applied to transport within a Member State or to its export or transit traffic. In addition, the tariffs which the Commission considered to be discriminatory were also gradually amended or abolished.

All in all, therefore, the provisions of Article 79(2) have been complied with even though some criticism has been levelled against the pragmatic approach taken by the Commission, in particular by the European Parliament. Nevertheless the Commission's measures did comply with the Article as worded, which seems to suggest a non-binding procedure.

It is also worth pointing out that when the Commission submitted a proposal for a regulation, based on Article 79(2), on the abolition of discrimination other than that referred to in paragraph 1, the proposal, which was submitted as long ago as 24 October 1965, got stuck in the Council and has still not been adopted.

1.2.2.2 Prohibition of support tariffs

Pursuant to Article 80 of the Treaty, support tariffs were prohibited, as already described,[1] with effect from 1 January 1962 for the six original Member States, from 1 January 1973 for Denmark, Ireland and the United Kingdom and from 1 January 1981 for Greece. According to the Court of Justice, the Commission has considerable powers of discretion in this field, not only over which tariffs to authorize but also over how to authorize them within the framework of the EEC Treaty.[2] In the past, however, and more particularly before the merger of the executives of the three Communities, the Court ruled that the High Authority was not authorized under the ECSC Treaty to take account of regional policy requirements in order to authorize support tariffs until the Community had its own regional policy.[3] This interpretation no longer applies since in July 1967 a single Commission took over the powers of the High Authority within the framework of a Community which has put the implementation of a regional policy high on its list of priorities. Basically, it is true to say that the Commission has achieved the application of the provisions of Article 80 firmly and impartially, but with due caution. Many of the cases it has had to handle related

---

[1] See above, pp. 45-46.
[2] Court of Justice, 9 July 1969, 1/69, ECR 1969.
[3] *Idem,* 10 May 1980, 27-28-29/58, ECR 1960, p. 503.

to tariffs in Italy (Sardinia and the Mezzogiorno), France (Brittany and Corsica) and Germany (the tariffs applied by the Federal German railways for the Zonenrandgebiete, i.e. the areas along its Eastern border).[1]

1.2.2.3 Introduction of general rules on transport rates and conditions

Whereas the objectives of Articles 79 and 80 of the Treaty were achieved without too much difficulty, the Commission's proposals on the introduction of general rules on tariffs for the three modes of inland transport met with the firm opposition of the Member States.

Legally, the Commission was acting within its powers under Article 75(1)(c). The idea, therefore, was to reach agreement on an economically viable set of rules compatible with the objectives of the Treaty and taking into account the distinctive features of the various modes of transport. Politically, the system then had to meet with the approval of the Member States and since these were 'provisions concerning the principles of the regulatory system for transport', according to Article 75(3) this approval had to be unanimous, even after the second stage.

As early as 10 April 1961, in its Memorandum, the Commission had emphasized that the existence of very dissimilar tariff systems in the Member States constituted a major obstacle to the establishment of a common market in transport, particularly at international level. On 20 May 1963, therefore, it proposed that the Council apply a general system of bracket tariffs to the three modes of inland transport mentioned in the *lex specialis* on transport.

By bracket tariffs, the Commission meant a system whereby prices would have to be set between pre-established maximum and minimum limits. The upper limit was designed to prevent the abuse of dominant positions and the lower limit to prevent cut-throat competition. Prices could be set freely between these two limits in accordance with supply and demand. Thus only the upper and lower limits of the tariff scale would then have to be published.

The bracket tariff system was basically an act of faith in the principle of competition tempered by considerations regarding the special nature of the transport sector, particularly the carriage of goods. In itself it was not particularly revolutionary since the principle of bracket tariffs was not a new

---

[1] With regard to competitive rates which are not prohibited by Article 80, and in particular to potential competitive rates which were the reason for the controversy between the Commission and the German Government over the 'als-ob Tariffe' applied by the *Deutsche Bundesbahn* because of the potentially competitive effect of the proposed Sarre-Palatinate canal, see *La politique commune des transports de la CEE de janvier 1967 à fin mars 1968*, Studiecentrum voor de Expansie van Antwerpen, Antwerp, April 1968, p. 40.

one.[1] In France it already applied to road and rail transport, in the Federal Republic of Germany to short-distance road transport and in the Benelux to road transport between the three countries of the Union. Nevertheless, the Council found it impossible to reach a unanimous decision. The point at issue was not so much the principle of bracket tariffs as such, but rather the plan to apply them to all three modes of inland transport. Accordingly the Dutch Government refused to apply the system to the Rhine navigation in view of the country's obvious interest in maintaining a totally liberal approach to transport at Community level.

The reason the proposed system provoked such conflicting reactions was that it was essentially a compromise solution to satisfy both those who maintained that market forces should be left to determine how transport was organized and those who felt that some intervention was required. The road transport sector welcomed the proposed new tariff system and saw it as a way of moving beyond the continual state of crisis facing the industry. The railways too saw the general application of bracket tariffs as a way of obtaining some room for manoeuvre on prices in countries, like Italy, where there was very little play. They also felt it would help to limit excessively fierce competition from other modes of transport. However, all parties concerned with Rhine navigation were strongly opposed to a compulsory bracket tariff system, and in particular the Dutch Government and the Dutch railways, who had always been opposed to any form of price control.

As has been pointed out, it was only as a result of the Council agreement of 22 June 1965 on organization of the transport market that it was possible to reach a unanimous decision on tariffs by combining compulsory bracket tariffs with a system of reference tariffs. To this end the Commission subsequently forwarded a proposal for a regulation to the Council in October 1965 which, in view of the difficulties encountered with the proposed bracket tariff system, was designed, by way of amendment, to set up a system of reference tariffs for certain types of transport alongside the compulsory bracket tariff system. The system of reference tariffs is defined as a 'system of agreed bracket tariffs which are published but not obligatory'. Moreover, under certain conditions, it would have been possible to sign special contracts fixing rates outside the bracket tariff limits in accordance with the derogation already referred to in the 1962 action programme. The reference tariffs would thus act solely as guidelines, and transport operators would remain free to fix rates outside these limits.

Whereas the compulsory bracket tariff system required the publication of the upper and lower tariff limits and of any special contracts signed outside the compulsory bracket tariffs, under the reference tariff system it would have been compulsory to publish rates set outside the official tariff, the aim again being to ensure that services to which it was applied would operate economically.

---

[1] For further information on the whole subject of the bracket tariff system the reader is once again referred to F. Santoro, op. cit., pp. 148-158.

The proposal for a regulation also allowed Member States to take temporary safeguard measures to avoid serious and persistent difficulties in the transport sector, or in the event of difficulties which might affect the economic stability of a country. Provision was also made for the setting up of an advisory committee, consisting of government experts and chaired by the Commission, with the task of monitoring the market. The proposed system was to be set up gradually in three stages, and would ultimately result in the virtually complete liberalization of tariff arrangements through the step-by-step application of the Community tariff system, first to international transport and later to internal transport, through the adoption of the bracket tariff system and the reference tariff system and their application respectively to rail and road transport and inland waterway transport.

However, as a result of the institutional problems which arose in connection with the implementation of the CAP, but also because of the Council's perpetual inertia, the proposal in question met with only partial and extremely tardy success. It finally became Regulation (EEC) No 1174/68 of the Council of 30 July 1968 on the introduction - on an experimental basis incidentally - of a system of bracket tariffs for the carriage of goods by road between Member States.[1]

This Regulation was a long way from the Commission proposal since the system adopted applied only to the international carriage of goods by road, the sector where action was most urgently required, and paid no regard to the other modes of transport or to inland transport in general. The bracket spread was set at 23% of the maximum rate. Special contracts were allowed if the tonnage carried under such contracts was not less than 500 tonnes within any three-month period. Tariffs were to be agreed between the Member States directly concerned. The Commission would arbitrate in case of disagreement although appeals could be made to the Council.

The Regulation came into force only in 1971. The weak point of the whole tariff system was the fact that governments continued to exercise control and that the only penalties provided for were at national level.

The Regulation was originally adopted on an experimental basis for one year up to 31 December 1971 but its period of application was extended each year until 31 December 1977.[2]

After this date, the Regulation was replaced by Council Regulation (EEC) No 2831/77 of 12 December 1977 *on the fixing of rates for the carriage of goods by road between Member States*[3] which, for an experimental period - up to 31 December 1983 - establishes a system of reference tariffs for the carriage

---

[1] OJ L 194, 6.8.1968, p. 1.
[2] The Regulation was last extended by Council Regulation (EEC) No 3181/76 of 21 December 1976 (OJ L 359, 30.12.1976).
[3] OJ L 334, 24.12.1977, pp. 22-27.

carriage of goods by road as an alternative to the previous system of compulsory bracket tariffs, which had never been applied in Denmark, Ireland or the United Kingdom.

Article 2 of this Regulation allows Member States to replace the system of compulsory bracket tariffs which applies to the carriage of goods by road with reference tariffs or to introduce reference tariffs where no Community tariff rules previously applied. The idea was to provide a choice so as to bring about the gradual liberalization of transport rates on the international market in the carriage of goods by road. It gave rise to much controversy and was criticized by those who considered - and still consider - that a climate of competition is not particularly appropriate on the road haulage market. With regard to whether reference tariffs guarantee healthy competition on the international road haulage market, the Commission also published an interesting study on the three modes of inland transport.[1]

At the end of the period of application of Regulation (EEC) No 2831/77, the Council adopted Regulation (EEC) No 3568/83 of 1 December 1983 on the fixing of rates for the carriage of goods by road between Member States which confirms the system of reference tariffs but leaves Member States free to agree mutually, taking account of the economic and technical circumstances in the transport markets concerned, to introduce compulsory tariffs with a bracket spread from 15% below to 15% above the base rate instead of reference tariffs.[2] The Regulation came into force on 1 January 1984 and applies until 31 December 1988.

In support of the new trend towards deregulation of transport rates which began in 1977, it can be argued that in any case the original system of compulsory rates never had a significant effect on the fixing of rates for the international carriage of goods by road since in practice, unlike national transport rates, international rates are determined by market conditions.

---

[1] See R. Willeke, H. Baum and W. Hoewer, *References tariffs for goods transport*, Studies Collection, Transport Series No 6, Luxembourg, 1982.
[2] OJ L 359, 22.12.1983, p. 1.

2. Controlling the supply of transport services

2.1 Access to the market

There are two sides to the problem of access to the transport market. On the one hand, the Community guarantees freedom of establishment and freedom to provide services in the transport sector, principally by eliminating all forms of discrimination on grounds of nationality. On the other, at national level transport rates have been prevented from fulfilling their role as price regulators because supply and demand in respect of transport services are relatively rigid. Certain rules have had to be applied to the three inland transport modes concerning admission to the occupation of road transport operator and the supply of transport services.

2.1.1. *Right of establishment and freedom to provide services*

Article 3(c) of the EEC Treaty states as a principle the abolition, as between Member States, of obstacles to freedom of movement for persons, services and capital. Point (e) of the same Article lists the adoption of a common policy in the sphere of transport as a Community objective. Hence under the common transport policy, obstacles to the free movement of persons and services within the transport sector must be abolished. Moreover, Article 61(1) states that freedom to provide services in the field of transport shall be governed by the provisions of the Title relating to transport.

2.1.1.1 Abolishing restrictions on the freedom of establishment

The right of establishment is covered by the provisions of Articles 52 to 58 in Chapter 2 of Title III of the Treaty entitled 'Free movement of persons, services and capital'. According to Article 52 restrictions on the freedom of establishment should have been abolished during the transitional period. However, the elimination of discrimination on grounds of nationality is not enough to guarantee proper freedom of establishment since, again according to Article 52, this freedom of establishment shall include the right of nationals of a Member State established in the territory of another Member State to take up and pursue activities as self-employed persons under the conditions laid down for its own nationals by the law of the country where such establishment is effected. To this end, Article 57 provides for the mutual recognition of diplomas, certificates and other evidence of formal qualifications.

The fourth title of the general programme for the abolition of restrictions on freedom of establishment adopted by the Council on 18 December 1961 in accordance with the provisions of Article 54 of the Treaty concentrates on the transport sector, taking special account of the considerable uncertainty surrounding the application to transport of regulations not included in the *lex specialis*.

The programme included measures to abolish restrictions on freedom of establishment and measures to coordinate rules on taking up and pursuing the occupation of road transport operator for the different modes to be taken during the first two years of the third stage of the transitional period, in other words between 1 January 1966 and 31 December 1967.

In 1970 the Commission, on the basis of Article 54 of the Treaty, presented the Council with proposals for directives to abolish restrictions on freedom of establishment in two sectors, the carriage of goods by road and the carriage of goods and passengers by inland waterway. In addition there were proposals for regulations on coordination designed to abolish restrictions on freedom of establishment as referred to in Article 57. These measures concerned in particular the mutual recognition of national diplomas and certificates and the rules on admission to the occupation, i.e. the conditions to be met individually by road transport operators and the rules in force on the different transport markets governing their activities.

However, as none of these measures were adopted by the Council, the only positive effects with regard to the abolition of restrictions on freedom of establishment came from the above-mentioned judgment handed down by the Court of Justice on 21 June 1974, which stated that after the end of the transitional period the provisions of Article 52 were directly applicable in the Member States.[1] However this was a solution only to the problem of the right of establishment and did nothing about the lack of any regulations for implementing the provisions of Article 57 in order to make it easier to take up and pursue these occupations.

It was not until 1974 that the Council adopted the first measures proposed by the Commission to abolish restrictions on freedom of establishment. These were Council Directive 74/561/EEC of 12 November 1974 on admission to the occupation of road haulage operator in national and international transport operations[2] and Council Directive 74/562/EEC of 12 November 1974 on admission to the occupation of road passenger transport operator in national and international transport operations.[3]

These Directives specify the conditions to be met by those who wish to be admitted to these occupations and the qualifications they will require. They must be of good repute and of appropriate financial standing, and must possess

---

[1] Case 2/74 *Reyners* v *Belgian State* [1974] ECR 631.
[2] OJ L 308, 19.11.1974, p. 18.
[3] *Idem*, p. 23.

the requisite professional competence. The communication which the Commission forwarded to the Council on 1 October 1975[1] included a proposal for a similar directive to establish rules on admission to the occupation of carrier of goods or of passengers by waterway in national and international transport[2] and a second directive, based on Article 57, aiming at the mutual recognition of diplomas, certificates and other evidence of formal qualifications for road or waterway passenger transport and goods haulage operators, including measures intended to encourage these operators effectively to exercise their right to freedom of establishment.[3]

More recently, on 7 December 1983, the Commission sent the Council a proposal for a Council Directive on access to the occupation of carrier of goods by waterway in national and international transport and on the mutual recognition of diplomas, certificates and other evidence of formal qualifications for this occupation.[4] The aim of the proposal was to increase the qualifications of carriers as a way of improving the market and the quality of the services provided.

It is quite obvious, however, that in the inland waterway transport sector the Community has made no progress whatsoever - let alone in connection with the right of establishment - over the last five years. The only piece of legislation of any significance, as rightly observed by Parliament,[5] was the Directive of 4 October 1982 laying down technical requirements for inland waterway vessels.[6]

Still with the Council is an important new proposal for a directive on the conditions under which non-resident carriers may operate certain national transport services within a Member State,[7] which the Commission put before the Council on 16 December 1982. This has already met with the basic approval of the Economic and Social Committee[8] and the European Parliament.[9]

Finally, the right of establishment of freight forwarders is covered by the provisions of Title IV.

---

[1] Doc. COM(75) 490 final.
[2] OJ C 1, 5.1.1976.
[3] *Idem.*
[4] COM(83) 720 final, OJ C 351, 24.12.1983, p. 5.
[5] European Parliament, proposal for a resolution under Article 47 of the Regulation on Community measures concerning inland waterway transport, Doc. 1-263/83 of 4 May 1983.
[6] Council Directive 82/714/EEC (OJ L 301, 28.10.1982).
[7] OJ C 18, 22.1.1983, p. 3.
[8] OJ C 211, 8.8.1983, p. 37.
[9] OJ C 307, 14.11.1983, p. 135.

2.1.1.2 Abolishing restrictions on the freedom to provide services

For road transport the freedom to provide services is governed by Article 61 of the Treaty and for Rhine navigation by the Mannheim Convention. For transport on the other inland waterways in France and Germany, this freedom has not yet been established.

Subparagraph (a) of Article 75(1) specifies that common rules shall be laid down for international transport to or from the territory of a Member State or passing across the territory of one or more Member States; subparagraph (b) stipulates that the conditions under which non-resident carriers may operate transport services within a Member State shall also be specified.

So far, the only Commission proposals adopted by the Council concerning the freedom to provide transport services relate to the carriage of passengers or goods by road. These are examined below.

2.1.1.3 Regulations on passenger transport services

Since the Member States of the Community already had national regulations covering these services and since a set of international regulations had already been adopted within the ECE, the Community's task was relatively easy. The rules on passenger transport laid down by the Community include a number of regulations on international services but do not cover national services, as might reasonably be expected in the goods transport sector.

Community regulations on passenger transport are more limited in scope than the regulations on goods transport because passenger services usually meet a direct need and therefore have less impact on the establishment of the common market than does goods transport, and hence there is less need to standardize rules on competition between different transport undertakings at Community level.

Listed below are the relevant regulations adopted to date.

Regulation No 117/66/EEC of the Council of 28 July 1966 on the introduction of common rules for the international carriage of passengers by coach and bus[1] *(and implementing Regulation No 1016/68 of the Commission of 9 July 1968*[2]*)*

The rules contained in this Regulation are based on the principle, which is commonly followed in the sector, of a specific authorization for each regular service, i.e. it has to be approved by the Member States concerned. In the case

---

[1] OJ 147, 9.8.1966.
[2] OJ L 173, 22.7.1968.

of 'occasional' services, only the Member State where the vehicle is registered has to authorize the service.

Regulation (EEC) No 516/72 of the Council of 28 February 1972 on the intro-duction of common rules for shuttle services by coach and bus between Member States.[1]

This Regulation - which is certainly not one of the most important - contains detailed rules on international shuttle services. Shuttle services are 'services whereby, by means of repeated outward and return journeys, previously formed groups of passengers are carried from a single place of departure to a single destination'.

Regulation (EEC) No 517/72 of the Council of 28 February 1972 on the intro-duction of common rules for regular and special regular services by coach and bus between Member States

This Regulation supplements the rules on scheduled passenger transport between Member States.[2]

2.2 Controlling the supply of road and inland waterway goods services

As we have already pointed out, the Member States found spontaneous adjustment in inland transport very difficult because of the considerable rigidity of supply and demand in respect of transport services, which would make it somewhat difficult for prices effectively to fulfil their function as market regulators. This consideration was of particular importance as regards the carriage of goods by road, since the vast majority of such transport undertakings were very small. Therefore, the Commission's activities - based as always on principles of fair competition - have been directed towards creating a climate of healthy competition between transport undertakings, in particular by means of regulations to prevent the emergence of cut-throat competition on markets where there is a structural supply surplus.

Community action to regulate the haulage market has concentrated both on the conditions which road hauliers must meet to be admitted to the occupation and on those areas of activity which come under the heading of 'market diversity'. As we have seen, the Community has also been active on transport rates (compulsory bracket tariffs and reference tariffs) precisely in order to prevent abuse of dominant positions and, at the other end of the scale, cut-throat competition. After examining the Community's action on transport rates and

---

[1] OJ L 67, 20.3.1972.
[2] *Idem.* Later amended by Council Regulation (EEC) No 3022/77 of 20 December 1977 (OJ L 358, 31.12.1977).

access to the market - right of establishment and freedom to provide services - we should now look at how capacity, i.e. the supply of transport services, is controlled.

In fact, all Member States have rules on access to the transport market governing the number of undertakings and their sizes. Railway undertakings normally operate under concession and in many cases have a monopoly.

Road transport services, on the other hand, have to be authorized by the Member State in advance in order to adjust supply to demand and thus avoid surplus capacity. The position obviously varies according to whether these services are on own account or for hire or reward. At international level the quotas governing supply of services are determined by bilateral agreements, while the Benelux countries have an arrangement whereby all traffic within the area is quota-free. The inland waterways have a system of licences or permits, with special arrangements for the Rhine navigation system under the Mannheim Convention, which provides for free movement throughout the system for holders of licences issued by any Member State of the CCR.

2.2.1 *Controlling capacity in the road haulage sector*

2.2.1.1 **Bilateral agreements and Community quotas**

As regards the road haulage sector within the Community, the common transport policy is concerned primarily with bilateral quotas, since the regulations which apply in the Member States are actually intended to authorize transport services within the limits set by agreements signed from time to time between two and sometimes more countries (bilateral or multilateral agreements). Under these agreements quotas are established for road haulage from the outset. However the Community was faced with a dilemma: for the reasons given above it was impossible to deregulate international traffic completely because of past experience and the policies adopted by the majority of the Member States: but it was also impossible to allow the bilateral quota system to continue since it severely restricted the development of the road haulage market. This in turn constituted an obstacle to the free movement of services, a Treaty objective.

It was therefore decided at Community level that even if, while taking into account the distinctive features of road transport, it was not possible to abolish bilateral quotas at a stroke - in fact for a transitional period at least they would have to be maintained - it was nevertheless essential gradually to take the tonnage quota system under the Community's wing. Thus in 1963 the Commission put a proposal to the Council for a regulation to establish, alongside the bilateral and multilateral quotas which would be kept to a reasonable level, a system of Community quotas for the carriage of goods by road within the Community for hire or reward. This quota would gradually be increased to replace the existing bilateral and multilateral quotas and would eventually become the general instrument for regulating the number of road vehicles used within the Community. Personal non-transferable Community licences would be granted to authorize the free movement of vehicles - laden or unladen - on the whole Community road network without restrictions on journeys, loads or activities.[1] The Commission proposal led in 1968 to the Council adopting Regulation (EEC) No 1018/68 on the establishment of a Community quota for the carriage of goods by road between Member States.[2] In adopting this Regulation the Council radically departed from the Commission's original proposal by making the Community quota system merely experimental and not a system designed gradually to replace bilateral quotas. This was because the Council considered it essential to balance the introduction of tariff measures to control freight services with deregulation of the tonnage quota on the supply of services. However, even though to some extent emasculated, the Community quota system was still an important step towards establishing the freedom to provide services in the international road haulage sector, except that the system was not to apply to transport services operated exclusively within the Member States, thus creating a dangerous discrepancy between the national and international markets.

Quotas are fixed each year by the Council according to the requirements of each Member State and they are adjusted to actual needs on the road transport market. The 1968 Regulation - which was to apply for three years - established an initial quota of 1 200 authorizations in all and covered only those services operated by professional carriers (for hire or reward). It did not apply to services provided within an individual Member State. Moreover, if Community authorizations were under-used or used solely for bilateral operations, they could be withdrawn; in fact, account was to be taken of the use made of previous authorizations when deciding on a new Community quota. The Community quota system was subsequently continued and extended by a series of measures which did take account of the actual use made of authorizations granted in the past.

The Regulations in question were: Commission Regulation (EEC) No 1224/68 of 9 August 1968 implementing Council Regulation No 1018/68; the Commission recommendation to Member States of 9 June 1969 concerning implementation of Article 6 of Regulation No 1018/68 and Article 5 of Commission Regulation No 1224/68; Council Regulation (EEC) No 2829/72 of 28 December 1972 on the Community quota for the carriage of goods by road between Member States; Council Regulation (EEC) No 2063/74 of 1 August 1974 amending Regulation No 2829/72; Regulation (EEC) No 3256/74 of 19 December 1974 extending and amending the Community quota system; Council Regulation (EEC) No 3331/75 of 18 December 1975 extending the period of validity of Regulation No 2829/72; Council Regulation

---

[1] On the problem of controlling the supply of road haulage services see F. Santoro, op. cit., pp. 205-227.
[2] OJ L 175, 23.7.1968, p. 13.

1976; Council Regulation (EEC) No 3024/77 of 21 December 1977; Council Regulation (EEC) No 3062/78 of 19 December 1978; Council Regulations (EEC) Nos 2963/79 and 2964/79 of 20 December 1979; Council Regulation (EEC) No 305/81 of 20 January 1981 amending Regulation (EEC) No 3164/76; Council Regulation (EEC) No 663/82 of 22 March 1982 amending Regulation No 3164/76; Council Regulation (EEC) No 3515/82 of 21 December 1982 amending Regulation (EEC) No 3164/76 and Regulation (EEC) No 2964/79 which came into force on 1 January 1983.

The following table shows how the distribution of the Community quota changed over the period until 1 January 1983.

	Reg. (EEC) No 1018/68	Reg. (EEC) No 2829/72	Reg. (EEC) No 3256/74	Reg. (EEC) No 3024/77	Reg. (EEC) No 2963/79	Reg. (EEC) No 633/82
	(a)	(b)	(c)	(d)	(e)	(f)
	1969/72	31.12.1973	1975	1978	1980	1982
B	161	191	265	318	413	433
DK	—	68	169	203	286	305
D	286	321	427	512	689	727
GR	—	—	—	—	—	88
F	286	313	409	491	627	656
IRL	—	23	50	60	76	88
I	194	230	319	383	539	567
LUX	33	45	70	84	106	111
NL	240	279	382	458	597	626
UK	—	114	272	326	418	436
Total authorized	1 200	1 584	2 363	2 835	3 751	4 038

(a) OJ L 175, 23.7.1978
(b) OJ L 298, 31.12.1972. The above-mentioned increase was put at 15% for 1973 and 1974.
(c) OJ L 349, 28.12.1974. The number and allocations of authorizations provided for in this Regulation remained unchanged until 31 December 1977 (see Regulation (EEC) No 3164/76 of 16.12.1976, OJ L 357, 29.12.1976).
(d) OJ L 358, 31.12.1977.
(e) OJ L 336, 29.12.1979.
(f) OJ L 78, 24.3.1982. A 15% increase in the quota of Community authorizations for Greece and Ireland and a 5% increase for the other Member States.

The Community quota system still applies only to a very small proportion - approximately 5% - of all road haulage traffic.

On 15 June 1983, in an attempt to bring about a substantial increase in the Community quota, the Commission sent the Council a proposal for a regulation to the effect that each year for five years the Community quota would be increased by five times the rate of increase in the road haulage traffic between Member States 'in the latest year for which adequate statistics are available' whereas a reduction in road haulage traffic between Member States would not affect the Community quota. Under the proposal, if the Council decides to postpone the proposed extension of the Community quota system until 1 January 1992, each year during a transitional period the Community quota would be increased by 10 times the rate of increase in road haulage traffic between Member States.[1] On 26 October 1983 the ESC voted broadly in favour of this proposal.

2.2.1.2 Deregulation of the carriage of certain goods by road and harmonization of bilateral quotas

In addition to the introduction of the Community quota system, it is worth mentioning a number of measures which have helped to deregulate approximately 35% of all goods traffic carried by road between Member States by exempting certain types of carriage of goods by road from authorization or quota,[2] and by establishing common rules for the fixing of bilateral quotas.[3]

However, although these measures did to some extent help to improve competition and the operation of the international road haulage market, they had virtually no effect on national traffic. Commercial road transport operations continue to be governed to a large extent by bilateral quotas whereas the whole 'cabotage' market is still monopolized by national hauliers.[4]

2.2.2 *Controlling inland waterway capacity*

Over-capacity is one of the basic problems in inland waterway transport. This is an important sector within the Community but one which faces economic difficulties and is hampered by the constraints placed upon it by the Rhine navigation system, which affects attempts at improvement.

---

[1] Proposal for a Council Regulation (EEC) amending Regulation (EEC) No 3164/76 on the Community quota for the carriage of goods by road between Member States (submitted to the Council by the Commission on 15 June 1983) (OJ C 179, 6.7.1983, p. 6).

[2] These include cross-frontier transport operations (for hire or reward) in a zone extending 25 km on either side of the border as the crow flies, transport operations between one Member State and the frontier zone of another Member State, road transport operations between certain coastal regions separated by a stretch of sea, the carriage of damaged or broken-down vehicles, the carriage of spare parts for ships or aircraft, the carriage of items or exhibits for commercial or artistic exhibitions and, in certain cases, all road haulage operations conducted by undertakings on their own account. For further details see the First Council Directive of 23 July 1962 on the establishment of certain common rules for international transport (carriage of goods by road for hire or reward) (OJ 70, 6.8.1962) and subsequent amendments, the most recent of which are Council Directive 78/175/EEC of 20 February 1978 (OJ L 54, 25.2.1978), Council Directive 80/49/EEC of 20 December 1979 (OJ L 18, 24.1.1980) and Council Directive 82/50/EEC of 19 January 1982 (OJ L 27, 4.2.1982). More recently, Council Directive 83/572/EEC of 26 October 1983 (OJ L 332, 28 .11.1983, p. 33) introduced a multilateral authorization for intra-Community removals carriage by road. Finally, the Commission has presented a proposal for a directive which meanwhile has been approved by the European Parliament (Doc. 1-921/83 of 28 October 1983) designed to abolish restrictions in certain Member States on the use of hired vehicles for the carriage of goods by road for hire or reward and on own account (Doc. COM(78) 772 of 31 January 1979).

[3] Council Decision 80/48/EEC of 20 December 1979 on the adjustment of capacity for the carriage of goods by road for hire or reward between Member States (OJ L 18, 24.1.1980).

[4] See Communication from the Commission to the Council of 11 February 1983, op. cit., p. 5.

Basically, many of the vessels are old and operated by small or family firms. Since these old vessels are often surplus to requirements, they ought to be scrapped and suitable compensation provided. There is also a temporary imbalance between supply of vessels and demand which has only recently improved, although not by much. This could cause serious disruption on the market, although one solution would be temporarily to lay up superfluous vessels, once again providing compensation.[1]

Because of the constraints imposed by the Rhine navigation system only a few of the measures were adopted in spite of repeated attempts by the Commission to tackle the whole range of problems concerning the operation of the market, the setting of rates and social and technical matters.

The measures adopted concern:

(i) reciprocal recognition of navigability licences for inland waterway vessels;[2]

(ii) a Commission recommendation on the scrapping of old vessels no longer used which has been followed by the Member States;[3]

(iii) Community participation in the drafting of a protocol to amend the Mannheim Convention as regards access to the market in the Rhine navigation system;[4]

(iv) technical requirements for inland waterway vessels.[5]

Proposals on the dismantling of barges were discussed and obtained the approval of a large number of the economic operators concerned, but not that of the Council. On the Rhine navigation system there were still no restrictions, which prevented any action at Community level and foiled the Commission's attempts to set up a European Fund for the laying-up of inland waterway vessels.[6]

The situation is somewhat better on the inland waterway system which links Belgium, France and the Netherlands (the Meuse and the Scheldt) since at least it is better controlled.

---

[1] In its document 1-263/83 of 4 May 1983, the European Parliament lists a number of difficulties facing the inland waterway market, including relatively low profitability, lack of competitiveness with the other modes of inland transport, the high level of dependence on water levels and seasonal fluctuations, which means in many cases that the supply of vessels cannot cope with demand, and in addition serious bottlenecks on the inland waterway network, infrastructure deficiencies and failure to apply a minimum level of social legislation.

[2] Council Directive 76/135/EEC of 20 January 1976 (OJ L 21, 29.1.1976) as amended by Directive 78/1016/EEC of 23 November 1978 (OJ L 349, 13.12.1978).

[3] Commission recommendation of 31 July 1968 (OJ L 218, 4.9.1968).

[4] Council Decisions of 19 December 1978 and 24 July 1979 (not published in the Official Journal).

[5] Council Directive 82/714/EEC of 4 October 1982 (OJ L 301, 28.10.1982).

[6] See the Council's most recent decision of 20 February 1978 on the temporary laying-up of inland waterway vessels used for the carriage of goods on certain waterways in which the Council authorizes the Commission to re-negotiate with Switzerland to this end, on the basis of the draft agreement amended to take account of the observations made by the Court of Justice on 26 April 1977 on the protocol agreement already granted (OJ C 107, 3.5.1977).

Compared with the Commission's five proposals[1] on inland waterway transport (concerning access to the occupation of inland waterway carrier, harmonization of social conditions, the introduction of a system of reference tariffs, access to the goods transport market (cabotage) and conditions of access to the Rhine navigation system) which are still before the Council - and some of them have been for years - the Commission's recent action programme in fact contains very few measures, although they are effective. They concern: access to the occupation and the mutual recognition of diplomas, certificates and other formal qualifications; the implementation by the Community of the second additional protocol to the Mannheim Convention which specifies conditions of access to the Rhine navigation system by operators belonging to non-Community non-riparian States; preparing a Community strategy for setting up and operating breaking-up funds, together with a ban on state aids for the construction of new vessels, at least as regards vessels used in international transport; an initial look at the problem of charging users of the Rhine in order to allocate infrastructure costs between users.[2]

Finally, on 12 October 1983, the Commission submitted to the Council a proposal for a decision on common action by certain Member States within the Central Commission for the Navigation of the Rhine on the adoption of measures to eliminate the structural over-capacity of the Rhine fleets. The Commission proposes that the five Member States which belong to the CCR should proceed by common action in accordance with the provisions of Article 116 of the Treaty.[3]

---

[1] See the Commission's Communication to the Council of 11 February 1983 (OJ C 154, 13.6.1983, p. 28).
[2] *Idem*, pp. 14-16 and 20.
[3] COM(83)582 final.

3. Harmonization of conditions of competition

In order to lay the foundations for healthy competition within each mode of transport and between the various modes of transport - both within Member States and in transport between Member States - in accordance with the objectives stated in the 1961 Memorandum and re-stated in the Commission's Communication of October 1973, it was essential to harmonize at Community level certain provisions which have a real effect on competition. The idea of harmonizing the legislation, regulations and administrative provisions of the Member States is quite compatible with the Treaty establishing the EEC. Article 3(h) mentions 'the approximation of the laws of Member States to the extent required for the proper functioning of the common market' as a way of achieving the objectives of the Community. Article 99, dealing with indirect taxation, also states in its first paragraph that the legislation of the various Member States can be harmonized in the interest of the common market. Similarly, Article 100 requires the Council to 'issue directives for the approximation of such provisions laid down by law, regulation or administrative action in Member States as directly affect the establishment or functioning of the common market'. In the Title on social policy, Article 117 states, in its second paragraph, that Member States believe that improvements in standards of living for workers and working conditions will ensue from the 'approximation of provisions laid down by law, regulation or administrative action'.

Without launching into a somewhat theoretical argument about the exact meanings of the terms 'approximation' and 'harmonization', the fact remains that these Articles do constitute the legal basis for those harmonization measures designed to ensure healthy competition within and between the different modes of transport which the Community institutions are authorized to take by Articles 75(1)(c) and 189.

Accordingly, at its meeting on 13 May 1965, the Council of Ministers approved part of a Commission proposal submitted in May 1963 on the basis of the 1962 action programme by adopting Decision 65/271/EEC 'on the harmonization of certain provisions affecting competition in transport by rail, road and inland waterway'.[1] This Decision recognized that one of the objectives of the common policy must be 'to eliminate disparities liable to cause substantial distortion in competition in the transport sector' and specified that the Council should take measures on the harmonization of taxation, on State intervention in transport and on social legislation in the Member States. However, the Council did not agree to take the measures proposed by the Commission concerning the insurance

---

[1] OJ 88, 24.5.1965, p. 1500.

sector[1] and the adjustment of specific systems of transport taxation in order to achieve a fair allocation of transport infrastructure costs.

Apart from being legally binding on the Member States, since it imposed upon them the obligation not to take measures at national level which were contrary to the provisions of the decision itself,[2] the Decision also embodied the principle, which had always been upheld by the Commission, of parallelism between harmonization measures and measures to deregulate transport within the Community.

Various specific points mentioned in the Council's framework Decision of 13 May 1965 have since formed the subject of Council measures or Commission proposals. These are examined below.

3.1 Tax harmonization

In order to ensure that conditions of competition are the same both within and between the different modes of transport, the first step is to establish a generally neutral tax situation, in respect not only of relationships between modes and categories of transport but also of relationships between the transport sector as a whole and other sectors of the economy.

To this end, the Second Council Directive of 11 April 1967 on the harmonization of legislation of Member States concerning turnover taxes makes road haulage, but not passenger transport, subject to the common value added tax system. The Sixth Council Directive 77/388/EEC of 17 May 1977,[3] defines the uniform basis of assessment for the common value added tax system and in Article 28(3)(b) states that during a transitional period of five years the Member States may continue to exempt passenger transport from VAT. For the purposes of the Community budget, Regulation (EEC, Euratom, ECSC) No 2892/77 of 19 December 1977[4] states that Member States shall calculate the VAT own resources basis as if these passenger transport operations were taxed.

The fact that haulage services are subject to VAT means that they are not subject to other taxes and thus puts road haulage on an equal footing with other sectors of the economy. However, the normal system of taxation specific to transport includes road taxes, and possibly other road haulage taxes, and

---

[1] Nevertheless, Council Directive 72/166/EEC of 24 April 1972 (as later amended on 19 December 1972) based on Article 189 of the Treaty abolished checks on green cards as of 1 July 1973 in the six original Member States and as of 15 May 1974 in the three new Member States. Since then checks have also been abolished in Austria, Finland, Norway, Sweden and Switzerland.

[2] See in this connection the judgment handed down by the Court of Justice of the European Communities in Case 9/70 on 6 October 1970 [ECR 1970].

[3] OJ L 145, 13.6.1977.

[4] OJ L 336, 27.12.1977.

fuel tax. These specific taxes are often set by governments to meet budgetary requirements rather than specific national transport policy objectives.

The Community has still to decide on rules for charging for the use of transport infrastructure which can reconcile the somewhat incompatible objectives of making conditions of competition comparable within and between the various modes of transport, optimizing the use of infrastructure and balancing the budgets of the authorities managing this infrastructure. In the meantime, the Commission has prepared a number of specific proposals on tax harmonization.

The first of these — on the standardization of provisions regarding the duty-free admission of fuel contained in the fuel tanks of commercial motor vehicles[1] — was to be submitted to the Council on 20 July 1966. It specified a quantity of 200 litres as the maximum quantity of motor fuel which Member States were required to admit duty-free. This proposal later became Council Directive 68/297/EEC[2] of 19 July 1968, which introduced this measure with effect from 1 February 1969 but reduced the maximum quantity from 200 to 50 litres. In actual fact, the Directive applied solely to France and the Federal Republic of Germany since none of the other Member States had ever imposed restrictions.

A proposal was subsequently made to amend this Directive and has recently been adopted by the Council.[3]

On 18 March 1964 the Commission submitted a proposal on commercial vehicle taxation which stated that vehicles registered in one Member State and used in other Member States in international transport should be subject to the taxes and duties applicable in the country of registration, and should be totally exempt from the taxes and duties imposed in other Member States.

Another Commission proposal also designed to avoid double taxation on vehicles used in international transport was based on the principle of territoriality, i.e. vehicles should be taxed according to the amount of time they spent in the territory of each Member State. Although the Council accepted this principle it never managed to reach any final decisions, since it considered that the adoption of measures designed to apply the principle of *non bis in idem* to taxation specifically on motor vehicles should be linked to the harmonization of taxation in general and to rules on charging for the use of infrastructure. In the meantime, the principle was broadly applied through reciprocal bilateral agreements between Member States.

Another important Commission proposal suffered a similar fate. In 1968 the Commission proposed a directive on the adjustment of national systems of commercial vehicle taxation,[4] and this is still before the Council.

[1] OJ 185, 17.10.1966.
[2] OJ L 175, 23.7.1968.
[3] OJ C 104, 13.9.1974.
[4] OJ C 95, 21.9.1968 and OJ L 91, 9.4.1983. With effect from 1 July 1984 at the latest, the duty-free limit was raised to 200 litres, as specified in the original proposal.

3.2 **Harmonization of State intervention**

The measures to harmonize national legislation on State intervention set out in Decision 65/271/EEC basically reflect the need to allow the railways to compete on an equal footing with the other modes of inland transport.

3.2.1 *The problem of the railways*

A vital aspect of the common transport policy is that it should help to solve the problem of the railways and in particular to reduce their deficits and, in the long term, to bring about a certain financial stability.

In fact, since the Member States of the Community had different attitudes to the organization of their national railway undertakings, the central States depending to a somewhat larger extent on the railways than the peripheral Member States, the railways' deficits had increased to such an extent that in some Member States subsidies and compensatory payments to the railways were on the point of becoming an uncontrollable financial liability. As a result, since some governments were finding their financial commitment to the railways increasing all the time, the problem of the railways eventually became so acute that it affected virtually all general transport policy decisions and acceptance of policies regarding the other modes of transport was governed by potential effects on the railways. As a result most other considerations regarding transport became subordinated to the overriding interests of the railways.[1] It therefore became essential for the common transport policy, if it was to develop harmoniously, to take account of the concerns of many of the Member States regarding their rail networks and the enormous financial burdens of the railways.[2] In fact, although the Commission's Communication to the Council on the further development of the common transport policy of 24 October 1973 stressed the urgent importance of attempting to define the future role of the railways in the transport system and of solving their financial problems, it is quite clear that more than 10 years later, the problem of competition between rail and road and, to a lesser extent, the inland waterways remains central to any attempt to make progress on the common transport policy. In practice, because the Member States have to bear the heavy cost of the railways and because they are subject to moral constraints which prevent them, for social reasons, from substantially cutting rail services on less productive lines, they finish up by imposing restrictions on other modes of transport (in particular road transport) in an attempt to avoid further deterioration in the financial position of the railways.

It is therefore essential to improve the situation of the railways if attempts to revive the common transport policy are to be effective.

---

[1] See 'Community rail policy: review and outlook for the 1980s', Commission Communication to the Council, Doc. COM(80) 752 final of 12 December 1980.
[2] See the Council Resolution of 15 December 1981 on Community railway policy (OJ C 157, 22.6.1982, p. 1).

The present unsatisfactory financial position of the railways is the result of a number of complex factors which to some extent condition the way the railways are run. In fact, in many respects, the railways have distinctive features of their own which clearly set them apart from the other modes of inland transport.

Firstly, the railways enjoy various forms of protection by the public authorities in the Member States. They are also subject to public service obligations, which have an important effect on their economic management of railway operations and put railway undertakings at a competitive disadvantage with regard to the other modes of inland transport. The other problem is that the railways themselves have to pay all the costs of the infrastructure they use whereas, with the other modes of inland transport, some or all of the infrastructure charges are met by the public authorities, since even where systems exist for charging for the use of transport infrastructure they do not allocate all costs between users. This is the case with road transport and, in particular, with the inland waterways.

Secondly, in most Member States, railway staff generally enjoy better conditions than the staff working in other modes of inland transport in terms of salaries, working conditions and pension schemes. This naturally places an additional financial burden on railway undertakings compared with road and inland waterway undertakings.

3.2.2 *Community action on State intervention*

In the context of Community action on rail transport, beginning in 1969 the Council adopted a series of proposals on State intervention, and on the independent commercial management of railway undertakings and improving cooperation between them. However, for the reasons given above, it was not possible to achieve the ambitious objective of improving the financial situation of railway undertakings and, in particular, of establishing rules to govern all financial relations between the railways and the State, i.e. the delicate matter of institutional reform of the railways.

3.2.2.1 Public service obligations

Council Regulation (EEC) No 1191/69 of 26 June 1969[1] was adopted to implement the Council Decision of 13 May 1965 and was based on Articles 75 and 77 of the Treaty. It establishes new rules on the conduct of governments in the field of public service obligations, an area of considerable importance for the transport sector as a whole. Under the Regulation Member States are required to terminate all obligations inherent in the concept of a public service imposed on inland transport (which in practice means primarily the railways) and to take

---

[1] Regulation (EEC) No 1191/69 of the Council of 26 June 1969 on action by Member States concerning the obligations inherent in the concept of a public service in transport by rail, road and inland waterway (OJ L 156, 28.6.1968, p. 1).

and to take upon themselves the financial burdens resulting from those obligations still imposed. Exceptions are allowed, however, since such obligations may be maintained insofar as they are essential in order to ensure the provision of 'adequate' transport services. The Regulation does make a distinction between the different types of public service obligation: 'the obligation to operate', 'the obligation to carry' and 'tariff obligations'. It leaves it up to transport undertakings to apply to the competent authorities of the Member States for the termination in whole or in part of any public service obligation which entails economic disadvantages for them.

If the supervisory authority considers that certain public service obligations must be maintained in order to ensure the provision of adequate transport services, compensation is granted to transport undertakings for the corresponding financial burden in accordance with common compensation procedures.

Although this Regulation has a somewhat limited scope in that it applies only to the main national rail networks and not to secondary or local networks and includes interregional haulage services but excludes local services and most regional road and inland waterway transport services, it has obviously brought considerable advantages, primarily to the railways, since they are more seriously affected by public service obligations than other modes.

It is worth pointing out that during the time this Regulation has applied, its basic principle as set out in Article 1, namely the termination of all obligations inherent in the concept of a public service, has not yet been put into practice. However, the principle of providing financial compensation for the maintenance of such obligations insofar as they are essential in order to ensure the provision of adequate transport services has been recognized.

3.2.2.2 Normalization of the accounts of railway undertakings

The idea of putting the railways accounts in order, referred to as normalization, is an old idea which first emerged in the UIC. It was adopted by the Community and made the subject of a Council Regulation which was also adopted on 26 June 1969.[1]

The Regulation is in fact based on the Council Decision of 13 May 1965 and takes account of the fact that one of the objectives of the common transport policy is to eliminate disparities which arise by reason of the imposition of financial burdens on, or the granting of benefits to, railway undertakings by public authorities, which are liable to cause substantial distortion to the conditions of competition. It therefore contains common rules on the normalization of the accounts of railway undertakings which apply to certain types of

---

[1] Regulation (EEC) No 1192/69 of the Council of 26 June 1969 on common rules for the normalization of the accounts of railway undertakings (OJ L 156, 28.6.1969, p. 8).

burden (i.e. burdens other than those imposed by public service obligations) or benefits, whenever the Member States decide in favour of normalization of the accounts of railway undertakings in connection with the proposed gradual harmonization of rules governing the financial relations between railway undertakings and Member States. As with the Regulation on public service obligations, this Regulation sets out ultimately to eliminate situations which give rise to the adjustment of items in the railway budget and in any case to ensure that financial compensation is granted taking account of the burdens, or benefits, concerned. There are fifteen different classes of burdens (or benefits) which include payments which railway undertakings are obliged to make but which are borne by the government for the rest of the economy, social expenditure incurred by railway undertakings in respect of family allowances, pensions, expenditure on crossing facilities, the obligation to recruit or retain surplus staff, and the conditions imposed in respect of public works or supply contracts. In practical terms, this Community Regulation helped in particular to clarify the nature of certain subsidies paid by governments to railway undertakings. From a strictly economic point of view, however, differences of interpretation between the Member States regarding the amount of financial compensation which should be paid and hesitations regarding the hidden dangers of, as it were, questioning the acquired rights of railway staff rather undermined the application of the basic principle contained in the Regulation.

3.2.3 *Financial relations between railway undertakings and governments*

With Decision 65/271/EEC of 13 May 1965 the Council established the principle of harmonizing the rules which govern financial relations between the railways and the State, as part of the general objective of improving the situation of the railways. If the aim is to organize transport in such a way that there is competition not only within each mode of transport but also between the different modes of transport, the first task is clearly to ensure effectively that undertakings are actually financially independent. This applies in particular to the railway undertakings since they normally come under the supervision of the Member States and are governed by the general or regional economic policy objectives followed by the Member States themselves. Hence the need to allow railway undertakings once again to manage their own economic and commercial affairs properly, in particular by harmonizing rules governing financial relationships between railway undertakings and the State so that railway undertakings actually have to face up to the responsibilities of their financial performance. In a proposal for a Council Decision submitted on 18 August 1971 on the improvement of the situation of railway undertakings and the harmonization of rules governing financial relations between such undertakings and States, the Commission set out its objective of proper institutional reform of the railways by allocating to undertakings, given legal personality, more extensive powers in respect of management, administration and economic and financial control as a means of ensuring proper financial equilibrium.

The proposal sets out to achieve a proper distribution of responsibilities between the undertaking and the State and to define the obligations and rights which result from this distribution, in particular by clearly specifying the 'supervisory' powers which the State has the right to exercise over railway undertakings. On the one hand, as the proprietor, the State must provide the undertaking with the financial resources it requires to carry out its activities properly and, on the other, the State must treat the undertaking in the same way as undertakings operating other modes of transport by allowing it the fullest possible independence in the management of its affairs, and by treating it as a commercial operator, which nevertheless has certain responsibilities towards the public.

3.2.3.1 Community legislation on improving the situation of railway undertakings and on their commercial independence

On 27 June 1974, on the basis of the abovementioned proposal, the Council published a resolution setting out guidelines concerning financial relations between the national railway undertakings and the Member States, although the financial independence of railway undertakings was in fact defined in a more restrictive sense than in the proposal in order to make it possible for the Member States to reach unanimous agreement.[1]

The Council used this resolution as a basis for the important Council Decision 75/327/EEC of 20 May 1975 on the improvement of the situation of railway undertakings and the harmonization of rules governing financial relations between such undertakings and States.[2]

In the preamble to the Decision it is stated that the gradual improvement of the financial situation of railway undertakings could appreciably improve the situation on the transport market. This improvement should in turn help to improve the financial results of these undertakings as a basis for achieving financial balance, although this balance could be achieved only by increasing their financial independence and commercial responsibility. Accordingly, within the framework of the overall policies laid down by each State and the discharge of public service obligations by the undertaking, each railway undertaking, by 1977, was to have sufficient independence as regards management, administration and internal control over administrative, economic and accounting matters to enable it to achieve financial balance. This independence should include in any event the separation of its assets, budgets and accounts from those of the State. Railway undertakings were to be managed in accordance with economic principles and thus each railway undertaking was to submit its business plans, including its investment and financing programmes within the framework of the overall policies laid down by the State, after agreement had been reached by the State and the undertaking. In order to enable the undertaking to carry out its

---

[1] OJ C 111, 23.9.1974, p. 1.
[2] OJ L 152, 12.6.1975, p. 3.

activities, the State could guarantee loans obtained by the undertaking, or give loans or direct grants, and could also grant compensation for financial charges resulting from public service obligations imposed on the undertakings.

Before 1 January 1978 the Council, acting on a proposal from the Commission, was to adopt the necessary measures to achieve comparability between the accounting systems and annual accounts of all railway undertakings and was to lay down uniform costing principles. Within the framework of general policy on prices and taking into account both national and Community rules on transport rates and conditions, railway undertakings were to determine their own rates, with the aim of achieving optimum financial results and financial balance.

Pursuant to Article 3(2) of Regulation (EEC) No 1107/70, which we shall examine later, compensation could be made in respect of tariff obligations which could not be classed as public service obligations. Acting on a proposal from the Commission to be submitted not later than 1 January 1978, the Council would harmonize the procedures for granting such compensation. Lastly the Decision states that, before 1 January 1979, the Commission would submit to the Council a report on the objectives to be pursued in the long term and the measures to be taken to promote partial or total integration of railway undertakings at Community level. Every two years the Commission would submit to the Council a report on the implementation by the Member States of this Decision and before 1 January 1980 the Commission would submit to the Council such proposals as it deemed necessary to fix the time limit and conditions for achieving the financial balance of the railway undertakings.

To date, the programme set out in this Decision has been implemented only partially by two Council Regulations: the first on the measures necessary to achieve comparability between the accounting systems and annual accounts of railway undertakings[1] and the second laying down uniform costing principles for railway undertakings.[2]

In addition there was a Council Decision of 19 July 1982 which states that the railway undertakings shall, in accordance with their commercial interests and taking account of costs and the market situation, fix the rates and conditions for the international carriage of goods between Member States according to the principle of commercial management of the carriage of goods by rail within a framework of sufficient commercial independence.[3]

Basing itself on the Council resolution of 15 December 1981, in which the Council in particular expressed its own concern to improve cooperation between railway undertakings in international transport, the Commission put forward an action programme which provides the basis for a number of specific proposals presented in 1982 and 1983.

[1] Council Regulation (EEC) No 2830/77 of 12 December 1977 (OJ L 334, 24.12.1977, p. 13).
[2] Council Regulation (EEC) No 2183/78 of 19 September 1978 (OJ L 258, 21.9.1978, p. 1).
[3] Council Decision 82/529/EEC of 19 July 1982 (OJ L 234, 9.8.1982, p. 5).

A first proposal adopted by the Council concerned the commercial independence of the railways in the management of their international passenger and luggage traffic.[1] According to this Decision, the railway undertakings are free to establish common tariff scales offering rates for the whole journey, to offer all-in package services, on their own or in cooperation with other transport undertakings or the tourist industry, to create revenue pools within the framework of communities of interest and to delegate powers among themselves to make joint offers to customers.

Within the framework of the Community rules applicable and in particular of Article 9(1) of Decision 75/327/EEC, railway undertakings are to fix the rates and conditions for the international carriage of passengers and luggage between Member States in accordance with their commercial interests and taking account of costs and the market situation. They must apply rates intended both to ensure that the assignable costs specific to the traffic concerned by this Decision are covered and to make a positive contribution to covering joint costs.

With regard to Italy in particular, mention should also be made of the Commission's recommendation of 22 February 1982 to the Italian Republic inviting it to continue its measures in the most effective manner possible to find a solution to the problems existing in respect of rail transport operations between Italy and the other Member States, notably the North-South traffic link, and to take into consideration when carrying out the Italian Railways' integrated investment programme the fact that measures relating to rail transport to and from Community tates should have priority.[2]

According to the Commission's latest paper on inland transport,[3] ultimately the Community's railways are likely to be helped more by improving the attractiveness and efficiency of their services and by supporting their efforts to adapt themselves to market requirements than by attempts to stifle other modes of transport, which is the case in many of the Member States. To this end it is the Community's job to press on with the railway cooperation programme as a way of helping to remove the various obstacles which at present inhibit the railways from benefiting from the longer distances and the greater scale of a Community market. The Council resolution of 15 December 1981 had already demonstrated what could be achieved. Again, it would also be worthwhile to continue to develop combined transport since this is an area where the interests of the railways could be combined with those of other modes of transport and one which could make a contribution towards improving the financial situation of the railways. The Commission also considers that it would be helpful to give priority to those infrastructure projects of Community interest which the Council has agreed to support which are designed to facilitate the transfer of traffic from road to rail where this is economically justified. While on the subject of

[1] Council Decision 83/418/EEC of 25 July 1983 (OJ L 237, 26.8.1983, p. 32).
[2] Commission recommendation 82/172/EEC of 22 February 1982 to the Italian Republic concerning measures to improve the transport of goods by rail to and from Italy (OJ L 78, 24.3.1982, p. 24).
[3] Commission communication to the Council of 11 February 1983, op cit.

infrastructure, distortions between railways and the other modes of inland transport could easily be eliminated if the railways were put on the same footing as the other two inland modes. In particular, the costs of providing and maintaining rail infrastructure should be the financial responsibility of the State. In turn, as with the other modes of transport, the railways should pay for the use of infrastructure in the form of a fee reflecting at least the short-term marginal costs. This would enable the railways to develop costing and pricing methods more in line with the commercial principles of their competitors. Finally, a clearer distinction should be made between the railways' responsibilities and rights as commercial undertakings on the one hand and their rights and responsibilities in relation to the public on the other. In the Commission's opinion, there was thus a good case for recommending to Member States that the various public service obligations should be reduced or abandoned, in particular with regard to goods transport.

3.2.4 *Aid granted in the transport sector*

There is a special Regulation on the aid allowed by Article 77 of the Treaty.[1] It provides for the granting of aid in accordance with Articles 77, 92 and 93 of the Treaty and on the basis of the provisions of Articles 75 and 94.

The Regulation starts by stating that Articles 92 to 94 of the Treaty shall apply to aids granted for transport by rail, road and inland waterway, in respect of aids which distort competition in the transport sector, even if they do not affect trade between Member States.

The only exception to this general principle concerns local or regional transport services. The Regulation goes on to outline further rules on the aids referred to in Article 77 of the Treaty and lists those types of aid which meet the needs of coordination of transport and are thus compatible with the Treaty.

Briefly, the Regulation considers compatible those aids intended as compensation for certain financial burdens borne by those railway undertakings which are not covered by the system for normalizing railway accounts, aids granted to ensure that each sector is charged for the infrastructure which it uses, aids granted to promote research into and the development of transport systems and technologies more economic for the community in general at the experimental stage, and aids granted as an exceptional and temporary measure in order to eliminate excess capacity causing serious structural problems. Under the same heading come aids intended as reimbursement for the discharge of obligations inherent in the concept of a public service which are not included in the Regulation on public service obligations and those aids granted to transport undertakings or transport activities to which that Regulation does not apply. Regulation

---

[1] Regulation (EEC) No 1107/70 of the Council of 4 June 1970 on the granting of aids for transport by rail, road and inland waterway (OJ L 130, 15.6.1970) as amended by Council Regulation (EEC) No 1473/75 of 20 May 1975 (OJ L 152, 12.6.1975).

No 1107/70 allowed each Member State to establish its own system of aids in accordance with its own national policies.

The granting of aid is normally covered by the Community procedure in Article 93. However, the Council has adopted a simplified procedure for aids granted to railway undertakings which also applies to the types of aid covered by Council Regulation No 1473/75 of 20 May 1975.[1] Nevertheless, the most important issue which the Regulation had to settle was that of the state of railway finances since the ultimate aim of all the legislation is to restrict all the various reimbursements by the State to the railway organizations, so that they themselves are left to achieve their own financial equilibrium.[2]

In 1982, a Regulation was adopted which amends the Regulation of 4 June 1970. It contains provisions designed to encourage investment in the development of combined transport and particularly in infrastructure and the fixed and movable transfer facilities required.[3] This shows how important intermodal transport has become at Community level in recent years. We shall examine the various reasons for this later.

3.3 Harmonization of social legislation

The legal basis for the Community's social policy is Title III - 'Social policy' - in Part Three - 'Policy of the Community' - of the Treaty (Articles 117 to 128). Although some articles deal with very specific points like the principle that men and women should receive equal pay for equal work (Article 119), paid holiday schemes (Article 120) and social security for migrant workers (Article 121), the articles which go furthest towards defining a Community social policy are Articles 123 to 128 on the European Social Fund.

Although the rules contained in the Treaty are rather restrictive, the Community has managed to develop its social policy satisfactorily using the legal basis in the Treaty and the institutional procedure provided. This task was facilitated in particular by the reform of the Social Fund set in motion by the Council Decision of 1 February 1971 and subsequent implementing regulations.[4]

In its efforts to establish a common transport policy, the Commission has always been concerned to combine and to balance gradual economic deregulation with further social progress. It was inevitable, therefore, that the adoption of measures designed to make conditions of competition between transport undertakings comparable should go hand in hand with efforts by the Commission to

---

[1] OJ L 152, 12.6.1975.
[2] See F. Santoro, op. cit., p. 267-268.
[3] Council Regulation (EEC) No 1658/82 of 10 June 1982 supplementing by provisions on combined transport Regulation (EEC) No 1107/70 on the granting of aids for transport by rail, road and inland waterway (OJ L 184, 29.6.1982, p. 1).
[4] See D. Strasser, op cit., pp. 200-225.

guarantee conditions of social security with an eye to the possible consequences of such measures. Social measures relating to transport are thus the logical consequence of the adoption of the economic measures we have already examined.

Subsequently, the Commission set up joint advisory committees to examine the social problems of the three modes of inland transport as a means of establishing closer contact with the economic interests concerned. These were the Advisory Committee on Road Transport, set up in 1965, followed by the Advisory Committees on Inland Waterway Transport (1967) and Rail Transport (1972). In December 1963, in fact, it had organized an important round-table discussion on social policy in transport which examined the main issues relating to the harmonization and coordination of working conditions, vocational training and employment, social security and health at work. A fact-finding survey of salaries in the road transport industry was organized in 1966 in accordance with Council Regulation (EEC) No 100/66 of 14 July 1966,[1] which is based on Article 213 of the Treaty.

The provisions of the Council's framework decision of 13 May 1965, to which we have already referred[2] included the harmonization for the three modes of transport of rules on driving times and rest periods, manning and overtime arrangements, and a system for checking compliance with provisions concerning working periods.

The sector most urgently in need of regulation was road transport, and in fact a Regulation was adopted on 25 March 1969[3] designed to harmonize the rules on competition between the modes of transport and in international transport, to promote social progress and to improve road safety. The Regulation contains provisions on the minimum ages for drivers, the composition of crews, driving periods and rest periods. Provisionally, compliance with these provisions was to be controlled by crew members themselves by filling in an individual control book.[4]

Regulation No 543/69 was last amended by Council Regulation (EEC) No 2827/77, in order among other things to adjust the rules to combined road-rail and road-ferry transport and to allow Member States exemptions in the case of

---

[1] OJ 134, 22.7.1966, p. 2538.

[2] OJ 88, 24.5.1965, p. 1500/65.

[3] Regulation (EEC) No 543/69 of the Council of 25 March 1969 on the harmonization of certain social legislation relating to road transport (OJ L 77, 29.3.1969, p. 49).

[4] This Regulation was originally intended to come into force on 1 October 1969 for international transport and on 1 October 1970 for road transport as a whole. Its implementation was delayed because of difficulties at international level following the signing at Geneva, on 1 July 1970 within the framework of the ECE, of the AETR Agreement, five Member States of the Community being participating States. As a result it was necessary to harmonize the provisions of this Regulation with those of the Agreement, particularly as regards the transit of vehicles from non-Community states through Community territory. Accordingly, the Regulation was amended by Council Regulation (EEC) No 514/72 of 28 February 1972 (OJ L 67, 20.3.1972).

specific national transport operations,[1] and by Council Regulation (EEC) No 2829/77 which is designed to take account of the provisions of the abovementioned European Agreement concerning the work of crews of vehicles engaged in international road transport (AETR) which entered into force on 5 January 1976 - and which, in its recommendation of 23 September 1974, the Council invited the Member States to ratify - with regard to traffic between Member States and third countries which are not party to the Agreement. The Regulation also provides that, by way of exception, the Member States of the Community shall be authorized to deposit the instruments of ratification or accession individually, even though the power to negotiate and conclude the Agreement lies with the Community, since the subject-matter of the AETR Agreement falls within the scope of Regulation (EEC) No 543/69.[2]

The fact that it was the responsibility of the crew itself to enter driving periods and rest periods into an individual control book was certainly not a cast-iron guarantee of compliance with this social legislation. Since it was often in the interests of crews not to comply with the rules on rest periods in order to obtain bonuses the control book was often referred to as 'a book of lies'.

Not long afterwards, a Council Regulation of 20 July 1970 prescribed the installation of recording equipment in vehicles used for the carriage of passengers or goods by road. The equipment was intended to record driving periods, working periods, rest periods and breaks, vehicle speed and distance travelled.[3] There were a few exceptions however: vehicles suitable for the carriage of passengers provided there were no more than nine seats; vehicles used for regular passenger services over distances not exceeding 50 km and vehicles used for the carriage of goods, the permissible maximum weight of which did not exceed 3.5 tonnes.

A subsequent Council Regulation of 28 February 1972 states that this recording equipment, meeting certain specifications, must compulsorily replace the individual control book, since it had been established that the tachograph would be introduced on 1 January 1980 for vehicles registered before 1 January 1975 and used for the carriage of goods or passengers in order to provide enough time

---

[1] Council Regulation (EEC) No 2827/77 of 12 December 1977 amending Regulation (EEC) No 543/69 on the harmonization of certain social legislation relating to road transport (OJ L 334, 24.12.1977, p. 1). On the basis of this Regulation the Commission took decisions to authorize certain Member States (notably the United Kingdom and Ireland) to apply certain measures by way of derogation from Regulation No 543/69, particularly as regards the transport of milk from farms to a dairy or to a reloading point. See Commission Decision of 18 December 1981 (OJ L 29, 6.2.1982, p. 15) and of 31 March 1982 (OJ L 123, 6.5.1982, p. 46).
[2] Council Regulation (EEC) No 2829/77 of 12 December 1977 on the bringing into force of the European Agreement concerning the work of crews of vehicles engaged in international road transport (AETR) (OJ L 334, 24.12.1977, p. 11). A revised version of Regulation (EEC) No 543/69 incorporating various subsequent amendments is given in OJ C 73, 17.3.1979.
[3] Regulation (EEC) No 1463/70 of the Council of 20 July 1970 on the introduction of recording equipment in road transport (OJ L 164, 27.7.1970, p. 1).

for fitting the new instrument. In the case of transport operations carried out within a radius of less than 50 km, however, Member States are authorized to grant exemptions nationally provided driving and rest periods are observed.[1]

On 25 June 1973 the Council adopted the first amendment to Regulation No 1463/70 which states that vehicles registered before 1 January 1975 (1 January 1976 for the new Member States) and fitted with recording equipment of a type which has received national approval shall not be required to install and use 'Community' recording equipment until 1 January 1980.[2]

Council Regulation (EEC) No 2828/77, which takes account of experience gained in the application of Council Regulation (EEC) No 1463/70 on the construction and use of the tachograph, makes it compulsory to install and use recording equipment at the time of entry into service of vehicles registered for the first time on or after 1 January 1975 (1 January 1976 for the new Member States), or in the case of vehicles used for the carriage of dangerous goods, whatever the date of registration, and for all other vehicles with effect from 1 January 1978. Member States are required to grant type-approval for recording equipment to be used in vehicles registered in those Member States.[3]

Recently, Council Regulation (EEC) No 3281/85[4] repealed Regulation (EEC) No 1463/70 and replaced it by provisions introducing a procedure for EEC type approval of recording equipment and listing detailed requirements for construction, testing, installation and inspecting of this equipment.

In the same way, Council Regulation (EEC) No 3820/85[5] repealed Regulation (EEC) No 543/69. Although the new Regulation lays down precise rules on certain aspects of social legislation - minimum ages for crew members, driving periods, breaks and rest periods, prohibition of certain types of payment and control procedures - it also allows for greater flexibility than did the previous Regulation. On the subject of the AETR Agreement, it is interesting that the Regulation confirms the principle that the power to negotiate and conclude the Agreement lies with the Community.

However, the Member States are still allowed, by way of exception, to follow the derogation procedure provided for by Regulation (EEC) No 2829/77. In addition, Member States should enter a reservation when depositing their instruments of ratification or accession in order to ensure the supremacy of Community law in intra-Community transport.

---

[1] Regulation (EEC) No 515/72 of the Council of 28 February 1972 (OJ L 67, 20.3.1972, p. 11).
[2] Regulation (EEC) No 1787/73 of the Council of 25 June 1973 (OJ L 181, 4.7.1973, p. 1).
[3] Council Regulation (EEC) No 2828/77 of 12 December 1977 amending Regulation (EEC) No 1463/70 on the introduction of recording equipment in road transport (OJ L 334, 24.12.1977, p. 5).
[4] Council Regulation (EEC) No 3821/85 of 20 December 1985 on recording equipment in road transport (OJ L 370, 31.12.1985, p. 8).
[5] Council Regulation (EEC) No 3820/85 of 20 December 1985 on the harmonization of certain social legislation relating to road transport (OJ L 370, 31.12.1985, p. 1).

It is true to say that, taken together, these social harmonization measures effectively solve the problems which arise in road transport, although the social regulations adopted have not so far had an appreciable effect on actual conditions of competition, partly because the rules have not been properly applied in certain Member States, particularly the rules on the use of the tachograph, and this has created considerable distortion. The fact that the tachograph is not used properly is largely due to the fact that national regulations on penalties have not been harmonized. It is to be hoped that current discussions between the parties concerned may go a long way towards achieving agreement on a solution to the problem of the actual implementation of Community social legislation by the Member States.

As regards inland waterway transport, presumably it should be possible in the future to bring about harmonization similar to that achieved in the road transport sector. The problem of harmonization in the railway industry is different altogether since the railway undertakings of the Member States have their own statutes. However, there is no reason why these different statutes could not be harmonized by means of Community regulations. Unfortunately, there is little prospect at present of more extensive Community action in this field.

4. Transport infrastructure

The 1961 Memorandum already referred to transport infrastructure in the Community. It mentioned two aspects: charging for the use of infrastructure and coordinating the action required to ensure that the resources set aside for the maintenance and construction of infrastructure are put to the best economic use.

The aspect with which the Community authorities first concerned themselves, since it was a precondition for achieving full tax neutrality within the transport sector, was charging for the use of transport infrastructure. From 1964 onwards extensive studies and surveys were devoted to this topic.[1]

4.1 Charging for the use of infrastructure

In its Agreement of 22 June 1965 on organization of the market in transport and in its Resolution of 10 October 1966, the Council confirmed the need to settle the problem of charging for the use of infrastructure, even if only provisionally. In a subsequent Decision 67/790/EEC of 14 December 1967 on certain measures of common transport policy[2] the Council also specified a timetable and general guidelines for the first measures to be adopted with a view to establishing a system for charging for the use of infrastructure.

In 1970 a Regulation was published which introduced an accounting system for expenditure and use of infrastructure. It contained standard rules on investment expenditure (expenditure on new construction, extension, reconstruction and renewals), current expenditure (expenditure on maintenance and operation) and general expenses.[3] Lastly, on 24 March 1971, the Commission published a Memorandum[4] in which it proposed the introduction of a system of infrastructure charging for the three modes of inland transport based on the allocation of the marginal social costs arising from the use of infrastructure, adding on where necessary extra charges to ensure the financial equilibrium of the public undertakings responsible for managing this infrastructure.

---

[1] See Council Decision 64/389/EEC of 22 June 1964 on the organization of a survey of infrastructure costs in respect of transport by rail, road and inland waterway (OJ 102, 29.6.1964) - Commission Decision of 27 April 1965 on the surveys and studies to be conducted in 1966 on the use of transport infrastructure (OJ 82, 12.5.1965) - M. Allais, M. del Viscovo, L. Duquesne de la Vinelle, C. Oort, H.S. Seidenfus, *Options in transport tariff policy*, EEC, Studies collection, Transport series, No 1, Brussels, 1965.

[2] OJ 322, 30.12.1967.

[3] Regulation (EEC) No 1108/70 of the Council of 4 June 1970 introducing an accounting system for expenditure on infrastructure in respect of transport by rail, road and inland waterway (OJ L 130, 15.6.1970).

[4] Memorandum from the Commission to the Council on charging for the use of infrastructure, 24 May 1971, Doc. COM(71) 268 final.

It is common knowledge that certain Member States, particularly those in Central Europe which have a very extensive railway network, have always maintained that the problem of allocating the costs of using the different transport infrastructure systems must be solved before they are prepared to make further efforts to deregulate road transport, arguing that road and inland waterway transport, unlike the railways, do not make a fair contribution towards covering the cost of use of their infrastructure.

The need for proper allocation of infrastructure costs thus arose from the need to ensure equal conditions of competition not only between the different modes of transport but also, within each mode of transport, between undertakings operating in different countries. This would put an end to the disparities occurring because, often solely for budgetary reasons, the Member States tended to arrive at different solutions to the problem of indirect taxation specifically of transport. The system adopted would have to take account of the substantial differences between the modes of transport. In other words, whereas it was inevitable that all expenditure for the use of rail infrastructure was exclusive to the railways and that the problem would have to be solved primarily by establishing a proper balance between the railway undertakings and the public authorities in order to guarantee the financial equilibrium of the undertakings responsible for managing the infrastructure, with the other modes, since the infrastructure did not belong to transport operators, a solution would have to be found by applying a specific tax system to ensure that the cost of using infrastructure was allocated equally between the different users.

If establishing total parity of competition within each mode of transport and between the different modes of transport had been the only requirement at Community level, it would have been possible to find a fair solution to the infrastructure charging problem by taking the total cost, which would include expenditure on current infrastructure investment and the investment required to maintain the existing network, and allocating it between users. However, there was another economic aim, namely to optimize the use of the infrastructure. For this purpose, it was no longer the total cost which was most important, as with the theory of resource allocation, but the marginal cost of using infrastructure, which was taken as the criterion for allocating public infrastructure expenditure in accordance with the objective of optimizing the distribution of resources.

The marginal cost of use, defined as the increase in the total cost resulting from one additional vehicle of the type concerned, can be taken as the wear and tear on infrastructure caused by one individual vehicle and corresponds to the increase in the costs of maintenance, renewal, operation and management caused by this vehicle, which should be charged to users. In cases where potential traffic exceeds available capacity, a dissuasive element should be added to this in order to prevent saturation of the infrastructure and hence congestion. We are now moving towards the concept of marginal social costs. To cover these the user should pay a fixed 'economic charge', in other words a price which includes not only the charge to cover the costs mentioned above but also a single charge in the case of economic saturation in order to keep demand compatible with available capacity.[1]

Although marginal social costs do include negative effects like the increased probability of accidents and disturbance and pollution caused by heavy traffic, which are referred to as marginal external costs, they consist chiefly of the Community and social costs - the marginal costs of congestion - which each additional road-user causes to the other users of the same service in that his presence may cause delays, with consequent increases in cost (because of the extra time the vehicle and the goods carried are held up, which will also increase maintenance expenditure) and journey time for other users of the same service. It has therefore been suggested that there should be a kind of efficiency or anti-congestion payment.[2] In spite of the obvious difficulties, attempts have been made to estimate a charge for each type of vehicle, which is translated or should be translated into increased income for the undertaking managing the infrastructure (but not for those users which suffer inconvenience, for whom there is no compensation mechanism) by means of precise adjustments in road taxes or fuel taxes.[3] However, because the small proportion of costs accounted for by use is small, and because a system of charges based on marginal social costs would obviously not enable undertakings managing infrastructure to balance expenditure against revenue, it seems reasonable instead to impose this as a further condition on the public authorities responsible for managing infrastructure and to add an item to the marginal social cost so that the deficit is covered by the charges paid by users. In fact, it is only possible to allocate the total cost of infrastructure between the various types of users according to objective economic criteria if the total cost is covered by revenue from the charges referred to above. However, these criteria cannot be applied to the resulting deficit which may have to be borne by the undertaking managing the infrastructure so an extra amount would have to be added to the marginal social cost in order to balance the books, i.e. a balancing charge. By means of a proper system of charges it would therefore be possible, on the one hand, to encourage the best use to be made of existing infrastructure, by channelling demand into infrastructure which provides the same quality of service but at reduced cost to society and, on the other, to allocate between users the total cost of constructing and operating transport infrastructure.

However, this system of charging for the use of infrastructure at Community level obviously did not solve the problem of deciding upon infrastructure investment. Accordingly there were plans for introducing a scheme for coordinating investment, which we shall examine shortly.

---

[1] See M. Allias et al, op. cit., p. 126, which is a very useful reference work on the whole subject of charging for the use of transport infrastructure at Community level.
[2] See U. Marchese, *Aspetti economici e territoriali del sistema dei trasporti,* ECIG, Genoa, 1980, p. 285.
[3] An interesting pilot study was conducted by the Community on Paris and Le Havre regarding the costs which can be attributed to the various types of vehicle, see *Rapport sur l'étude pilote,* EEC No 270 of 13 May 1965.

According to the Memorandum, infrastructure expenditure means, for the reference period, financial burdens incurred in respect of: construction, reconstruction and renewals (investment expenditure); maintenance and operation of installations and management (current expenditure); depreciation and financial charges in respect of loans contracted during previous periods in order to finance investment expenditure and allocated to the reference period (financing expenditure).[1]

Two considerations follow from the application of the above principles:

    (i)   each mode of transport, and each user category within it, must cover all the costs allocated to it out of its own resources;

    (ii)   all revenue obtained from charging for the use of infrastructure must be used to manage and improve that infrastructure, a practice which although legally permissible, constitutes, under Community public law, an exception to the principle set out in Article 3 of the Financial Regulation of 1977 applicable to the general budget of the European Communities which states that all revenue and all expenditure shall be entered in full in the budget and in the accounts.[2]

4.1.1 *Applying infrastructure charging to the three modes of inland transport*

According to the 1971 proposal, infrastructure charging was to be applied to the three modes of inland transport as follows :

4.1.1.1 **Railways**

There was a direct link between efforts to balance the infrastructure budget and attempts at general improvements in the financial situation of the railways, which were running huge deficits in all the Member States. The whole issue of infrastructure charging thus amounted to a rational reappraisal of financial relationships between the railways and the State to which the infrastructure belonged so that ultimately the railways' operating account could take over all expenditure on the infrastructure it used, while users would cover the total operating cost.

---

[1] A valid objection to this formula was that, in the case of reconstruction or renewal of installations, the expenditure incurred was still allocated as a total amount, irrespective of whether or not it had been backed up by loans or other types of financing (see F. Santoro, op. cit., p. 360).
[2] OJ L 356, 31.12.1977, p. 3.

4.1.1.2 **Inland waterways**

A system of navigation dues would have to be introduced as a means of balancing the budget for infrastructure charging purposes.

Of all the modes of inland transport, inland waterway transport was the mode which made the smallest contribution to covering its infrastructure costs.

In order to balance the budget, therefore, there would certainly have to be an increase in freight rates, which might also cause serious economic difficulties for inland waterway traffic on certain networks. It was therefore considered essential to attempt to put waterways on a more equal footing, perhaps by establishing economically and technically homogeneous categories of waterways. It was possible that certain legal difficulties might arise with regard to the introduction of infrastructure charging for the use of inland waterways in connection with certain provisions of the Act of Mannheim, since problems of compatibility could arise if the infrastructure charging system applied to Rhine navigation.

4.1.1.3 **Roads**

This is the sector where it proved most difficult to introduce an infrastructure charging system, principally because of interference with existing taxation systems. It was also the area where congestion and pollution were most serious and the area where most money was needed.

Therefore, on the one hand, infrastructure charging should make it possible to ensure that users bear all the social costs which they occasion for society. On the other hand, in some sectors, and particularly in urban areas, the allocation of infrastructure costs should be designed to direct the consumer's choice towards the mode which is most economically beneficial to society as a whole. In practice, it is possible only to achieve a reasonable compromise between the economic objective and the practicalities of collecting charges for the use of infrastructure, although there are, in fact, several ways of charging for the use of roads: tolls, taxes on motor vehicles, taxes on fuel and even taxes on transport services (direct infrastructure charging measures).[1]

4.1.2 *Taxes and direct infrastructure charging*

Although in order to achieve total parity within and between modes of transport it would be necessary to harmonize general taxation as well, in practical terms, it is easier to adjust the specific taxes which the different Member States apply to transport activities. This was the aim behind the abovementioned proposal

---

[1] For an excellent and detailed study of the whole issue of road infrastructure charging see R. Malcor, *Problems arising in the practical application of charges for the use of road infrastructures*, EEC, Studies Collection, Transport series, No 2, Brussels, 1970.

for a Council Directive of 1968 on the adjustment of national taxation systems for commercial road vehicles. This Directive is obviously closely linked with the 1971 Memorandum although their respective scopes are very different and in the case of commercial road vehicles could have very different results. In fact, the 1968 proposal sets out to harmonize the structure of taxes specifically on commercial road vehicles whereas the Memorandum lays down general principles which each Member State should use as the basis for working out its own infrastructure charging system. In some respects, if adopted, the 1968 proposal could, since it specifies a uniform tax structure specific to commercial road vehicles, constitute the preliminary stage in the application of the broader tax system set out in the Memorandum. The proposal is based on three fundamental principles:

(i)   the different existing tax systems should take account of the need to cover road infrastructure costs;

(ii)   the proposed tax system would be based on the number and distribution of axles and the total weight of the vehicle, thus putting vehicles into different categories for tax purposes;

(iii) the proposed tax system would be based solely on the criterion of marginal cost of use (and not on marginal social cost), i.e. the cost of controlling traffic and of maintaining and renewing infrastructure, which can be calculated on the basis of the wear and tear on infrastructure caused by the weight of the vehicle on each axle.

It also proposed to introduce, in addition to fuel taxes, a specific tax on the use of road infrastructure to replace existing motor vehicle taxes (road taxes and, in some cases, taxes on transport services).

After this brief look at the 1968 proposal and the similarities with and differences from the 1971 Memorandum, we shall now consider the changes to the specific tax system which the infrastructure charging system proposed in the Memorandum would entail.

The proposed use of taxes on fuel and motor vehicles as instruments of infrastructure charging means that they would no longer serve a fiscal purpose but rather that their structure and level would be set solely as a function of the infrastructure charging system.

4.1.2.1 Fuel taxes

The relative proportions of tax on petrol and on diesel fuel would have to be specified in such a way as to ensure that tax has absolutely no effect on the choice of one fuel or the other and that costs per kilometre were the same for vehicles in the same category irrespective of the fuel used. In theory, absolute tax levels would have to be harmonized at Community level in order to avoid creating tax obstacles to trade within the Community. These levels would be established with reference to infrastructure costs and taking into account revenue obtained from other systems of charging.

4.1.2.2 Motor vehicle taxes

Obviously fuel taxes could not be used as the sole means of charging for the social cost of using infrastructure. The component of social cost accounted for by the marginal cost of use alone varies a great deal, as tests conducted by the ASHO have shown, according to the number of axles of each vehicle and the weight on each axle, factors which in particular govern wear and tear on the road. Since, however, these factors have very little effect on fuel consumption, motor vehicle taxes would have to be used as a correcting mechanism.

Motor vehicle taxes would therefore be set as a function of fuel taxes. Their level would depend on how far it were possible to extend the use of direct infrastructure charging.

4.1.2.3 Problems involved in applying a direct infrastructure charging system

Even if a direct infrastructure charging system were required to include infrastructure charging measures such as taxes on fuel or motor vehicles so that the prices paid by users corresponded more closely to actual costs to society in terms of congestion and pollution and thus contained a real element of dissuasion, there is no denying that in practical terms these measures would be very difficult to apply and might even impede traffic. Just as in urban areas payment for parking is now a common method of charging, the tolls which for some time now certain Member States have been collecting directly on some motorways might be a useful way of charging for the use of infrastructure if they could be integrated into the direct tariff system and adjusted according to traffic volumes (rush hours, night traffic, etc.).

However, although there was some agreement on certain aspects of the infrastructure charging system proposed by the Commission, in political, practical and administrative terms it would clearly have been very difficult for the Member States to apply the system as a whole and for this reason they took great care not to reach any final decisions within the Council.

Thus even if the Commission endeavours to come up with new proposals for a Community system for allocating infrastructure costs, there is every reason to suppose that the Community will not achieve the momentum for introducing such a system for some time. Moreover, unlike at the beginning of the 1970s, the governments of the Member States are now subject to permanent budgetary constraints and these certainly do not favour harmonization of taxation specifically on transport, which is one of the main instruments used by Member States to balance national budgets weakened by the financial consequences of the structural economic crisis facing Europe at the moment.

4.2 Coordination of investment

If one considers what transport infrastructure basically is, namely the essential medium for the movement of persons, goods and factors of production between the different production activities and between the production sector as a whole and centres of population, it is easy to see why it is so important to coordinate transport infrastructure investment in an area, like the Community, where the economies are gradually being integrated.

Nor is it enough to establish rules on charging for the use of infrastructure. This alone will not solve the infrastructure problem since there is also the matter of selecting investment projects, which in turn raises the problem of evaluating the total benefit to the Community of each individual project compared with its construction and operation costs.

Quite rightly, therefore, the 1961 Memorandum subdivided the Community infrastructure problem into (a) charging for the use of infrastructure in order to allocate the costs of using infrastructure equally between those who use it, and (b) the coordination of investment considered essential in order to allocate resources earmarked for the maintenance and construction of infrastructure on the basis of sound economic principles. According to the Memorandum, the principle of coordinating investment could be thought of initially in terms of harmonizing national decisions on investment of Community interest and ultimately in terms of the general coordination of transport investment projects at Community level.

In practical terms, it is particularly important for the Community and for the Member States to coordinate investment projects, not only in order to distribute resources more effectively and to improve the use of facilities already available but also, more broadly, to promote the adoption of a coherent transport policy properly linked to policies in the other sectors of the economy. Finally improving Europe's infrastructure network should help to give it a real sense of unity and integration.[1]

The preparatory studies on infrastructure carried out between 1964 and 1965 clearly showed how communication networks had been designed and constructed solely as a function of national objectives which varied considerably from one Member State to another and developed according to criteria which were not always consistent with their transport policies. It was felt necessary, therefore, in 1965 to propose a programme for improving the infrastructure of the three modes of inland transport. With the railways this involved harmonizing electrification programmes in order to link up the electrified networks of the

---

[1] See K.M. Gwilliam, S. Petriccione, F. Voigt, J.A. Zighera, *Coordination of investments in transport infrastructures, Analysis - Recommendations - Procedures*, EEC Studies collection, Transport series, No 3, Brussels, 1973; Communication to the Council on action in the field of transport infrastructure approved by the Commission on 30 June 1976, Bull. EC 6-1976; 'The role of the Community in the development of transport infrastructure', Memorandum adopted on 7 November 1979, Bull. EC Supplement 8-1979.

various Member States and to increase capacity on certain lines. With the roads the objective was to create a system of major through-routes to a specific standard and with the inland waterways it was to improve links between seaports and their hinterlands and to establish links between the waterway systems of the Community suitable for use by 'European class' waterway vessels.[1]

In 1966, consistent with the objective of working out common rules on the choice of infrastructure investment projects, the Council on a proposal from the Commission instituted a procedure for consultation in respect of transport infrastructure investment projects of Community interest.[2] In some ways this procedure is an extension of the consultation procedure adopted in 1962 with regard to measures taken by Member States in the sphere of transport policy[3] except that the Commission's powers are restricted solely to making recommendations. In fact, the attempts made by the Commission to make this procedure into an effective instrument for coordinating investment at Community level met, in the initial stages at least, with the staunch resistance of certain Member States reluctant to relinquish national powers in this area and afraid of seeing coordination of investment projects at Community level become an irreversible process whereby certain infrastructure decisions would no longer be taken within the framework of national transport policy.

However, apart from this extremely blinkered view, which in certain circumstances may have been a case of appealing to the masses, there were real issues to be contended with: the development of transport between Member States, which was increasing at a faster rate than national transport within Member States, the increasing interdependence of networks, the key role of infrastructure in determining the future development of transport and the increasing difficulties facing national public authorities in obtaining financing for their own infrastructure projects. All these factors prompted the Commission to continue with a perfectly coherent policy designed not only to improve the procedure for coordinating investment projects of Community interest but also to evolve instruments for granting Community financial support for certain types of major transport infrastructure project.

---

[1] In Italy, for example, the 1965 programme mentioned the following infrastructure improvements:
   (a) converting the Genoa-Modane and Bolzano-Brenner lines to direct current;
   (b) doubling the track on those sections of the Genoa-Modane and Genoa-Ventimiglia lines where this was still to be done;
   (c) building a road tunnel through the Alps between Turin and France;
   (d) linking up the 'Autostrada del Sole' with the Brenner Pass;
   (e) building a tunnel north of Milan to make it easier for road traffic heading for Northern Europe to get across the Alps;
   (f) building a waterway link between the River Po and Lake Maggiore (see F. Santoro, op. cit., footnote on p. 26).
[2] Council Decision 66/161/EEC of 28 February 1966 instituting a procedure for consultation in respect of transport infrastructure investment (OJ 42, 8.3.1966, p. 583).
[3] Council Decision of 21 March 1962 instituting a procedure for prior examination and consultation in respect of certain laws, regulations and administrative provisions concerning transport proposed in Member States (OJ 23, 3.4.1962) as amended by Decision 73/402/EEC (OJ L 347, 17.12.1973).

4.2.1 *Improving the consultation procedure*

Between 1973 and 1976 the Commission conducted intensive studies into requirements in respect of the carriage of passengers between the major towns of Europe for the period from 1985 to 2000.[1] In 1977 it began a forward study on requirements in respect of the carriage of goods, again for 1985-2000,[2] and other studies on infrastructure capacity and evaluation of Community interest. Together with its action programme, it put forward a proposal designed to improve the consultation procedure established in 1966 and to create a Transport Infrastructure Committee.[3]

The proposal was extremely well received by the European Parliament[4] and by the ESC[5] and was adopted as the Council Decision of 20 February 1978 instituting a consultation procedure and setting up a committee in the field of transport infrastructure.[6]

This was an extremely important Decision both because of its political scope and because of its technical content. As has rightly been pointed out,[7] the Decision showed that the Council was convinced that transport infrastructure measures should play an important part in the future development of the common transport policy. Moreover, according to the Decision - and this was certainly a step forward compared with the previous consultation procedure - Member States were to notify the Commission of projects of Community interest and of plans and programmes they had drawn up for developing transport infrastructure which might form the subject of consultation, i.e. examination and discussion with representatives of the other Member States. The Commission also set up a Transport Infrastructure Committee consisting of representatives of the Member States, which had wide-ranging responsibilities and in particular the task of examining any question concerning the development of a transport network of benefit to the Community.

The Committee has already achieved some encouraging results and, as we have already mentioned, the Commission has completed a number of studies aimed at identifying the Community's infrastructure requirements and developing criteria for the determination of the Community interest in infrastructure projects. However, it is also true that the Council, to the Commission's chagrin, has yet to take a decision on the key questions of complementing the development of national transport infrastructures by a Community procedure

---

[1] COST 33 study in the *Tenth General Report on the Activities of the European Communities*, Brussels, Luxembourg, 1977, point 445.
[2] Eleventh General Report, Brussels, Luxembourg, 1978, point 372.
[3] OJ C 207, 2.9.1976.
[4] OJ C 183, 1.8.1977.
[5] OJ C 56, 7.3.1977.
[6] OJ L 54, 25.2.1978.
[7] See Bull. EC, Suppl. 8/79, p. 13.

designed to coordinate national planning more effectively with a view to developing a Community infrastructure network, and to plan, evaluate and finance specific projects of Community interest.[1]

4.2.2 *Financial support for projects of Community interest*

The second objective of the Community's action programme was the granting of financial support for projects of Community interest. To some extent this aim had already been anticipated by the Commission's Memorandum on infrastructure charging which made provision for the setting up of bodies to manage infrastructure which would have sufficient financial independence and would be free to establish their own investment programmes and take out loans to finance them.[2] On 5 July 1976 the Commission presented the Council with a proposal for a Regulation along these lines.[3]

According to the proposal[4] the aim of Community financial support was to give assistance with the implementation of transport infrastructure projects of Community interest under the following headings:

(i)   projects in the territory of a Member State designed to eliminate bottlenecks in Community traffic;

(ii)   cross-frontier projects which are not sufficiently economic to qualify as projects to which a Member State is prepared to allocate available resources;

(iii)   projects which, socio-economically, are not sufficiently important at national level to justify implementation but which, from the Community's point of view and from the point of view of the Community's specific objectives, are relatively much more important;

(iv)   projects which help to standardize equipment and synchronize work on the Community communications network.

Insofar as the consideration of benefits to the Community can positively influence national decisions and make possible the implementation of projects which are of relatively greater interest to the Community than to the Member State directly concerned, the system proposed by the Commission for granting financial support for a limited number of projects of importance to

---

[1] See the Commission's Communication to the Council of 11 February 1983 on *progress towards a common transport policy - inland transport* (OJ C 154, 13.6.1983, p. 7).

[2] Doc. COM(71) 268 final, p. 50.

[3] Proposal for a Council Regulation (EEC) on support for transport infrastructure projects of Community interest submitted by the Commission to the Council on 5 July 1976 (OJ C 207, 2.9.1976, p. 9).

[4] Later amended by a proposal submitted by the Commission on 4 March 1980 designed to extend the application of Community financial support to include infrastructure projects to be undertaken within a non-member country but of benefit to the Community (OJ C 89, 10.4.1980, p. 4).

the Community should make it possible to apply to transport infrastructure the whole range of financial instruments which exist within the Community, as shown in Annex. Briefly, these are EIB loans, the New Community Instrument (NCI), also called the Ortoli facility, which since 1979 has enabled the Commission to contract loans to finance investment projects in energy, industry - particularly small businesses - and infrastructure, the European Regional Development Fund (ERDF)[1] and the interest subsidies which are available to the less-prosperous Member States (currently Ireland and Italy) which are full members of the European Monetary System (EMS).

There would seem to be some justification for the introduction of the system proposed by the Commission, which is in keeping with the distinctive features of Community action on transport infrastructure,[2] if one considers the specific limitations of existing instruments with regard to financial support for transport infrastructure projects designed to help create an organized European network of communications.[3]

It is also worth mentioning that, while awaiting a Council Decision on its proposal for financial support for projects of Community interest, the Commission has prepared a detailed list of short-term and long-term transport infrastructure objectives, summarized below.[4]

(a) *Short-term objectives*

    (i)   Determination of bottlenecks likely to hinder traffic between the Member States.

    (ii)   Identification and examination of projects of Community interest.

    (iii)   International links between major centres (e.g. the following rail links: Brussels-Cologne, Utrecht-Cologne-Frankfurt, Amsterdam-Brussels-Luxembourg-Strasbourg).

    (iv)   Links with peripheral regions (e.g. in Ireland: Dublin-Derry and Dublin-Cork/Galway; in the United Kingdom, links with East Anglia; in Italy links with the Mezzogiorno and the islands).

    (v)   Links where an increase in traffic is expected following the accession of Greece and, later, Spain and Portugal.

---

[1] Council Decision 83/595/EEC of 29 November 1983 enabling the ERDF to exceed the 70% limit for infrastructure investment projects for the period 1981 to 1983 (OJ L 340, 6.12.1983).

[2] See the Communication to the Council on action in the field of transport infrastructure, Bull. EC 6-1976, points 1401 to 1404.

[3] In fact there are specific geographical restrictions on two of these instruments: the ERDF and the interest subsidies granted under the EMS; non-repayable subsidies may be granted only by the ERDF and EMS interest subsidies granted on EIB and NCI loans only for projects in the less prosperous countries of the Community; lastly the EIB and the NCI grant loans, the terms of which depend on those prevailing on the capital market. For further information see the *special report of the Court of Auditors on loans and borrowings* (OJ C 319, 6.12.1982).

[4] Bull. EC, Suppl. 8/79, pp. 14-15.

(vi)   Links overcoming natural obstacles (e.g. the Channel crossing,[1] the link between the Federal Republic of Germany and Denmark, the Alpine links between the Federal Republic of Germany and Italy and the Apennine crossings).

(vii)   'Missing links' between existing networks. A prime example for the motorway network is the Thionville-Luxembourg-Trier link; the inland waterways need a link between Belgium and France (to handle large vessels) and between the North Sea and the Mediterranean via the Rhine-Rhône Canal.

(b) *Long-term objectives*

(i)   Definition of a network of major links of Community interest and evaluation of investment needs.

(ii)   Research into criteria for selecting between investment projects and cost/benefit analysis to determine on an objective basis criteria for assessing the Community interest of a project.

After the Commission had published the 1979 Memorandum on the role of the Community in the development of transport infrastructure,[2] which was favourably received by the European Parliament[3] and by the ESC,[4] it went on to draft two sets of reports on bottlenecks[5] and criteria for assessing the Community interest of transport infrastructure investment projects.[6] On the basis of these reports the Council, at its meeting on 15 December 1981, asked the Commission to cooperate with the Transport Infrastructure Committee in applying the methods for assessing Community interest on an experimental basis to a limited number of specific projects and to submit its conclusions before 1 October 1982. Within this deadline, the Commission submitted to the Council a Communication concerning an experimental transport infrastructure programme[7] on which Parliament and the ESC have given their opinion. The Communication lists the projects previously selected by the Member States, compares them and decides which could be considered to be of overriding Community interest. In the Communication the Commission estimates that the Community budget will have to provide approximately 300 million ECU for infrastructure projects in the three years from 1984 to 1986 and that on average the maximum financial

---

[1] On a number of occasions the European Parliament has argued in favour of a fixed link across the Channel. See the recent interim report by the Committee on Transport on the possibilities of providing Community support for a fixed link across the Channel, Doc. 1-372/83, 30.5.1983 and the Resolution of 10 June 1983 (OJ C 184, 14.7.1983).

[2] Doc. COM(79) 550 final, 14.11.1979.

[3] Opinion of 7 May 1981 (OJ C 144, 15.6.1981).

[4] Opinion of 26 February 1981 (OJ C 138, 9.6.1981).

[5] 'Report on bottlenecks and possible modes of finance', requested by the Council in November 1978 and forwarded by the Commission on 19 June 1980.

[6] 'Community assistance for transport infrastructure: the evaluation of Community interest for decision making', document of 16 September 1981 sent to the Council on 29 September 1981; 'Report from the Commission to the Council: the Community interest of transport infrastructure investments: practical experience with the evaluation methodology', document of 7 December 1982.

[7] Doc. COM(82) 828 final.

the maximum financial support for each project should work out at 20% of its total cost, so that the total cost of the experimental programme could be put at 1 500 million ECU.

Although the Council has still not reached a decision on the experimental programme, the Economic and Social Committee emphasizes in its opinion the need to create new structures for financing transport infrastructure investment projects, in particular by setting up a special Community financial instrument, in the form of a fund for the development of transport infrastructure within the Community (Infrafonds).[1] This fund could be financed from national charges for the use of infrastructure.

For its part, the European Parliament advocates instead an intermodal approach based on complementarity which it feels is the only way of allowing each mode of transport, including combined transport, to play its proper part within the Community. It also complains that the list of sample projects compiled from Member States' contributions contains a majority of road projects and a large number of rail projects. In its opinion the interest shown by the Community in these types of infrastructure should on no account exclude other types of transport infrastructures, e.g. inland waterways, ports and airports.[2]

Subsequently, in 1983 the Commission came up with a proposal for a Regulation on financial support for a multiannual transport infrastructure programme[3] which, if adopted, would go some way towards providing direct assistance for transport infrastructure projects of Community interest. This took the form of rules on a multiannual experimental programme to run until the Council adopted the basic proposal for a Regulation on Community support for transport infrastructure projects which was first submitted in 1976, and subsequently amended on several occasions.

The proposal covers Community finance for transport infrastructure over a period of five years. Apart from transitional rules which apply to 1983 and 1984, the proposal contains a number of general rules for deciding which projects are to be financed. On the basis of these rules, the Commission decides from a list of eligible projects on the financial support to be granted, the total amount of which may not exceed 70% of the cost of the individual project. Financial support is to take the form of a subsidy or interest rate reduction, and these may be combined with other forms of Community financial assistance for the same project. The list of projects is to be drafted by the Commission on the basis of information received from the Member States and taking account of the rules defining Community interest. The list is then put before the Council for its approval, after the European Parliament has given its opinion.

---

[1] See Opinion of the ESC on the Commission Communication to the Council on an experimental transport infrastructure programme (OJ C 341, 19.12.1983, pp. 4, 5 and 7).

[2] European Parliament Resolution closing the procedure for consultation of the European Parliament on the Communication on an experimental transport infrastructure programme (OJ C 184, 11.7.1983, pp. 136-137).

[3] Doc. COM(83) 474 final.

The European Parliament has published an opinion firmly supporting the proposal.[1] A striking feature of this opinion is its call on the Commission to extend its machinery for evaluating the importance to the Community of transport infrastructure projects when implementing the proposed multiannual programme and, in particular, to establish, during the two-year transitional period, adequate objective criteria for determining the benefit to the Community by means of a cost-benefit analysis using a standard procedure for all projects.[2] The Parliament was also in full agreement regarding the criteria for selecting the types of project to be financed, the priorities being to eliminate bottlenecks within the Community, to improve railway services on the main long distance routes, particularly combined transport, to improve links between the outlying Member States and the rest of the Community by the use of trunk routes, which may involve transit through a non-Community country, to improve transfer facilities between modes of transport within the Community - and here Parliament asks for particular account to be taken of those seaports and airports important for traffic between Member States - and to modernize the inland waterway system.[3]

In addition to the experimental programme and the multiannual programme, a third venture of the Commission, in a somewhat more limited field, was to propose limited financial support for transport infrastructure designed to make full use of the administrative appropriations available under the 1982 Budget (as adopted by the European Parliament) which amount to 10 million ECU.[4] Accordingly, on 20 July 1982, the Commission submitted a proposal for a Regulation on the granting of Community financial support, not to exceed 20% of the cost of the project, for work on modernizing sections of, or stations on, transalpine rail links, provided that the work in question is compatible with the long-term development alternatives for these links, and for preparatory work which will speed up the transition to the construction phase of projects affecting traffic between Member States.[5] This proposal subsequently became the only actual decision so far adopted by the Council on financial support for transport infrastructure projects of Community interest, namely Council Regulation (EEC) No 3600/82 of 30 December 1982 on the granting of limited support in the field of transport infrastructure.[6] On the basis of this Regulation the Council freed the appropriations available under the 1982 Budget in order to

---

[1] See EP Working Documents 1983-84, Report drawn up on behalf of the Committee on Transport on the proposal from the Commission of the European Communities to the Council for a Regulation on financial support for a multiannual transport infrastructure programme, Doc. No 1-979/83 of 8 November 1983.

[2] *Idem,* pp. 8 and 13.

[3] *Idem,* pp. 7-8.

[4] See Article 781 'Financial support for transport infrastructure projects' in the General Budget of the European Communities for the financial year 1982. The appropriation earmarked for this heading for 1983 is 15 million ECU. The financial support takes the form of subsidies or interest rebates for infrastructure projects of Community interest.

[5] Proposal for a Council Regulation on the granting of limited financial support in the field of transport infrastructure (submitted by the Commission to the Council on 20 July 1982) (OJ C 226, 31.8.1982, p. 14 and 15).

[6] OJ L 376, 31.12.1982, p. 10.

grant financial support to implement, in Italy, the 'marshalling yard and customs station at Domodossola' project and, in Greece, the 'Evzoni-Volos road-section between Kleidi and Axios' project. Support was also to be granted for the technical work being done by banking institutions on the appraisal of a fixed cross-Channel link project.

On the basis of this Council Regulation, the Commission subsequently decided to grant financial support of 7 million ECU for the Italian project[1] and 2.5 million ECU for the Greek project.[2] The money left over is to be used for studies on a fixed cross-Channel link but so far no decision has been taken by the Commission on the granting of financial support.

There is as yet no legal instrument which enables the appropriation of 15 million ECU entered in the 1983 Budget for financial support for infrastructure projects actually to be used. This is because, at its meeting on 7 June 1983, the Council did no more than discuss the problem of selecting projects to be financed, while the possibility of actually adopting a proposal for a Regulation on the granting of limited financial support in the field of transport infrastructure from the amounts allocated in the 1983 Budget, which the Commission had meanwhile put forward, came to nothing because of a difference of opinion between the Council and the Commission on the period of application of the Regulation. The Council considered that only one-year programmes should be envisaged while the Commission - and its opinion was shared by the ESC and the Parliament - felt that action on infrastructure would necessarily have to come within the framework of a multiannual programme.

In the meantime, no decision has been taken by the Council on the crux of the whole matter of infrastructure, in other words on the basic Regulation to grant Community support for transport infrastructure projects of Community interest proposed by the Commission[3] and repeatedly called for by the European Parliament as being the most effective instrument for a Community transport infrastructure policy.[4]

---

[1] Commission Decision 83/474/EEC of 12 September 1983 (OJ L 260, 21.9.1983, p. 23).
[2] Commission Decision 83/472/EEC of 12 September 1983 (OJ L 259, 20.9.1983, p. 32).
[3] OJ C 207, 2.9.1976, p. 7, as subsequently amended in OJ C 249, 18.10.1977, p. 5 and OJ C 89, 10.4.1980, p. 4.
[4] See EP, Doc. No 1-979/83, 8.11.1983, cit. p. 11.

ANNEX B

Existing sources for infrastructure financing in the Community[1]
(including transport infrastructure)

	European Regional Development Fund	European Investment Bank
Eligible infrastructure projects	Infrastructure investments which contribute to the development of certain regions	Investments in infrastructure projects of regional or Community interest
Geographical limits	1. Regions established by Member States in applying their systems of regional aids and for which State aids are granted 2. Participation of the Fund in the financing of specific measures: regions to be determined by the Council	1. Community 2. Outside the Community (ACP and Mediterranean countries)
Forms of intervention	1. Subsidies 2. Interest rebates of 3 points on EIB loans	1. Loans 2. Guarantees
Resources	— Fund budget for 1983: 1 909.5 million ECU (Not including 100.5 million ECU for specific measures). Probably available for infrastructure projects: 70%, a condition which did not apply for the period 1981-83 under the Council Decision of 29.11.83 — Distribution of the Fund's resources between the Member States according to quota[2] (95% of the budget) — Specific measures: distribution to be determined by the Council (5% of the budget)	Loans and guarantees granted in 1982: 4 244.2 million ECU, of which 682.2 million ECU for transport infrastructure projects within the Community
Financial conditions	1. Investments must exceed 50 000 u.a. 2. — Investments < 10 million u.a.: maximum Fund contribution 30% of national aid — investments > 10 million u.a.: maximum Fund contribution 10-30% — investments of particular importance: maximum Fund contribution 40% 3. Specific measures: conditions to be determined by the Council	1. Maximum contribution 50% of the cost of the project 2. Projects must offer prospects of a reasonable return (commercial criterion) 3. Guarantee of the State or other first-class security.
Procedures	1. Member State submits request to the Commission 2. Consultation of Fund Committee 3. Consultation of Regional Policy Committee projects ⩾ 10 million u.a. 4. Commission decides; if its decision is not in accordance with the Committee's, the Council decides	1. Member State, Commission or undertaking submits request to the Bank 2. Consultation of Commission and Member State 3. Bank decides (acting unanimously if the Commission's opinion is unfavourable)
Legal bases	1. Council Regulation (EEC) No 724/75 of 18 March 1975, as amended by: 2. Council Regulation (EEC) No 214/79 of 6 February 1979 3. Council Regulation (EEC) No 3325/80 of 16 December 1980	1. Treaty, Title IV, Articles 129 and 130 2. Protocol on the Statute of the EIB 3. EIB Annual Report

[1] Apart from infrastructure aids under Article 56 of the ECSC Treaty and Article 84 of the Budget (EAGGF) which are specifically aimed at particular sectors (coal and steel, and agriculture), the amounts in question are comparatively small.

[2]
Belgium	1.11%	Greece	13.00%
Denmark	1.06%	Italy	35.49%
Federal Republic of Germany	4.65%	Luxembourg	0.07%
France	13.64%	Netherlands	1.24%
Ireland	5.94%	United Kingdom	23.80%

	New Community Instrument (NCI)	EMS interest rebates
Eligible infrastructure projects	Investments in infrastructure (and industrial and energy) projects which contribute to convergence and integration of the economic policies of the Member States, taking into account the regional and employment effects	Investments in infrastructure projects in the less prosperous countries participating in the EMS, taking into account the regional effects
Geographical limits	Community	1. Italy 2. Ireland
Forms of intervention	Loans	Interest rebates on 3 points on EIB and NCI loans
Resources	1 000 million ECU (NCI 1) 1 000 million ECU (NCI 2) 3 000 million ECU (NCI 3)[1]	1 000 million ECU (in five yearly tranches of 200 million ECU each) as interest rebates on EIB and NCI loans of 5 000 million ECU (in five yearly tranches of 1 000 million ECU each)
Financial conditions	In accordance with EIB conditions	In accordance with EIB conditions
Procedures	1. Council approves tranches and establishes regulations for the projects 2. Requests submitted to the European Investment Bank directly or through the Commission or Member State 3. Commission decides on the eligibility of the project 4. Bank decides on the granting and conditions of the loan	1. Commission and Member States prepare indicative programmes 2. Consultation of Member States 3. Commission decides on the eligibility of the project 4. Bank decides on the granting and conditions of the loans
Legal bases	1. Council Decision 78/870/EEC of 16 October 1978; Council Decision 79/486/EEC of 14 May 1979; Council Decision 80/739/EEC of 22 July 1980; Council Decision 80/1103/EEC of 25 November 1980; Council Decision 82/169/EEC of 15 March 1982; Council Decision 82/268/EEC of 26 April 1982; Council Decision 83/200/EEC of 19 April 1983; Council Decision 83/308/EEC of 13 June 1983 2. Cooperation agreement between the Commission and the Bank of 27 November 1978 3. Protocol on the Statute of the EIB	1. Council Regulation (EEC) No 1736/79 of 3 August 1979 2. Council Decision 79/691/EEC of 3 August 1979 3. Cooperation agreement between the Commission and the EIB of 17 September 1979

[1] Overall figures, including 624.6 million ECU invested by 30.9.1983 in transport infrastructure. See EIB 1982 Annual Report and EIB Information, No 31 of July 1982 and No 36 of October 1983.

5. Technical standardization

Although no mention was made of this subject in the framework Decision of 13 May 1965, the Commission considered it worthwhile proposing the harmonization of certain technical standards and regulations concerning road transport.

To begin with at least, the Commission's efforts in this area were designed to ensure the free movement within the Community of a specific finished product, the motor vehicle, and to eliminate technical barriers to trade within the Community resulting from different manufacturing standards for motor vehicles in different Member States. In many cases these differences prevented motor vehicle manufacturers from offering their products for sale in the other Member States or forced them to incur additional and unjustifiable extra costs in order to meet the manufacturing standards imposed in the other Member States. By harmonizing technical standards, it was the Commission's intention to encourage the free movement of motor industry products throughout the Community.

This was the aim behind the 'General programme for the elimination of technical barriers to trade which result from disparities between the provisions laid down by law, regulation or administrative action in Member States' which the Commission adopted on the basis of Article 100 of the Treaty on the approximation of legislation. It submitted the programme to the Council on 28 May 1969 and from February 1970 onwards proceeded within this framework to submit to the Council a series of measures to approximate highly technical legislation in the Member States, many of which have been adopted. These measures concerned the rules on the technical approval of vehicles, including tractors used in agriculture or forestry, noise levels, exhaust systems, fuel tanks, rear protective devices, the positioning and mounting of the rear registration plate, direction indicators, doors, audible warning devices, pollution caused by vehicles, the suppression of radio interference caused by spark-ignition engines, external projections, rear-view mirrors, braking devices, lighting devices, fog lights, safety glass, safety belts, field of vision, windscreen wipers, the strength of seats, the behaviour of steering wheels in accidents, speedometers and reversing lights.

Later on measures were adopted concerning the measurement of the capacity of the tanks of vessels,[1] the reciprocal recognition of navigability licences for inland waterway vessels,[2] the ratification of the International Convention for Safe

---

[1] Council Directive of 12 October 1971 (OJ L 239, 25.10.1971).
[2] Council Directive of 23 November 1978 amending Directive 76/135/EEC (OJ L 349, 13.12.1978).

Containers (CSC),[1] summertime arrangements,[2] the introduction of reduced rates for telephone calls within the Community,[3] roadworthiness tests for motor vehicles,[4] the limitation of noise emissions from subsonic aircraft[5] and first steps towards the introduction of a Community driving licence.[6]

Although the original purpose was to guarantee the free movement of goods, the new guidelines for the common transport policy set out in the October 1973 Memorandum extended the purpose of approximating the legislation of Member States on technical standards considerably, so that European standards for the manufacture of motor vehicles were subsequently recognized as being intended to improve road traffic safety, to help protect the environment and to safeguard the citizens of Europe.[7] It is worth mentioning, however, that the EEC is not the only body concerned with technical standardization. The ECMT also plays an important role in this area, although within a different context, particularly with regard to rail transport.

5.1 Weights and dimensions of commercial vehicles

It should be made clear from the outset that technical standardization at European level was never seen as a necessity in road transport as it was in rail transport. Only with commercial vehicles and only as international trade developed did different dimensions and construction features begin to create real problems. This prompted study on the adoption of European standards on dimensions, overall weight and axle weight.

Attempts were made in each Member State to come up with rules on weights and dimensions which constituted a satisfactory compromise between the two main requirements. On the one hand, it was necessary to ensure that light motor traffic continued to flow smoothly and generally to prevent congestion on the roads, while on the other hand, account had to be taken of the concern of transport operators to minimize operating costs per unit of load by achieving the maximum possible benefit from the economies of scale of their vehicles, hence their preference for high-capacity vehicles.[8] Furthermore, in order to protect road infrastructure, account had to be taken of the permissible weights of vehicles, in terms not only of overall weight but also of the weight on each

---

[1] Council Recommendation 79/487/EEC of 15 May 1979 on the ratification of the CSC (OJ L 125, 22.5.1979) and proposal for a Council Directive on the harmonized application of the CSC in the EEC (OJ C 228, 8.9.1980).
[2] Council Directive of 22 July 1980 on summertime arrangements (OJ L 205, 7.8.1980).
[3] EP, Report drawn up on behalf of the Committee on Transport on the introduction of reduced rates at weekends, on official holidays and after 8 p.m. for all intra-Community telephone calls, Doc. 1-502/83, 15.7.1983.
[4] Council Directive 77/143/EEC of 29 December 1976 (OJ L 47, 18.2.1977).
[5] Council Directive 80/51/EEC of 20 December 1979 (OJ L 18, 24.1.1980).
[6] Council Directive 80/1263/EEC of 4 December 1980 (OJ L 375, 31.12.1980).
[7] Internal EEC Memorandum No 68/75 of 19 December 1974.
[8] See Annex C.

axle, since the wear and tear on road surfaces was basically a function of the weight of the vehicles using them and in particular, as was shown by the well-publicized and much-discussed ASHO tests in America, the weight on the axles. Clearly, at Community level, rules on the weights and dimensions of commercial vehicles were bound to vary considerably depending on the emphasis which was placed on each of these factors. Furthermore, in international transport within the Community, not only are there differences in rules but there are also differences in the conditions under which the transport operators belonging to the various Member States operate. Obviously those operators belonging to countries with more liberal rules will enjoy a comparative advantage. At present, rules within the Community vary considerably, as is shown in the Annex at the end of this chapter,[1] both in terms of maximum permissible weight, where the range is from 32 to 44 tonnes for five-axle semi-trailers and in terms of maximum weight per axle - from 10 to 13 tonnes.

It is worth pointing out that, on the basis of a proposal originally presented by the Commission on 7 December 1962[2] and subsequently amended by the addition of some further technical conditions,[3] the original six Member States managed, in a Council Decision of 17 May 1972, to agree on a maximum weight per axle of 11 tonnes and a maximum overall weight of 40 tonnes (for five-axle semi-trailers).[4]

Unfortunately, the accession of the three new Member States postponed the prospect of an agreement indefinitely since they rejected the compromise reached by the Six as unacceptable, the weight on each individual axle being 8 tonnes in Denmark, 10 tonnes in Ireland and the United Kingdom and the maximum overall weight 32 tonnes in all three countries.

Thus, as regards standardization of the weights and dimensions of commercial vehicles, the enlargement of the Community clearly made the already complex harmonization problem facing the six founder members considerably more complicated.

---

[1] See Annex C.
[2] Doc. COM(62) 244 final.
[3] Proposal for a Council Directive of 21 May 1971 on the weights, dimensions and certain other technical characteristics of commercial road vehicles (OJ C 90, 11.9.1971).
[4] See Annex D.

ANNEX C

Breakdown of transport costs relative to payload depending on total weight (38 t vehicle)

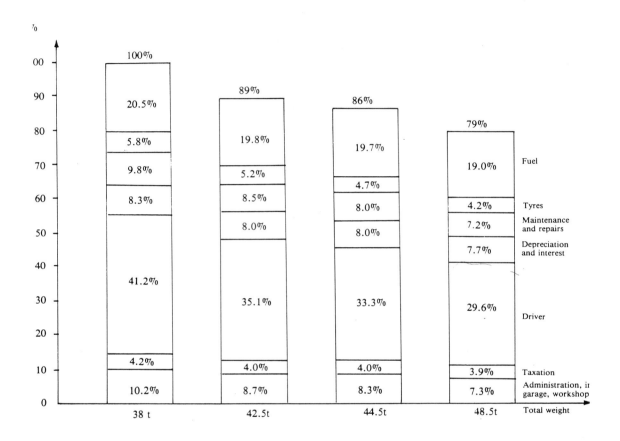

Source: Institut für Verkehrswesen, Universität (TH) Karlsruhe, Darstellung der Systemkomponenten und Elemente des zu optimierenden System Güterfernverkehr auf Bundesautobahnen. Systemmodel, unpublished preliminary study commissioned by die Forschungsvereinigung Automobiltechnik e.V. (FAT), Karlsruhe 1977. Figure 3.23.

ANNEX D

Maximum permissible total weights in the Member States of the European Community and the Commissions's harmonization proposal

B	D	DK	F	UK	EEC		I	IRL	L	NL
26	22	24	26	24	2 4		24	22	26	24
26	22	32	26	30	3 0		24	28	26	—
38	32	38	38	32	3 5		40	32	38	34.5
38	38	42	38	32	4 0		44	32	38	40.5
38	38	44	38	32	4 2		44	32	38	42.5
38	38	44	38	32	4 4		44	32	38	48.5
39	32	38	38	32	3 5		40	32	40	36.5
40	38	42	38	32	4 0		44	32	40	42.5
40	38	44	38	32	4 2		44	32	40	42.5
40	38	44	38	32	4 4		44	32	40	50

Source : Journal of the Federal Association of German Long-distance Transport (BDF).

6. Combined transport

Since the mid-1970s increasing interest has been shown within the Community in the development of intermodal operations which combine rail transport with other modes. Although previously the Commission had been concentrating on the problem of harmonizing conditions of competition within each mode of transport and between the different modes of transport, the October 1973 Memorandum clearly recognized the interdependence in the Community between transport policy and other Community policies designed to improve living and working conditions while at the same time recognizing the importance of the public authorities in the transport sector. The most important aspect of this new attitude to the common transport policy was the emphasis placed on integrating national transport systems into a Community system, a process requiring intervention by the Community in many different areas in order to make the best use of the resources of the transport sector.

It is not surprising, therefore, that from 1975 onwards a number of Community measures were taken to encourage combined road/rail transport (sometimes referred to as 'piggyback transport') in view of its many advantages in terms of improving the use of existing infrastructure, swift and regular service, energy saving and environmental protection. The aim was to increase the efficiency of the various types of service and transport operation in order both to improve the financial situation of railway undertakings and to promote uses which would help to improve rail services.

Thus the first Council Directive[1] of 17 February 1975 freed certain types of combined road/rail carriage of goods between Member States from all quota systems and systems of authorization. This applied to the carriage of goods by road (on own account or for hire or reward) where the tractor unit, lorry, trailer, semi-trailer or their swop bodies (including containers of 20 feet or more according to the amendments contained in Directives 79/5/EEC and 82/3/EEC) are transported by rail between the nearest stations and the points of loading and unloading. A subsequent Council Resolution[2] of 15 December 1981 on the Community's rail policy placed particular emphasis on the development of combined transport as a means of improving the efficiency and hence the financial position of the railways and asked the Commission to submit proposals on, in particular, a suggested network of rail links and transfer terminals to handle the future development of combined transport in the context of more intensive cooperation between railway undertakings. A Council Directive of 28 July 1982 later extended the scope of Directive 75/130/EEC to include

---

[1] Council Directive 75/130/EEC on the establishment of common rules for certain types of combined road/rail carriage of goods between Member States (OJ L 48, 22.2.1975, p. 1) as subsequently amended by Council Directive 79/5/EEC (OJ L 5, 9.1.1979).
[2] Council Resolution of 15 December 1981, op. cit., p. 2.

combined transport by inland waterway and also included a provision to reduce vehicle excise duties in proportion to the journeys they undertake by rail.[1]

More recently, the Commission forwarded to the Council a proposal for a recommendation concerning the International Company for Piggyback Transport (Interunit) which was set up to encourage the development of piggyback transport, of railway networks in the Community and of piggyback companies in the Member States.[2] Then in 1983, the Commission sent the Council a draft recommendation on improving the structure of railway tariffs for international transport by container and piggyback techniques by combining the scales for the national sections by means of through tariffs involving a decreasing scale of charges.[3] According to these through tariffs, rates would be set from the point of departure to the point of arrival and would decrease as a function of the total distance. They would be set at a level which would take sufficient account of the existing competitive situation and in particular the through rates charged by road hauliers on the traffic links concerned. On 18 October 1983 the Commission sent the Council a report on the conclusion of negotiations with a view to signing the Agreement between the European Economic Community and Spain on the international combined road/rail carriage of goods. This Agreement is intended to free terminal road sections following a rail section from all quota and authorizations restrictions.[4]

---

[1] Council Directive 82/603/EEC of 28 July 1982 amending Directive 75/130/EEC on the establishment of common rules for certain types of combined road/rail carriage of goods between Member States (OJ L 247, 23.8.1982).
[2] Proposal for a Council recommendation concerning the International Company for Piggyback Transport submitted by the Commission to the Council on 15 June 1983 (OJ C 179, 6.7.1983, p. 4).
[3] Draft Council recommendation on railway tariffs for international transport by container and piggyback techniques submitted by the Commission to the Council on 24 June 1983 (OJ C 187, 13.7.1983, p. 7). ESC opinion (OJ C 23, 30.1.1984).
[4] COM(83) 590 final.

7. Sea and air transport

We have already discussed the problem of interpreting paragraph 2 of Article 84 of the Treaty and the judgment handed down by the Court of Justice on 4 April 1974 to the effect that the provisions of the Treaty outside Title IV also apply to sea and air transport. We have also explained the reasons which, at the time of the negotiations, prompted the drafters of the Treaty to limit the scope of the *lex specialis* devised for transport only to inland modes.

To a Community which had set itself as an immediate objective the creation of a customs union, and thus to some extent was taking a 'continental' view since its first concern was to eliminate barriers to trade between the Member States within it, the fact that, compared with inland transport, sea and air transport had special problems because of the world-wide scale of their market was a decisive factor at the time the Treaty was signed. It was felt that attempts by the Community to regulate these two sectors would run up against problems since the fleets of the Member States operated in a world market alongside countries which had no ties with the Community, but also alongside other countries which accounted for a considerable volume of the Community's trade. It could fairly be argued at the time, therefore, that Community regulations might serve to discriminate against non-Community countries since not all of them were trading partners of the Community.

Problems like flags of convenience, flag discrimination, the harmonization of working conditions of crews and State aid to the shipbuilding industry played, and continue to play, a by no means insignificant role in creating potential distortions of competition on the market and making it difficult to compare the operating conditions of shipping fleets in the various countries.[1] However, since it would have to consider competition on a world-wide basis, the Community felt that these admittedly important problems affecting the shipping market could not be tackled directly by the Treaty itself, not only because of the 'continental' view taken by the drafters of the Treaty but also because of the course the negotiations had taken and the fact that transport had been recognized as a separate economic sector very late on in the negotiations.

In any event, the wording of Article 84(2) of the Treaty prompted discussions as to whether the general rules of the Treaty outside Title IV should apply to sea and air transport, before such time as the Council reached a unanimous decision. From the outset the Commission had argued that the Treaty provisions were universally applicable, but certain governments, particularly the French Government, took an opposing 'minimalist' view arguing that because of the distinctive features of transport, provisions devised for industrial and commercial activities which had none of these distinctive features could not automatically be applied to transport.

---

[1] See B. Minoletti, *Trasporti marittimi e Mercato Comune,* cit., in F. Santoro, op. cit., p. 387.

Thus it was only after the important judgment handed down by the Court of Justice in 1974 that the problems of sea and air transport, the importance of which had already been stressed by the Commission in its Communication to the Council of October 1973, became the province of the Community. We should not forget, however, that in its Memorandum of 12 November 1960, the Commission had already made clear its opinion on the applicability of the Treaty to sea and air transport. It reiterated this opinion in its Memorandum of 10 April 1961.

The Commission argued that the Community would benefit from the application to sea and air transport of Treaty provisions on the free movement of workers, the right of establishment, the approximation of legislation, regulations and administrative provisions, and the harmonization of taxation, social provisions and commercial policy. However, it felt that considerable caution should be exercised in applying the rules on competition to these two sectors because of the strength of the competition at world level (particularly from the USA, the USSR and Japan as far as shipping was concerned).[1] On air transport, the Commission wanted to see a coordinated policy and concentrated efforts to put an end to the cut-throat competition between national airlines, particularly on trans-Atlantic routes. Finally, the Commission considered it particularly important to establish a common policy on investment and standardization of civil air fleets. Another reason for including air and sea transport within the scope of Community activities was the Community's commercial policy. Since Articles 113 and 114 state that the Community's trade agreements with non-member countries shall be negotiated by the Commission and concluded by the Council and since, in fact, most of these agreements are commercial and navigation treaties, it was difficult to envisage how the Community could conclude international agreements in sectors in which only the Member States were competent to negotiate.

7.1 Sea transport

On 4 June 1970, i.e. before the Court of Justice handed down its judgment of April 1974, Victor Bodson attended his last Council meeting as the Member of the Commission responsible for transport. On behalf of the Commission, he presented to that meeting a full report on the action to be taken at Community level on sea and air transport.[2]

In the Bodson report the Commission was not proposing that the Council adopt a full and proper policy on shipping. In view of the unanimity provision of

---

[1] In actual fact, the abovementioned Council Regulation No 141 of 26 November 1962 had exempted sea and air transport from the application of the rules on competition in Articles 85 and 86 of the Treaty for an unlimited period.

[2] For a summary of the report see V. Bodson, 'Le prospettive della politica commune dei transporti', in *Automobilismo e Automobilismo industriale*, Nos 5-6, 1970. As well as levelling some detailed criticism against the European transport policy followed in the past, the Bodson report contained a number of important innovatory proposals which were later taken up in the Communication of 24 October 1973.

Article 84(2) of the Treaty it instead listed a number of problems on which a swift Community decision would be desirable. These can be summarized as:

(i) the need to establish proper links between the Community's commercial policy and action on shipping when it comes to negotiations on agreements with non-member countries based on Article 113 of the Treaty, a particularly important point in respect of those non-Community countries which reserve cargo for ships of their own flag;[1]

(ii) the adoption of a common approach towards international economic organizations like Unctad and the OECD, in accordance with the provisions of Article 116;

(iii) the establishment of a procedure for cooperation between Member States in order better to protect their interests against flag discrimination by non-Community countries against the fleets of Member States;

(iv) the adoption of a common policy (harmonized at Community level) to policy on State aid for shipping aimed at improving the competitiveness of the fleets of the Member States and maintaining services felt to be essential;

(v) the standardization of working conditions of crews.

On 12 April 1972 the European Parliament adopted a resolution based on the Seefeld report accepting the objectives proposed by the Commission. The report pointed out that with the forthcoming enlargement of the Community it was increasingly urgent for the Community to work out and implement a common policy on shipping pursuant to Article 84(2) of the EEC Treaty.[2]

Once this programme had been worked out, the Commission did in fact attempt to stamp out flag discrimination by entering into various trade negotiations, particularly with Argentina, Brazil and Uruguay. In the end, however, no tangible results were achieved, principally because of vigorous opposition by the French to any mention of shipping in Community agreements on the grounds that this conflicted with the provisions of Article 84(2) of the Treaty.

Shipping became a new area of Community concern after the Community was enlarged and the Court handed down its judgment of 4 April 1974 taking the French Republic to task for maintaining shipping rules benefiting French seamen which were tantamount to discrimination on grounds of nationality. The judgment also confirmed the principle that the Treaty applied to sea and air transport in the same way as to the other three modes of inland transport provided they did not contravene the special provisions of the *lex specialis*.

---

[1] It is worth remembering that on 9 October 1961, when the USA adopted the Bonner Act which provided for somewhat oppressive inspection procedures for all vessels calling at American ports, the Community had failed to agree on any concerted action, whereas the USA had adopted joint measures with other European countries and with Japan within the framework of the OECD.

[2] EP Working document No 10/1972.

In any case the Commission's Communication to the Council of 24 October 1973 had already reiterated the importance of sea and air transport within the framework of the new approach to the common transport policy. However, it was principally in the second half of the 1970s that a particular effort was made by the Community on shipping.

We have already seen how this renewed interest mirrored the concerns of Member States such as Germany, the United Kingdom and the Netherlands in the face of unfair competition on certain trading routes from the Eastern bloc fleets. Another factor was the spate of serious oil spills which re-alerted governments to the need for Community action to safeguard against the dangers to public safety and the environment resulting from inadequate international regulations in this field.

The Commission took the view that it was still possible to take *ad hoc* Community action in specific areas, even if the Member States could not reach the minimum level of agreement required to start work on an overall plan of action on shipping.

A Community consultation procedure was actually adopted by the Council on 28 June 1977, which would apply to relations between Member States and non-Community countries and to action on shipping within international organizations.[1] Even though this Decision reflected only part of the Commission's proposal - the Commission wanted prior consultation in respect both of bilateral shipping agreements concluded between Member States and non-Community countries and of shipping matters discussed in international organizations, whereas the Council authorized consultation only in respect of the former, and after the event at that[2] - it nevertheless constituted the legal instrument which would serve as a basis, at Community level, for discussion of the most urgent problems facing sea transport without raising the thorny matter of the unanimous decisions required under Article 84(2). There is no denying that from 1978 onwards the fact that the Community had this institutionalized instrument for a consultation between Member States went some way towards speeding up Community action on the major shipping problems facing the Member States. These problems included:

(i)   relations with State-trading countries;

(ii) the organization of liner shipping and, in particular, defining the EEC's position on the 1974 Geneva Convention on a code of conduct for liner conferences;

(iii) safety of shipping and prevention of marine pollution,

---

[1] Council Decision 77/587/EEC of 13 September 1977 setting up a consultation procedure on relations between Member States and third countries in shipping matters and on action relating to such matters in international organizations (OJ L 239, 17.9.1977).

[2] And in fact came in for criticism from the European Parliament: see the Seefeld report on the present state and progress of the common transport policy, Doc. EP No 512/78 of 5 January 1979, p. 54.

(iv)   the application to shipping of the rules on competition.

We shall now examine these problems in detail.

7.1.1   *Relations with State-trading countries*

In 1978 the Council adopted two important Decisions in response to the acute concern shown by Member States in the face of the increasingly serious threat to the future of their merchant fleets from the unfair competitive practices used by the fleets of Comecon, and in particular the Soviet Union, the German Democratic Republic and Poland.

In an important document published in the same year,[1] the Commission analysed the way in which the fleets of the Socialist countries had rapidly penetrated the liner shipping market. This was seen as a growing threat to Community shipowners and one which was likely to become increasingly serious during the 1980s with the expected expansion of the liner fleets of the Comecon countries. The document showed that in 1976 the Netherlands' share of bilateral trade with the Comecon countries was barely 5% and that, of bilateral liner trade between the USSR and countries of the EEC, the Soviet fleet accounted for 64% with the United Kingdom (1976), 75% with Germany (1976) and 83% with Belgium (1975). Further, the Soviet Union's share of trade with non-Community countries had also reached alarming proportions as a result of the widespread dumping on the international market which is possible under a planned economic system by offering long-term freight rates which Western shipowners could not possibly match.[2]

The Commission therefore argued that in order to protect Community ship-owners it was essential to set up channels to provide regular information on market penetration by Comecon fleets so that, where necessary, appropriate countermeasures could be taken in good time. Accordingly, in April 1978, the Commission forwarded to the Council a proposal for a Decision asking each Member State to monitor the liner trade of the State-trading countries and authorizing each Member State, where necessary, to implement national legislation in retaliation. The substance of this proposal was embodied in a Decision taken by the Council on 19 September 1978 although - in order to placate the French representative, a loyal supporter of the Giscardian policy to maintain special relations between the Soviet Union and France - the document speaks in general terms of collecting information on the activities of third countries whose

---

[1] Commission of the European Communities, *Les transports maritimes des pays à commerce d'État et la Communauté,* Brussels, 1978.
[2] The study included some extremely interesting statistics: in 1976 the USSR accounted for 28% and 25% of trade on the west-east and east-west North Atlantic routes respectively; in the same year, the USSR accounted for 97% of bilateral liner trade with Japan and Comecon fleets accounted for 35% of the tonnage carried in liner trade between Northern Europe and the Mediterranean.

practices are harmful to the shipping interests of the Member States, but does not refer directly to State-trading countries.[1]

Later, however, the Decision was amended by the Council at its meeting on 23 November 1978 by extending the information system to include the activities of transport operators of Member States and non-member countries even if they are not prejudicial. The aim was to improve information on specific trade routes and to determine the importance and composition of those fleets which adversely affect the activities of other carriers and shipping in general.

However, since the scheme was primarily aimed at the Soviet fleet, the Commission proposal[2] listed the areas of operation for which information was to be collected. These were, in fact, the four areas where the Soviet fleet was most in evidence, in other words between the Member States and the United States of America (excluding the Pacific Coast), East Africa, Central America and the Far East.

In the amending Decision[3] which the Council adopted on 23 November 1978 only two of the four areas of operation proposed were finally adopted in order not to overburden the Member States with surveillance activities. These were:

(i)   between the Member States and East Africa (Somalia, Kenya, Uganda, Zambia, Tanzania and Mozambique);

(ii)   between the Member States and Central America (East and West Coasts- from Mexico's southern frontier to Panama inclusive, excluding the West Indies).

The information to be collected for all carriers serving the ports of the Member States engaged in liner trade in each of the two areas of operation concerned the details of the liner services operated, the liner cargo carried and transport rates.

According to Article 3 of Decision 78/774/EEC of 19 September 1978, the information collected between 1 June 1979 and 31 December 1980 by the information system established by the Member States was to be examined regularly by the Member States and the Commission together. Finally, under Article 4, the Council, acting unanimously, could decide on the joint application by Member States, in their relations with a third country of group of third countries, of appropriate countermeasures forming part of their national legislation.

---

[1] Council Decision 78/774/EEC of 19 September 1978 concerning the activities of certain third countries in the field of cargo shipping (OJ L 258, 21.9.1978).
[2] OJ C 259, 1.11.1978.
[3] Council Decision of 19 December 1978 on the collection of information concerning the activities of carriers participating in cargo liner traffic in certain areas of operation (OJ L 5, 9.1.1979).

In the wake of this Decision Belgium, Germany, Italy and the United Kingdom set up control mechanisms, which varied as to their degree of efficiency and their degree of precision.[1]

A later Council Decision of 4 December 1980 extended the collection of information to 31 December 1982 and included a third area from the Commission's original proposal, namely the Far East: Japan, Taiwan, Hong Kong, Malaysia, Singapore, the Republic of Korea, the Philippines and Thailand.[2]

Yet another Council Decision established detailed rules for the collection of information concerning the activities of carriers participating in cargo liner traffic between the Member States and the Far East.[3] The following year the Council extended the information collection system until 1984.[4] Nevertheless, the effectiveness of this commendable Community surveillance scheme depends entirely on the willingness of each Member State to set up suitable workable schemes to safeguard the interests of its national fleet against unfair competition from the fleets of State-trading countries. One positive sign was the Council's Decision 83/573/EEC to define an appropriate Community procedure concerning countermeasures which could be taken by the Member States in the field of international merchant shipping.[5]

7.1.2 *The Unctad Code of Conduct and the EEC*

When the Convention on a Code of Conduct for Liner Conferences was signed in Geneva in 1974 under the auspices of the United Nations Conference on Trade and Development (Unctad), it created a new climate (which is what the developing countries had been pushing for) which greatly reduced the freedom of scope which Conferences had enjoyed hitherto. The idea had been advocated by the developing countries in an attempt to break what they considered to be the monopoly of the industrialized countries in liner traffic by creating their own national shipping lines.

We do not intend here to examine the scope of the Convention in detail. In any case it is already widely discussed at international level because of the world-wide interests at stake. Instead, we shall consider the positions of the Member States of the EEC with regard to the problems it raised.

---

[1] See *L'action de la CEE en matière de transport maritime,* Studiecentrum voor de Expansie van Antwerpen, Antwerp, June 1979, p. 11-15.

[2] Council Decision 80/1181/EEC of 4 December 1980 amending and supplementing Decision 79/4/EEC on the collection of information concerning the activities of carriers participating in cargo liner traffic in certain areas of operation (OJ L 350, 23.12.1980).

[3] OJ L 88, 2.4.1981.

[4] OJ L 368, 28.12.1982.

[5] OJ L 332, 28.11.1983.

First of all, however, although no doubt going over familiar ground, we shall summarize the main new points contained in the Code of Conduct which would directly affect the interests of carriers in the Member States.[1]

The first point concerns the right to be a full member of a conference which, according to Article 1, is enjoyed by any national shipping line which serves the foreign trade of its country. According to the definition, a 'national shipping line' must have its head office of management and its effective control in that country and must be recognized as such by an appropriate authority of that country or under the law of that country. In order to become a full member of a conference, a national shipping line must furnish evidence of its ability to operate a regular, adequate and efficient service on a long-term basis.

The second point concerns the right of veto allowed to national shipping lines. This implies the *de facto* introduction of the unanimity rule for conference decisions, for Article 3 of the Code states that a decision relating to the trade between two countries cannot be taken without the consent of the national shipping lines of those two countries. Clearly this means that unanimous agreement is required.

A third point regards the reservation of trade for national shipping lines on the basis of the 40/40/20 rule for determining participation in trade. According to this rule, in trade between two countries the national shipping lines of these two countries shall each have 40% of the trade and the remaining 20% is left to 'cross traders' (or shared between the two shipping lines in the absence of cross trade). This rule did, of course, prompt some angry reactions from shipowners in the industrialized countries, who saw their share of conference trade reduced in order to benefit the shipping lines of the developing countries.

Another important innovation is the machinery referred to in Article 11 of the Code for consultation between a conference and the shippers. In addition there is a compulsory conciliation procedure which, with only a few exceptions, enables carriers to have a say in the setting of rates by conferences, which was not the case in the past.

We should add that, for the Convention on a Code of Conduct for Liner Conferences to come into force, it has to be ratified by at least 24 States representing at least 25% of world cargo tonnage.

Of the non-Community countries, the developing countries (the Group of 77) unanimously welcomed the Convention for obvious reasons. The USA, on the other hand, was clearly opposed to it since, although conferences are allowed under the Shipping Act of 1916 as amended by the Bonner Act of 1961, shippers

---

[1] For a summary of the main points relating to this topic see the report by L.M. Bentivoglio, F. Berlingieri, S.M. Carbone, C. Degli Abbati, R. Luzzatto and U. Marchese entitled *La ripartizione e la disciplina del traffico marittimo internazionale: la soluzione adottata in sede ONU e le reazioni CEE* presented to the Ninth Round Table on Community Law of 13 December 1975 organized by the International Law Institute of the University of Genoa and by the CCIA of Genoa and published in *Il Diritto Marittimo*, October-December 1975.

are fundamentally opposed to the type of cartel generated by the conference system. The attitude of the State-trading countries was basically ambivalent; officially they were in favour of the Convention because of the obvious propaganda advantage of supporting the Third World countries but in practice they were much less enthusiastic about the Convention since it would certainly limit the scope for the sharp practices they had been using to compete with the shipowners of Western Europe.

Let us now turn to the Member States of the EEC. Two Member States, Denmark and the United Kingdom, voted against ratifying the Convention while three others, Belgium, France and Germany, came out in favour. These different attitudes obviously reflected differences in interest between those countries which felt the Code of Conduct threatened their already consolidated positions and those countries which felt the Code provided an opportunity for their fleets to obtain a greater share of conference trade.

Right from the start, however, the Community emphasized the importance of organizing world liner trade properly. Neither should we forget Community concern at the unfair practices adopted by the shipping lines of State-trading countries, particularly the Soviet fleet, on routes of considerable importance for Community shipowners. In November 1976, the Council expressed the hope that the countries of the EEC would manage to take a common line on the Code of Conduct before the Unctad Conference to be held in Manila in 1979. In a working paper sent to the Council in April 1977, the Commission suggested a number of options for a common approach by the Member States: either they should do nothing, or they should ratify the Code of Conduct unconditionally, or they should negotiate a new Code, or they should accept the Code after it had been amended to make it more compatible with the interests of the Member States and the provisions of the Treaty of Rome, particularly in respect of the right of establishment.

This last option was made the subject of a proposal for a Regulation which the Commission submitted to the Council on 15 December 1977 concerning accession to the United Nations Convention on a Code of Conduct for Liner Conferences.[1]

The proposal contained some important points regarding the establishment of a common position on the Convention by the Community as a whole.

We should make it clear from the start that the Commission was proposing accession to the Code of Conduct and advanced some cogent arguments. It considered that ratification of the Convention would establish a universal instrument for regulating liner shipping and would put an end to the increasing tendency to sign bilateral international agreements in this field. Further, the amendments proposed by the Community would make it possible to reconcile the concern of the developing countries to guarantee themselves a proportion of

---

[1] OJ C 35, 11.2.1978.

trade with the concern of the Member States to prevent an excessive share of trade being reserved for the national shipping lines of the developing countries, as it would be under the 40/40/20 rule, while at the same time ensuring that liner shipping retained sufficient commercial freedom, within the framework of the OECD. Moreover, this rule of the Code would obviously serve to limit aggressive competition by the fleets of the State-trading countries. In the run-up to the Council meeting of 20 February 1979, in fact, there were two basic points at issue which served to split the Member States on the question of whether or not to sign the Code.

The first point concerned the conditions under which OECD countries which did not belong to the EEC would be allocated a share of the re-distributed trade, the Member States having decided between themselves how the Community's total share within the OECD (60% or 50%) would be redistributed.[1]

In fact, although all Member States agreed that the principle of reciprocity should be applied to redistribution and that the share of an OECD country which did not belong to the EEC should also be pooled, the Member States in favour of the Code (i.e. all of them except Denmark and the United Kingdom) still felt that the OECD country in question should accede to the Code of Conduct as a condition for having a share of this re-distributed trade.

The second point concerned trade between countries of the OECD. Although Member States agreed that the 40/40/20 rule should not apply to liner shipping between OECD countries, there were considerable differences of opinion on how to treat carriers belonging to non-Community non-OECD countries. So whereas the United Kingdom specified that the 40/40/20 rule should not be applied to these countries, the other Member States felt that it should.

Just before the Council meeting of 20 February 1979 at which the Community was to decide on its common approach, the French President of the Council, with the Commission's help, came up with a general compromise proposal designed to settle the dispute. The proposal was in two parts:

(a) the OECD countries and the other industrialized countries would not apply the Code of Conduct to their own trade but would agree to allow the developing countries to benefit from the 40/40/20 rule in trade with OECD countries;

(b) the other OECD countries would be allowed to take part in the redistribution of trade even if they had not acceded to the Code of Conduct.

At the meeting of 20 February 1979, contrary to all expectations, this compromise proposal aroused the strong opposition not only of the United Kingdom, as might be expected, but of Denmark and Italy too.

---

[1] The member countries of the OECD were the States which formerly belonged to the OEEC which was set up in 1948 to coordinate use of the aid granted under the Marshall Plan, namely Austria, Belgium, Denmark, France, Federal Republic of Germany, Greece, Iceland, Ireland, Italy, Luxembourg, Netherlands, Norway, Portugal, Spain, Sweden, Switzerland, Turkey and the United Kingdom, and, in addition, Canada, Japan, Malta and the USA.

Denmark's objection lay in the fact that, since 90% of its shipping trade was cross trade, particularly on routes between the United States and Japan, it wanted to know the attitudes of these two countries before accepting the compromise agreement. This was a perfectly legitimate concern. Since the USA was known to be hostile to the Code of Conduct, the Kingdom of Denmark wanted to protect itself against any retaliatory measures taken by the USA against European shipping lines, if the Americans decided that the Nine's agreement on the French proposal for a Regulation was against their interests.

The Danish authorities also wanted to know whether, if Japan acceded to the Code, it too would also be prepared to accept the Regulation and to take the appropriate measures.

The Danes finally lifted their reservation, but only after Richard Burke, the Member of the Commission then responsible for transport, had conducted a series of negotiations with the US authorities, who went some way towards allaying the fear that the Americans might take measures against the interests of European shipowners in general, or measures affecting the share of cross trade between the USA and Japan accounted for by Danish shipping lines in particular. Negotiations were also arranged with the Japanese authorities who seemed prepared to accept the Community Regulation and to take a liberal attitude on the question of liner trade within the OECD.

Italy's reservation (which was the same as the Belgian reservation although, as we shall see, the latter was later withdrawn in return for concessions) was founded on the general fear that the adoption of the proposed Regulation would adversely affect national shipowners. Italy therefore requested a guarantee that its trade share would not be substantially reduced following the current round of trade negotiations. The reservation was set aside when, after a number of meetings between Mr Burke and the Italian authorities, it was agreed that when the Regulation was adopted the Council would issue a declaration - which in fact was rather general - that it recognized the importance of the interests of those countries which generate trade.

Thus, once Coreper recognized that a consensus had been reached, the Council of Ministers was in a position to adopt the Regulation concerned,[1] which it did on 8 May 1979.

The Regulation, which reproduced the French compromise proposal in full, had the merit of reconciling the need for commercial freedom expressed by the United Kingdom and the Scandinavian countries with the preference of Belgium, France and Germany for a Code and with the valid expectations of the developing countries to establish their own national shipping lines. However, the Regulation could obviously only prove its worth if the Member States also

---

[1] Council Regulation (EEC) No 954/79 of 15 May 1979 concerning the ratification by Member States of, or their accession to, the United Nations Convention on a Code of Conduct for Liner Conferences (OJ L 121, 17.5.1979).

decided to abandon once and for all the practice of bilateral agreements on the distribution of trade.

The Regulation contains a set of measures specifically designed to maintain the commercial rather than the arithmetical approach to the problem of allocating cargo within conferences of shipping lines belonging to the OECD countries and in respect of liner traffic between OECD countries.

Following the lines of the French proposal, the Council Regulation contains the following points:

(a) in trade between the Community and States which are not OECD countries, the volume of cargo to which the shipping lines of the Member States are entitled under the Code shall be redistributed on a commercial basis between their various companies; operators from other member countries of the OECD may participate in the redistribution subject to reciprocity;

(b) the provisions in the Code which relate to shares of cargo (the 40/40/20 rule) shall not apply to trade between the Member States or more generally within the OECD area, although operators based in the developing countries shall be allowed to take advantage of this rule in trade between the Member States and, subject to reciprocity, in trade between the Member States and other member countries of the OECD;

(c) in order to make the 'national shipping line' concept compatible with the provisions of the Treaty governing the right of establishment, Article 2(3) of the Regulation states that 'each Member State shall ensure that all vessel-operating shipping lines established on its territory under the Treaty establishing the European Economic Community are treated in the same way as lines which have their management head office on its territory and the effective control of which is exercised there';

(d) the right of veto provided for by Article 3 of the Code in respect of national shipping lines shall not be applied in conference trades between Member States or, on a reciprocal basis, between such States and other OECD countries (Article 4(4) of the Regulation);

(e) Article 14(9) of the Code shall not be applied in conference trades between Member States and, on a reciprocal basis, between such States and other OECD countries which are parties to the Code (Article 4(4) and (5) of the Regulation). Article 14 of the Code states that a conference shall give notice of not less than 150 days to shippers of its intention to effect a general increase in freight rates. Paragraph 9 of the same Article goes on to state that the minimum period of time between the date when one general freight-rate increase becomes effective and the date of notice for the next general freight-rate increase shall not be less than twelve months. Although this rule was designed to help stabilize freight rates, the Member States felt that the excessively long gap between two successive increases in freight rates (150 days plus 12 months) would be bound to result in big jumps and would thus have the opposite effect to that intended.

In order to comply with the wishes of the Belgian authorities, who had voiced the fears expressed by their national shipowners that the Community Regulation might nullify the advantages of the entry into force of the Convention, Article 3(1) of the Regulation states: 'Where a liner conference operates a pool or a berthing, sailing and/or any other form of cargo allocation agreement ..., the volume of cargo to which the group of national shipping lines of each Member State participating in that trade or the shipping lines of the Member States participating in that trade as third-country shipping lines are entitled under the Code shall be redistributed, unless a decision is taken to the contrary by all the lines which are members of the conference and parties to the present redistribution rules. This redistribution of cargo shares shall be carried out on the basis of a unanimous decision by those shipping lines which are members of the conference and participate in the redistribution, with a view to all these lines carrying a fair share of the conference trade'.

Paragraph 3 of the same Article states: 'If no agreement is reached on the redistribution of cargoes referred to in paragraph 1, the matter shall, at the request of one of the parties, be referred to conciliation in accordance with the procedure set out in Annex II.' The Annex states that the parties to a dispute shall designate one or more conciliators. Should they fail to agree on the matter, each of the parties shall designate a conciliator. Should a party fail to designate a conciliator or the conciliators designated by the parties fail to reach agreement on the chairman, the President of the International Chamber of Commerce shall, at the request of one of the parties, make the necessary designations.

The principle of basing the redistribution of cargo shares on a unanimous decision and the fact that the Regulation contained a compulsory conciliation procedure were regarded by the Belgian authorities as sufficient guarantees, and they therefore accepted the Regulation.

Annex I to the Regulation contains a reservation regarding the interpretation of the term 'national shipping line' in the case of a Member State of the Community, together with the reservations already alluded to which are designed to reassure Denmark and Italy.

Contrary to original expectations, the adoption of a Community Regulation on the application of the rules on competition in Articles 85 and 86 of the Treaty to conference agreements was not seen as a pre-condition for accession of the Member States to the Unctad Code. Two recitals, however, state, firstly, that the common position adopted by the Member States in relation to the Code 'should respect the principles and objectives of the Treaty', and, secondly, that 'whereas the stabilizing role of conferences in ensuring reliable services to shippers is recognized, ... it is nevertheless necessary to avoid possible breaches by conferences of the rules of competition laid down in the Treaty;' and '... the Commission will accordingly forward to the Council a proposal for a Regulation concerning the application of those rules to sea transport'.

We shall examine this proposal together with the Regulation ratifying the Code later.

The Regulation was adopted on 15 May 1979. Later, on 3 June 1979, at the end of the Unctad Conference in Manila a resolution was unanimously adopted which insisted that the Unctad Convention on a Code of Conduct for Liner Conferences adopted in Geneva on 6 April 1974 be applied.

Twenty countries voted at the Conference for ratification of the Code: the Community countries, China, Finland, the German Democratic Republic, Greece, Japan, the Republic of Korea, Liberia, Norway, Spain, Sweden and the USSR.

This made up the required tonnage (at least a quarter of world liner shipping) for the Code then to come into force, since the condition regarding the number of participating countries (at least 24) had already been met in March 1978.

7.1.3 *The application of the rules on competition to sea transport*

As we have just seen, Council Regulation (EEC) No 954/79 of 15 May 1979 concerning the ratification by Member States of, or their accession to, the United Nations Convention on a Code of Conduct for Liner Conferences was not, as originally intended, preceded by the adoption of a Regulation specifying how the Treaty rules on competition would apply to sea transport and in particular to conference agreements.

The proposal for a Regulation referred to in the last recital of Regulation No 954/79 was actually prepared by the Commission in 1979 after a long series of meetings with the organizations concerned - shipowners, shippers and forwarding agents - and submitted to the Council on 16 October 1981.[1]

The drift of the proposal is that the Council should empower the Commission directly to examine alleged infringements of Article 85, which prohibits agreements, and Article 86, which prohibits abuse of dominant positions, in respect of sea transport. It also suggests that the Commission should be empowered to take decisions and impose sanctions in order to allow it to put a stop to any infringements established.

---

[1] Proposal for a Council Regulation laying down detailed rules for the application of Articles 85 and 86 of the Treaty to maritime transport (OJ C 282, 5.11.1981).

Various arguments are put forward in the recitals to justify this proposal:

(i) the rules on competition form part of the Treaty's general provisions, which also apply to maritime transport;

(ii) according to Council Regulation No 141/62,[1] Council Regulation No 17/62[2] does not apply to transport, and Council Regulation (EEC) No 1017/68[3] applies to inland transport only; consequently the Commission has no means at present of investigating directly cases of suspected infringement of Articles 85 and 86 in maritime transport; moreover, the Commission lacks such powers of its own to take decisions or impose penalties as are necessary for it to bring to an end infringements established by it; this situation therefore necessitates the adoption of a Regulation applying the rules of competition to maritime transport similar to the Regulations covering other inland transport and other sectors of the economy;

(iii) Council Regulation (EEC) No 954/79 concerning the ratification by Member States of the United Nations Convention on a Code of Conduct for Liner Conferences[4] will entail application of the Code to a considerable number of conferences serving the Community, while many other conferences serving the Community probably will not come under the Code;

(iv) the Regulation must take account of the need to provide for implementing rules that enable the Commission to ensure that competition is not unduly distorted within the common market, and of the need to avoid excessive regulation of the sector, from which, in view of the Commission's experience, bulk transport is excluded.

The Regulation is based on Article 87 of the Treaty and lays down detailed rules for the application of Articles 85 and 86 of the Treaty to international maritime transport operations from or to one or more Community ports (Article 1).

Articles 2 and 3 of the proposal list a number of exemptions from the prohibition of agreements between undertakings set out in Article 85(1) of the Treaty.[5] These include:

(a) a statutory exception for technical agreements, in other words agreements, decisions or concerted practices whose sole object and effect is to achieve technical improvements or cooperation;

---

[1] OJ 124, 28.11.1962.
[2] OJ 58, 10.7.1962.
[3] OJ L 175, 23.7.1968.
[4] OJ L 121, 17.5.1979.
[5] This very important Article states: 'The following shall be prohibited as incompatible with the common market: all agreements between undertakings, decisions by associations of undertakings and concerted practices which may affect trade between Member States and which have as their object or effect the prevention, restriction or distortion of competition within the common market ...', and: 'Any agreements or decisions prohibited pursuant to this Article shall be automatically void'.

(b) an exemption for agreements between vessel-operating carriers providing liner services for the carriage of cargo or passengers on a particular route or routes within specified geographical limits and jointly fixing freight rates and any other conditions for those services. This exemption was granted for conferences because (eighth recital of the proposal) it was felt that, as stated in the last recital to Council Regulation (EEC) No 954/79, liner conferences have a stabilizing effect, assuring shippers of reliable services, and contribute generally to providing adequate efficient scheduled maritime transport services and give fair consideration to the interests of users.

The exemption includes (Article 3(2) of the proposal) the fixing of rates and conditions of carriage and rationalization agreements (coordination of shipping timetables, determination of the frequency of sailings or calls, coordination or allocation of sailings or calls among members of the conference, regulation of the carrying capacity offered by each member and allocation of cargo or revenue among members), but is subject to specific conditions and obligations as set out in Articles 4 and 5 of the proposal for a Regulation.

The conditions state in particular that:

(a) a conference shall respect the provisions of Article 79 of the Treaty, which prohibits discrimination which takes the form of carriers charging different rates and imposing different conditions on grounds of the country of origin or of destination of the goods in question (Article 4(1));

(b) where a conference offers shippers or forwarding agents the opportunity of entering into loyalty agreements, the conference shall not prohibit the shippers or forwarding agent from using modes of transport other than maritime transport, nor may it deprive them of the right to choose the port of consignment and the carrier from among the ports served by it and the vessels that it operates (Article 4(2)(e));

(c) again in respect of loyalty agreements, a conference may not impose on shippers or forwarding agents clauses or agreements which excessively restrict their freedom, but in each case must offer a system of immediate rebates or the choice between such a system and a system of deferred rebates. Under the system of immediate rebates each of the parties shall be entitled to terminate the loyalty agreement at any time without penalty and subject to a period of notice of not more than six months. Under the system of deferred rebates neither the loyalty period on the basis of which the rebate is calculated nor the subsequent loyalty period required before payment of the rebate may exceed six months (Article 4(2)(a));

(d) the conference shall draw up a list of circumstances in which shippers or forwarding agents are automatically released from their obligation of loyalty (Article 4(2)(c));

(e) a conference shall allow shippers, forwarding agents and consignees to approach the undertakings of their choice in respect of inland transport operations and quayside services not covered by the freight charge or charges agreed with the shipping line.

Obligations attaching to exemption include:

(a) allowing users at all times to acquaint themselves with the rates and conditions of carriage applied by members of the conference (transparency);

(b) immediately notifying the Commission of awards given at arbitration and recommendations made by conciliators that are accepted by the parties, so that the Commission can verify whether they exempt the conference from compliance with the conditions set out in the Regulation (Article 5).

Further, according to Article 6, the prohibition laid down in Article 85(1) of the Treaty shall not apply to agreements, decisions and concerted practices between shippers or forwarding agents, or between the latter or their associations, on the one hand, and conferences, on the other, concerning the quality, rates and conditions of scheduled maritime transport services.

Article 8 of the Regulation makes provision for a special consultation procedure in cases where the application of the Regulation to certain restrictive practices or clauses is liable to enter into conflict with the provisions laid down by law, regulation or administrative action of certain third countries, which could compromise important Community trading and shipping interest. In such cases - which are very likely to arise since the Regulation applies only to international maritime transport operations from or to one or more Community ports irrespective of the country in which the shipping line is registered - the Commission shall, at the earliest opportunity, undertake with the competent authorities of the third countries concerned, consultations aimed at reconciling as far as possible the abovementioned interest with the respect of Community law.

Moreover, within three years of the entry into force of this Regulation, the Commission shall report to the Council on experience gained in this regard and make proposals for such amendments to the Regulation as may be necessary in the light of that experience.

Furthermore, because of the specific role fulfilled by the conferences in the sector of liner services, it is considered that the reaction of the Commission to agreements, decisions or concerted practices which are found to infringe the Treaty or which contravene the conditions and obligations attaching to exemption must be progressive and proportionate.

Thus, according to Article 7, the Commission may, in order to put an end to those effects or breaches, first address recommendations to the persons concerned and, in the event of failure to observe such recommendations and depending on the gravity of the incompatible effects or breaches concerned, adopt an appropriate decision.

Finally, there are rules of procedure for the application of the Regulation contained in Articles 9 to 28 of the proposal. They take proper account of the distinctive features of transport operations viewed as a whole and therefore attempt to simplify as far as possible the administrative procedures required of undertakings or associations of undertakings. For the rest they reiterate the provisions of Council Regulation No 1017/68 applying rules of competition to the three modes of inland transport.[1] The proposal for a Regulation does not, therefore, make it compulsory to notify agreements which conform to the rules on competition, although there is a simplified procedure for those undertakings wishing to apply to the Commission for confirmation that their agreements are in conformity with the provisions in force.

7.1.4 *Safety of shipping and prevention of marine pollution*

Following the extensive environmental damage caused by the wreck of the *Amoco Cadiz* off the coast of Brittany, the European Council took a decision, at its meeting in Copenhagen on 7 and 8 April 1978, on the initiative of the President of the French Republic, that the Community should make the prevention and combating of marine pollution, particularly by oil, a priority objective. To this end it invited the Council, acting on proposals from the Commission, and the Member States forthwith to take appropriate measures and to adopt common attitudes in the competent international bodies concerning in particular the swift implementation of existing international rules, and especially those regarding minimum standards for the operation of ships, the prevention of accidents through coordinated action and the search for and implementation of effective measures to combat marine pollution.

Accordingly, in April 1978, the Commission sent the Council a communication on marine pollution arising from the carriage of oil[2] which starts by referring to previous action already taken by the Commission and goes on to survey international and Community action to combat pollution, noting that there is extensive regulation by convention, including regulations on the prevention of pollution by tankers, regulations on the safety of ships and of navigation and regulations on liability and compensation for damage caused by accidental pollution. In practice, however, the existing regulations have proved ineffective, partly because of lack of enforcement and partly because of some obvious omissions.

Although aware of the considerable economic and legal constraints, the Commission nevertheless proposed tougher action by the Community to combat

---

[1] OJ L 175, 23.7.1968.
[2] Doc. COM(78) 184 final. The Commission recalls in particular having sent the Council in 1977 a communication on the prevention, control and reduction of pollution caused by accidental oil spills, with draft resolution annexed, and on 6 December 1977 a second communication on reorganizing the shipbuilding sector, in which it reminded the Council of the need for stronger action, by appropriate measures, against ships not complying with the minimum social and safety standards.

pollution, in order to live up to the public's expectations. The action programme consisted of four proposals to the Council:

1. A draft Council Resolution on a programme of action by the European Communities to control and reduce pollution caused by oil spills at sea.

2. A proposal for a Council Decision to conclude the Protocol to the Barcelona Convention for the Protection of the Mediterranean Sea against Pollution of 16 February 1976 concerning Cooperation in Combating Pollution by Oil and Other Harmful Substances in Cases of Emergency.

3. A recommendation for a Council Decision concerning negotiation by the European Economic Community of its accession to the Bonn Agreement of 9 June 1969 on Cooperation in Dealing with the Pollution of the North Sea by Oil.

4. A recommendation for a Council Decision on extension to 12 miles of the breadth of the territorial seas of all Member States.

It had also sent the Council a proposal for a Directive[1] requiring the ratification by the Member States which had not already done so of two Inter-Governmental Maritime Consultative Organization (IMCO) conventions and one International Labour Office (ILO) convention. These are the 1974 International Convention for the Safety of Life at Sea (Solas) and the 1978 Protocol relating to the 1974 International Convention for the Safety of Life at Sea, the 1973 International Convention for the Prevention of Pollution from Ships (Marpol) as amended by the 1978 Protocol, and Convention No 147 concerning Minimum Standards on Merchant Ships adopted by the International Labour Conference on 29 October 1976.

The purpose of this proposal for a Directive was to constitute the quorum required for the entry into force of the various conventions by making all the Member States ratify them.

On 26 June 1978, as a result of the Commission's efforts, the Council of Ministers adopted a Resolution setting up an action programme on the control and reduction of pollution caused by hydrocarbons (i.e. oil) discharged at sea.[2]

In the Resolution, the Council undertook to take decisions within nine months on proposals submitted to it by the Commission after the completion of a series of preliminary studies on marine pollution and on a number of technical matters (computer processing of data on ways of dealing with marine pollution by oil, availability of data on tankers and on off-shore structures liable to pollute the

---

[1] OJ C 135, 9.6.1978.
[2] OJ C 162, 8.7.1978.

waters around the Community and the coasts of the Member States, the need for measures to enhance the effectiveness of emergency teams, a possible Community contribution to the design and development of clean-up vessels, amendments and improvements which may have to be made to the legal rules on insurance against the risks of accidental oil pollution, and the establishment of a proposal for a research programme on chemical and mechanical means of combating pollution due to oil discharged at sea and its environmental effects).

At the same meeting the Council decided that the Solas and ILO (No 147) Conventions could make a substantial contribution towards improving both technical and welfare standards affecting the safety of ships and the living and working conditions of their crews and therefore recommended that the Member States ratify them. The same applied to the Marpol Convention.[1] However, by converting the Commission's proposal for a Directive into a non-binding Recommendation, the Council to some extent emasculated the Commission's proposal, because, as usual, it was impossible to persuade all the Member States to reach agreement.

At its subsequent meeting on 23 November 1978 the Council took a number of decisions on safety in shipping:

(i)   the Council Recommendation of 21 December 1978 on the ratification of the 1978 International (IMCO) Convention on Standards of Training, Certification and Watchkeeping for Seafarers;[2]

(ii)   the Council Directive of 21 December 1978 concerning pilotage of vessels by deep-sea pilots in the North Sea and English Channel;[2] this was designed to ensure the availability of adequately qualified deep-sea pilots in these waters and to encourage vessels flying the national flags of Member States to avail themselves of these services;

(iii) the Council Directive of 21 December 1978 concerning minimum requirements for certain tankers entering or leaving Community ports;[2] this requires that the competent authorities be notified in advance in respect of oil, gas and chemical tankers of 1 600 gross registered tons and over, of any deficiency potentially deleterious to the safety of shipping and to the marine environment.

At the same meeting the Council also asked Ireland and Italy to accede to a Memorandum of Understanding signed by the other six maritime Member States and Norway and Sweden in the Hague on 2 March 1978 on the maintenance of standards on board merchant ships (on-board inspections of vessels calling at Community ports and barring or turning away those vessels which do not meet the required standards).

---

[1] Council Recommendation of 26 June 1978 on the ratification of Conventions on safety in shipping (OJ L 194, 19.7.1978).

[2] OJ L 33, 8.2.1979.

On the subject of combating marine pollution, the European Parliament stated its position in a report presented by Lord Bruce of Donington on behalf of the Committee on Regional Policy, Regional Planning and Transport, which basically supported the Commission's efforts and levelled criticism against the Council's lukewarm attitude. On the basis of the report, a resolution was adopted on 14 February 1979.[1] On 4 April 1979, on its own initiative, the Economic and Social Committee prepared an opinion on sea transport, adopted on the basis of the conclusions of the rapporteur Rouzier, which is a comprehensive analysis of the current problems facing Community policy on shipping safety, the role of the newly emerging maritime countries and the problem of flags of convenience and flag discrimination.[2]

Lastly, on 23 September 1980, the Council adopted a Recommendation[3] inviting the Member States to ratify the Torremolinos International Convention for the Safety of Fishing Vessels which was drawn up under IMCO and is designed to promote the safety of vessels in general, and fishing vessels and their crews in particular, or to accede to it before 31 July 1982.

Apart from the Commission proposals already referred to, there are another two important proposals still before the Council - a proposal for a Directive concerning the enforcement, in respect of shipping using Community ports, of international standards (IMCO and ILO) for shipping safety and pollution prevention,[4] and a draft Decision adopting a concerted action project for the European Economic Community in the field of shore-based maritime navigation aid systems[5] following on from the research and development programme in the field of environment adopted by the Council of Ministers in March 1981 and meeting the objectives set out in the final declaration of the Paris Conference of December 1980 on shipping safety and prevention of pollution. More recently, the European Parliament came up with a proposal on the creation of a European Foundation for Safety at Sea. The aim of this was to promote scientific research into safety and environmental protection, which would provide useful technical back-up when preparing IMCO proposals.[6]

---

[1] OJ C 67, 12.3.1979.
[2] ESC, Brussels, 1979.
[3] Council Recommendation of 23 September 1980 on the ratification of the Torremolinos International Convention for the Safety of Fishing Vessels (1977) (OJ L 259, 2.10.1980).
[4] OJ C 192, 30.7.1980.
[5] OJ C 256, 8.10.1981, as amended by OJ C 265, 9.10.1982. The proposal for a decision on this matter was adopted by the Council on 13 December 1982 (OJ L 378, 31.12.1982) and a Decision was adopted on 28 March 1983 on the conclusion of a Community-COST concertation agreement (OJ L 84, 30.3.1983).
[6] See the report by K. Kaloyannis on behalf of the Transport Committee on the creation of a European Foundation for Safety at Sea, Doc. EP No 1-773/83 of 10 October 1983.

7.1.5 *Recent developments on Community maritime transport policy*

In March 1985 the Commission published an important document[1] which provides a comprehensive summary of Community action to date together with a detailed analysis of changes in world and Community shipping over the last ten years and the reasons behind the relative decline of the Community fleet. In addition it proposes a whole set of new measures which, in the Commission's opinion, are required to promote the Community's trading and shipping interests. The Commission starts by recognizing that, although the maintenance of a multilateral and commercially-orientated Community shipping policy is still in the best interests of the Community's shipping industry, it is becoming more necessary than ever to come to grips with the growing threat to Community interests of the protectionist policies and practices adopted by other countries. Accordingly, the Commission proposes a number of practical measures which we shall now summarize.

1. A draft Regulation which will allow the Community to take action against the tendency to restrict access to bulk cargo which has, or could have, a serious effect on the trading interests of the Community (draft Council Regulation concerning coordinated action to safeguard free access to cargoes in ocean trades - Annex II-1).

2. A draft Regulation designed to apply the principle of freedom to provide services to the supply of artificial installations out at sea, trade between Member States and non-member countries, the carriage of goods wholly or partly reserved to ships flying the national flag and, with some specific exceptions, the carriage of passengers or goods by sea between ports in any one Member State, including overseas territories of that State (draft Council Regulation applying the principle of freedom to provide services to sea transport - Annex II-2, and the draft Council Decision amending Decision 77/587/EEC setting up a consultation procedure on relations between Member States and third countries in shipping matters and on action relating to such matters in international organizations - Annex II-3, providing for preliminary consultation between Member States and third countries in shipping matters).

3. A draft Directive suggesting a number of criteria for defining the concept of 'national shipping line' referred to in Council Regulation (EEC) No 954/79 of 15 May 1979 in order to avoid discrimination between the shipping lines of Member States and, provided that they grant reciprocal treatment, shipping lines of other OECD countries, without at

---

[1] Communication and proposals by the Commission to the Council - Progress towards a common transport policy - maritime transport (Doc. COM(85) 90 final of 15 March 1985).

the same time denying Member States the flexibility they need to take account of their own national circumstances (draft Council Directive concerning a common interpretation of the concept of 'national shipping line' - Annex II-4).

4. With regard to the application of the rules on competition to maritime transport, an amendment to the proposal for a Regulation submitted in 1981 which was designed in particular to counteract the negative effects of the increasing tendency to exclude foreign competition from trades operated by closed conferences (amendment to the proposal for a Council Regulation (EEC) laying down detailed rules for the application of Articles 85 and 86 of the Treaty to maritime transport - Annex II-5).

5. A proposal for a Regulation designed to give the Commission suitable powers to take action against unfair practices by shipping lines of non-Member States in order to ensure that Community liner shipping can compete with the shipping lines of non-Community countries in accordance with fair commercial principles (draft Council Regulation on unfair pricing practices in maritime transport - Annex II-6).

7.2 Air transport

7.2.1 Community action

7.2.1.1 The Air Union project

The history of air transport in a European Community context is similar in some ways, but not in others, to that of sea transport.

Air transport, too, is a world market with all the attendant difficulties with regard to Community regulations (which we discussed in the section on sea transport). A further problem is that air transport undertakings are operating on a much wider scale than just the Community.

One difference, however, is that access to the air transport market, particularly in Europe,[1] is subject to many more constraints and restrictions than is the case with sea transport.

With the existing system of prior authorization for intermediate stops, scheduled air services are, in fact, much more akin to inland transport services operated on a concessionary basis than to liner shipping, since they are regulated by States and are the subject of inter-governmental agreements. This comparison applies even if account is taken of liner conferences, which are cartel agreements that substantially restrict competition between carriers on liner shipping routes. Generally, therefore, it would be true to say that there are more restrictions and

---

[1] In the USA, the 1978 Airline Deregulation Act considerably liberalized the air transport market.

constraints on competition in the air transport market than is the case with sea transport. In fact, it was in the air transport sector, rather than in the sea transport sector, that Europe, and the European Community in particular, first felt the need for common action.

We have already mentioned the plan put before the Consultative Assembly of the Council of Europe by Count Carlo Sforza in 1951 on the setting up of a European Air Navigation Union, and the Bonnefous plan and the Van der Klieft report, both of which were submitted to the ECSC's Common Assembly in the 1950s.[1] We should now take a look at the project to set up the 'Air Union', a kind of European Civil Aviation Community.

The reason for the special interest shown in air transport is basically that for the Member States the establishment of the European Community provided the opportunity, through the transfer of some effective powers from the national level, to attempt to solve at Community level the more urgent problems facing air transport which it had not been possible to solve through general cooperation between States and national airlines within the framework of international associations such as the IATA. These problems were basically the need to develop air services within the Community and the need to improve the efficiency of undertakings operating air transport services, both by adjusting the sizes of flag-carriers[2] so that they could take advantage of the economies of scale allowed by rapid technological developments in the field of civil aviation after years of committing resources to military aviation, and by avoiding uneconomic duplication and interference with international air services.

Accordingly, the Commission of the EEC became directly involved in a plan drawn up by five flag-carriers of the Member States to set up a European Civil Aviation Community, an economic authority to regulate the activities of the airlines which would be called the 'Air Union'. In fact, from 1958 onwards, these airlines, Sabena (Belgium), Lufthansa (Germany), Air-France (France), KLM (Netherlands) and Alitalia (Italy), worked together to examine the prospects for cooperation, and possibly for a merger, in order jointly to take commercial advantage of scheduled and non-scheduled international air services (the agreement did not include domestic services). The prime objective of the agreement was to establish a common civil aviation policy by pooling the 'traffic rights' enjoyed by the various airlines, standardizing national regulations, coordinating the commercial management of airlines, including ground control services and organizing aircraft maintenance, particularly by standardizing

---

[1] For a more detailed study of the Sforza and Bonnefous plans and the Van der Klieft report, see F. Santoro, *op. cit.*, pp. 398-404.

[2] Some very small countries, e.g. Luxembourg, have national airlines operating international services. Even today Luxair, a company in which the State has a majority holding, has a fleet of only seven aircraft (five turboprop Fokker F 27s and two Boeing 737s).

fleets.[1] If this project had gone ahead it would have eliminated the cut-throat competition between airlines for international business and would have made it possible to negotiate the best possible conditions at international conferences and when signing bilateral agreements, particularly with the USA. International air services would have been allocated to individual airlines on a fixed percentage basis and those airlines would then have operated these services with their own aircraft. To begin with, these percentage shares would have been established on a provisional basis, based on the total production and potential of the individual airlines[2] and finalized only when total production had reached optimum levels. Overall profits would then have been distributed in proportion to the shares of each individual airline.

According to the basic principles set out in the draft agreement, there seemed to be two major problems: the problem of allocating shares of trade and the problem of aircraft orders which would affect the protection enjoyed by the aircraft industries in the various Member States.

In fact, in April 1959, KLM abandoned the negotiations because it would not accept the share it was to be given. The other four flag-carriers did manage to reach agreement, although it was not nearly as ambitious as had been hoped at the beginning. The body which was to be set up by this agreement - called the Air Union so as not to restrict membership solely to Member States of the EEC as would have been the case if 'Europair' (as originally proposed) had been adopted - was to reduce operating costs by centralizing air fleets and commercial services and to increase profits by coordinating schedules and increasing the frequency of flights. However, in October 1959, on the basis of a report by the respective Ministers of Transport, the governments of the four Member States involved decided on a different institutional approach, preferring to set up the Air Union by means of a multilateral inter-governmental agreement, since it had become clear that this inter-company initiative would be bound to involve governments directly.

Thus, 9 May 1962 saw the signature both of the Air Union pact between Sabena, Air-France, Lufthansa and Alitalia and of an inter-governmental agreement setting up the Air Union between Belgium, France, Germany and Italy. Later that year, however, on 29 December, the French Government came up with a new draft agreement. Typical of General de Gaulle's desire to see a Europe of nation States, the proposal was designed to prevent the loss of national sovereignty and to counter the move towards a supra-national Europe which lay behind the Air Union pact, a pact in which the carrier of the sacrosanct national

---

[1] For an appraisal of the Air Union project, see F. Santoro, op. cit., pp. 404-411. For a general examination of the problems surrounding the Air Union in the context of civil aviation in Europe, see *inter alia*, S. Weateraft, *The Economics of European Air Transport*, Manchester University Press, Manchester 1956; M. Duynstee, *Rapport sur certains aspects financiers et économiques des opérations de transport aerien*, Council of Europe, Strasbourg 1964; C. Delepiere-Nys, *Air Europe: La politique de coopération entre les compagnies aériennes de l'Europe des Six*, Ed. Université de Bruxelles, Brussels, 1974.
[2] By way of example, the share proposed for Alitalia was 26%.

flag, Air-France, played an important part. However, this new move also reflected the fears of a country which had always followed a policy of protecting its own aircraft industries instead of taking advantage of the wealth of aircraft from which it could have chosen under the pact establishing the Air Union. It was also an expression of the government's general reluctance to see airlines encroaching on areas of government responsibility, namely the planning of national airline schedules.

According to this French proposal, the basis for the operation of the Air Union should no longer be a pact between airlines but agreement between sovereign States. Following this attempt by France to bring the Air Union under government supervision, in November 1963 the Government of the Federal Republic of Germany came up with a new proposal, which in fact took considerable account of the general economic needs of the air transport sector within the Community.

From then onwards, contact between the Six (Luxembourg and the Netherlands had meanwhile asked to be included in the negotiations) continued at diplomatic conferences held in Brussels in 1964 and 1965 and chaired by Belgium. Since the negotiations were conducted inter-governmentally and not through Community institutions, on 20 October 1964 the EEC Commission presented to the Council its official reaction to the negotiations on the Air Union. This was a declaration on air transport policy in which the Commission expressed the opinion that any inter-governmental agreement concluded outside the institutional framework provided by the Treaty for the establishment of a common policy on air transport would have to be considered incompatible with the Treaty. It went on to argue that in a European context no benefits had been achieved - apart from some limited technical standardization - in terms of improving cooperation between airlines, and emphasized its earnest desire to continue with efforts to improve the competitiveness of Community airlines on the world market. Lastly, the Commission considered it essential that Member States should adopt a common approach to air transport and work towards establishing a common transport policy within the Community.

Although the declaration did not prompt the Council to stop negotiations at inter-governmental level, it nevertheless agreed to keep the Commission informed of the outcome of negotiations on the Air Union, which in any case came to an end in 1965 for the reasons outlined above.[1]

This episode showed - and unfortunately there were repetitions on other occasions in subsequent years - that the European Community as a whole, whether at government level or at individual company level, did not have sufficient political maturity to follow up the objectives set when the idea of the Air Union was proposed.

---

[1] In 1965 the Dutch Government submitted a new Air Union proposal arguing in favour of the geographical distribution of airline activities. This was rejected because several governments felt that it was based on excessively liberal principles.

7.2.1.2 Community action after the Air Union

At the Council meeting of 4 June 1970, Mr Bodson, the Member of the EEC Commission then responsible for the common transport policy, presented his report on, among other things, action to be taken on sea and air transport.[1]

The subsequent proposal for a Council Decision on the main aspects of common action on air transport which the Commission sent the Council in June 1972 - with an eye to the forthcoming enlargement of the Community - reiterates most of the points made in that declaration. The Commission's aim in submitting the proposal was to obtain authorization to adopt measures to promote cooperation between the airlines of the Member States and to take preliminary steps towards arriving at a general definition of the common air transport policy.

The proposal put before the Council paid due regard to the rigid set of bilateral agreements governing air transport between the Member States. Air transport was also subject to the new international regulations on air transport based on the strict bilateralism of the 1944 Chicago Convention. The proposal concentrated on three closely interrelated subjects:

(i)   improving scheduled services within the Community;
(ii) consultations on fares policy between the Member States;
(iii) consultations on policy to develop air links with non-member countries.

The improvements to scheduled services within the Community which the Commission had in mind concerned the 'second level' services, in other words, those services radiating out from the points served by 'first level' services on the main traffic routes between the major airports of Europe where intervention by the Community was unlikely to have much success. Thus the aim was to reorganize second level services for the benefit of users and to encourage more rational use of aircraft.

On air fares, the aim of the proposal was to bring about a common approach by Member States and their airlines to negotiating fares within IATA, the international association of airlines which the governments allow to set the level of fares.

For a clearer idea of the spirit of the proposal, we should remember that in 1967, very shortly after the Bodson declaration which formed the basis for the proposal, the effectiveness of the IATA cartel, with all its imperfections, and of its traffic conferences was enhanced in Europe by an inter-governmental agreement approved by the ECAC (European Civil Aviation Conference) which represented the public authorities responsible for civil aviation in the various countries of Western Europe. Under this agreement, the governments were to recognize the fares set by their own flag carriers in agreement with other carriers

---

[1] See A. Bodson, op. cit.

'possibly within IATA'.[1] The Commission took the view that something should be done to offset the risk that Member States might be prompted to take decisions - possibly using their flag carriers as a cover since in all Member States fares were (and still are) subject to government approval - relating to the level or structures of tariffs in respect not only of flights between one individual Member State and a non-member country but also in respect of flights between all Member States and the non-member country in question.

Lastly, on the subject of coordinating policy for the development of services to and from non-Community countries, the Commission felt that in order to increase the number of services of most economic benefit to airlines, i.e. long-distance intercontinental flights, it would be necessary to coordinate negotiations with non-Community countries.

To this end, the Commission came up with a way of getting round the delicate matter of the 'traffic rights' jealously guarded by certain flag-carriers: the airlines themselves would conduct preliminary negotiations with these non-Community countries and then the Community or the Member States would follow up with some real concerted negotiation on traffic rights.[2] Here again the strict bilateralism governing international air transport constituted for the Community an additional obstacle to the establishment of an air transport policy.

The Commission's commitment to air (and sea) transport was reaffirmed in the 1972 General Report on the Activities of the European Communities.[3] One paragraph states: 'The new dimensions of the Community transport market and the structural changes which will result from the access of the new Member States will make it necessary to go beyond the concept of a common transport policy limited to land transport and will require the establishment of a Community strategy for sea and air transport and in the matter of ports. One of the enlarged Community's essential tasks will therefore be to determine the nature and limits of action to be undertaken in this matter.'

7.2.1.3 Action taken by the Community since the judgment by the Court of Justice in Case 167/73 of 1974

It was not until after the important judgment handed down by the Court of Justice on 4 April 1974, or more precisely at the end of the 1970s, that renewed

---

[1] For an appraisal of the agreement see the *Report on Scheduled Passenger Air Fares in the EEC*, Commission of the EEC, Brussels, July 1981.

[2] For an analysis of the proposal and of the opinions expressed by the European Parliament and by the ESC, both of which basically accepted the proposal, see *La politique commune des transports de la CEE de novembre 1971 à fin décembre 1972*, Studiecentrum voor de Expansie van Antwerpen, Antwerp, March 1973, pp. 64-69.

[3] EEC Commission, *Sixth General Report on the Activities of the European Communities in 1972,* Brussels, 1973.

interest was shown in air transport within the Community. Thus in December 1979, the Council adopted a Decision setting up a Community consultation procedure on international action in air transport similar to that adopted two years previously (in September 1977) on sea transport.[1] Thus was created the instrument which would allow the Member States to encourage the development of air services on routes within the Community in accordance with the major guidelines set out in the Commission's Memorandum of July 1978.[2]

The proposed consultation procedure followed the lines laid down in the Council Decision of 13 September 1977 on sea transport. It consisted of prior consultation between Member States on any decisions to be taken within international organizations and a procedure whereby each Member State would inform the other Member States and the Commission of any developments occurring in its bilateral or multilateral relations with non-Community countries and the operation of bilateral or multilateral agreements relating to air transport.

The Memorandum itself took particular account of the fact that meanwhile the USA had deregulated air transport. Its main objectives were:

(i)   for consumers, new second and third level links designed to fill gaps in the Community's domestic network, efficient services and fares set as low as possible without discrimination;

(ii)   for the airlines, maintaining or restoring financial equilibrium by reducing operating costs and increasing productivity;

(iii)   for staff, removing obstacles to the free admission to the occupation throughout the Community;

(iv)   for the general public, improving safety, doing more to protect the environment, making more rational use of energy, developing Europe's aircraft industry and taking regional development objectives into consideration.

After examining the Memorandum, the Council asked the Commission to continue to look into problems connected with transfrontier inter-regional services within the Community and, by the first half of 1980, to come up with an action programme on this subject. However, the Council gave Coreper the task of continuing work on other priority problems (standards restricting the nuisance attributable to aircraft; simplification of formalities (facilitation), particularly those relating to air freight; implementation of technical standards (JAR); application to air transport of rules on competition, particularly those

---

[1] Council Decision 80/50/EEC of 20 December 1979 setting up a consultation procedure on relations between Member States and third countries in the field of air transport and on action relating to such matters within international organizations (OJ L 18, 24.1.1980). The same Official Journal contains Council Directive 80/51/EEC of 20 December 1979 on the limitation of noise emissions from subsonic aircraft. This states that 'noisy' aircraft, i.e. aircraft which have not been granted noise certification, may not be used after 31 December 1986.
[2] Commission Memorandum on the contribution of the European Communities to the development of air transport services (Doc. COM(79) 311 final of 6 July 1979).

on State aid; mutual recognition of qualifications of air crews and ground staff; working conditions; right of establishment; search, rescue and recovery operations and accident enquiries).

Complying with the consultation procedure introduced by the abovementioned Council Decision of 20 December 1979, the Commission presented the Council of Ministers in 1980 and 1981 with two proposals for Regulations and one proposal for a Directive. Meanwhile, in December 1980, the Council adopted a Directive on future cooperation and mutual assistance between the Member States in the field of air accident investigation, which took particular account of the fact that more than 90% of accidents involve aircraft of up to and including 5 700 kg.[1]

The first proposal for a Council Regulation concerned the authorization of scheduled inter-regional air services for the transport of passengers, mail and cargo between Member States.[2] The proposal was prepared in answer to a request made by the Council at its meeting of 20 December 1979. It sets out to deregulate international inter-regional third level flights, in other words flights between medium or small centres. Since the Commission was well aware that any attempt to introduce deregulation into the EEC would be a non-starter, its aim in presenting the proposal was to deregulate minor or third level international services over stages of no more than 200 km by aircraft with a capacity of less than 130 seats or a maximum take-off weight of less than 55 tonnes. To accept the proposal (and the German and Italian Governments in particular were extremely reluctant to do so) would have meant the liberalization of the system of traffic rights on international routes, with the result that these routes would no longer be considered in the context of bilateral negotiations.[3]

The second proposal for a Regulation prepared by the Commission concerned procedures for applying the rules on competition to the air transport sector.[4] If adopted, this Regulation would give the Commission powers to investigate cases, take decisions and impose sanctions in order to prevent agreements and abuses of dominant positions on the air transport market which would infringe

---

[1] Council Directive 80/1266/EEC of 16 December 1980 (OJ L 375, 31.12.1980).

[2] Doc. COM(80) 624 final of 27 November 1980. For a detailed examination of the content of this proposal see *La politique commune des transports de la CEE - Bilan de 1980-1981*, Studiecentrum voor de Expansie van Antwerpen, Antwerp, May 1982.

[3] This proposal was recently adopted as Council Directive 83/416/EEC of 25 July 1983 concerning the authorization of scheduled inter-regional air services for the transport of passengers, mail and cargo between Member States (OJ L 237, 26.8.1983). It provides for a Community authorization procedure which applies to journeys operated over stages of more than 400 km, or over stages of less than 400 km where air transport allows a substantial time saving by aircraft which have a capacity of not more than 70 passenger seats and a maximum take-off weight of not more than 30 tonnes (Article 1).

[4] Proposal for a Council Regulation of 31 July 1981 laying down the procedure for applying Articles 85 and 86 of the Treaty to the air transport sector, Doc. COM(81) 396 final (OJ C 317, 3.12.1982, p. 3).

Articles 85 and 86 of the Treaty. It would also have the right to examine the books of companies involved (or thought to be involved) in prohibited practices and to impose sanctions where necessary, thus extending to the air transport sector the powers of investigation and enforcement which the Commission already has in other sectors of the economy pursuant to the general principles on competition laid down in the Treaty.[1]

The proposal for a Council Directive[2] which the Commission put before the Council on 27 October 1981 concerns fares for scheduled air services between Member States and in particular the repealing of national regulations or rules set out in bilateral agreements which by prohibiting 'country of origin pricing' mean that tariffs have to be approved by both the governments of the Member States concerned in each particular case.

The effect of this provision should be to encourage more competition on tariffs since carriers will no longer be obliged to agree tariffs mutually between themselves. At present it is usually necessary, although not required by law, for carriers to bargain among themselves since many governments consult their own national airlines before taking decisions.

Apart from the proposals on inter-regional air services, this latest set of proposals has also run aground in the Council; in fact, these proposals were cited in the action brought by the European Parliament on 22 January 1983.

Accordingly in March 1984, the Commission, in answer to Parliament's request for a revised version of the Commission's work programme for 1984/85, submitted a second memorandum on civil aviation[3] designed to develop and expand on the objectives of the Commission's 1979 Memorandum in the light of the regulatory and economic changes which had taken place in the meantime and the renewed debate on possible improvements to the European air transport system in the general interests of consumers, airlines and workers alike. The document examines in some detail how competition policy affects air transport policy from the point of view of both governments and airlines. It also considers other aspects of air transport policy and in connection with a proposal on non-discrimination and standstill provisions, various schemes designed to help reduce airline's costs, ways of encouraging the activities of smaller airlines and charter

---

[1] The scope of this proposal is more limited than the similar proposal for a Council Regulation laying down detailed rules for the application of Articles 85 and 86 of the Treaty to maritime transport submitted by the Commission to the Council on 16 October 1981 (OJ C 282, 5.11.1981), since it contains only procedural arrangements but does not give a detailed list of agreements to which this Regulation does not apply.

[2] Proposal for a Council Directive on tariffs for scheduled air transport between Member States, Doc. COM(81) 590 final (OJ C 78, 30.3.1982, p. 6) drafted on the basis of the report adopted by the Commission on 15 July 1981 (COM(81) 398 final).

[3] Communication and proposals by the Commission to the Council - Civil aviation Memorandum No 2 - Progress towards the development of a Community air transport policy (Doc. COM(84) 72 final of 15 March 1984).

airlines and a proposal for the mutual recognition of licences. The Commission comes up with a number of measures for implementing these ideas and in particular the following proposals:

(i)   Proposal for a Council Decision (EEC) - based on Article 84(2) of the Treaty - on bilateral agreements, arrangements and memoranda of understanding between Member States relating to air transport (Annex I).

(ii)   Amended proposal for a Council Directive (EEC) - based on Article 84(2) of the Treaty - on fares for scheduled air transport between Member States (Annex II).

(iii)   Amendments to the proposal for a Council Regulation (EEC) - based on Article 87 of the Treaty - laying down the procedure for applying the rules on competition to undertakings in the air transport sector (Annex III A).

(iv)   Proposal for a Council Regulation (EEC) on the application of Article 85(3) of the Treaty to certain categories of agreements and concerted practices in the air transport sector (Annex III B).

(v)   Outline of a future Commission Regulation (EEC) exempting certain commercial agreements and concerted practices in the air transport sector (Annex III C).

(vi)   Proposal for a Council Decision (EEC) on non-discrimination and standstill provisions in air transport (Annex V).

Lastly Annex IV contains a policy paper and guidelines on State aids to air transport and Annex VI sets out a new programme of Commission initiatives in the field of civil aviation for the period from 1984 to 1986 which we give in Annex (p. 190).

Finally, a recent judgment by the Court of Justice[1] represents an important development as regards the applicability of the rules on competition to the fixing of air tariffs. After confirming that the general rules in the Treaty, and in particular those on competition, apply to air transport in the same way as to the other modes of transport, the judgment goes on to state that it is contrary to the obligations of the Member States under Article 5 of the EEC Treaty, read in conjuction with Articles 3(f) and 85, to introduce a compulsory national procedure for approving air tariffs where, in the absence of any rules adopted by the Council in pursuance of Article 87, it has been ruled or recorded by the national authorities or by the Commission, in accordance with the forms and procedures laid down in Article 88 or Article 89(2), that those tariffs are the result of an agreement, a decision by an association of undertakings or a concerted practice contrary to Article 85.

---

[1] Court of Justice of the European Communities, Cases 209 to 213/84, *Asjes and four other applicants* (30 April 1986 — not yet reported).

It is interesting that the same judgment also concludes that, in cases where there are no Community regulations, if such a ruling or recording has been made on the initiative of the national authorities or of the Commission, the national courts must draw all the necessary conclusions therefrom and in particular conclude that the concerted action on tariffs is automatically void under Article 85(2) of the Treaty.

This judgment clearly corroborates the proposals so far presented by the Commission, not only as regards tariffs specifically but also as regards the application of the rules on competition to air transport.

7.2.2 *Agreements between airlines*

7.2.2.1 **Bilateral agreements**

A large number of bilateral agreements exist between certain European airlines and are designed in particular to take advantage of 'pool' or 'joint venture' arrangements on certain routes and to combine forces on certain technical operations.[1]

7.2.2.2 **Multilateral agreements**

The main technical (i.e. not operational or commercial) agreements between European airlines are listed below. However, mention should be made of two successful agreements between non-Community airlines setting up consortia: Air-Afrique - a consortium of African flag-carriers, and SAS - Scandinavian Airlines System - which brings together the flag-carriers of Denmark, Norway and Sweden.

1. The KSSU consortium which was set up in 1967 and includes KLM, SAS and Swissair; joined in 1968 by the French UTA.

2. The Atlas consortium which was set up in 1967 and includes Alitalia, Air France, Lufthansa and Sabena, and was later joined by Iberia and, more recently, the Irish flag-carrier, Aer Lingus.

3. The Montparnasse Committee established in 1968 by those airlines which set up the KSSU and Atlas consortia. It was later joined by BOAC (which

---

[1] A 'pool' is an agreement between two (or more) carriers operating over the same route whereby all takings are pooled and later allocated according to specific formulae. In joint ventures, however, only the profits (or losses) are pooled; this offers less of an incentive to each carrier to operate efficiently (under a pooling agreement, an efficient company which has managed to contain its costs may make more of a profit than the other company even if, for instance, it accounts for only half of total takings).

is now British Airways) and Iberia. In 1971 the Committee decided to call itself the European Airlines Montparnasse Committee.

The main aim of these agreements was to pool technical expertise, standardize aircraft and coordinate long-term programmes. The fact that these agreements were concluded demonstrates the need for ever-closer cooperation between European airlines - although there is a possible risk of trusts emerging - particularly in order to tackle the serious problems currently facing these airlines in view of the climate of continuing recession, one example being competition between European airlines on the important North Atlantic routes.

7.2.2.3 Eurocontrol

The Convention establishing a European Organization for the Safety of Air Navigation (Eurocontrol) was signed in Brussels on 13 December 1960 by Belgium, France, Germany, Luxembourg, the Netherlands and the United Kingdom. In 1965 Ireland also became a full member of the Convention. Thus of the present Member States of the European Communities, only Denmark, Greece and Italy do not belong to Eurocontrol: Denmark because its flag-carrier (SAS) is a consortium with Norway and Sweden, Greece because it has only recently joined the Community and Italy because its air space is controlled by the military authorities. The main purpose of the Convention is to organize air traffic services in the upper air space jointly. The policies of the Organization are decided by a Commission composed of the Ministers of the Member States responsible for civil and military aviation. Eurocontrol has an Agency based in Luxembourg which is its executive and has the power to sign international agreements with third countries wishing to use the Agency's services. The basic objective of Eurocontrol is to guarantee the safety of air transport to the best of its ability. Some Member States, however, complain that the organization is inefficient and far too expensive and are thus reluctant to meet their own obligations, particularly financial obligations, *vis-à-vis* Eurocontrol, preferring to supervise their own national air space using their own resources. Particularly in recent years, this is putting the very future of the Agency in doubt.

This is yet another example of certain Member States being reluctant to entrust national responsibility for air navigation to an international institution, even an inter-governmental one.

7.2.3 *Concluding remarks*

After the failure of the Chicago Conference to establish multilateral regulation of air transport at world level, we now have a situation where international air traffic is organized on an extremely rigid bilateral basis.

Under bilateral arrangements - which, as we pointed out, put scheduled air services on the same level as inland transport services operated on a concessionary basis - governments reserve the right to determine the number of airlines, their operating capacity and the frequency of flights and to have the last word on tariffs, even though they are normally set by airlines within the IATA. Competition is further restricted by pooling and joint venture agreements between carriers relating, respectively, to overall takings and profits (or losses) resulting from the operation of services on specific routes. Alitalia, for example, operates all routes within Europe on a pool or joint venture basis, and also has pooling arrangements on many of its inter-continental routes.[1]

Although the 1978 Deregulation Act in the United States radically altered conditions of competition on the air transport market within the USA and the Bermuda II agreement signed in 1977 between the USA and the UK (later followed by bilateral agreements between the USA and Belgium, Germany and the Netherlands) gradually liberalized services on North Atlantic routes by allowing more airlines to fly them and by increasing the number of terminals within the USA, the position within the Member States of the EEC is clearly totally at odds with the rules on competition laid down in the Treaty.

There are strict bilateral governmental agreements governing air traffic between Member States and tariffs, which are either decided multilaterally within IATA or bilaterally, but always have to be approved by governments as well. Generally, the governments of the Member States are very loath to approve measures that will have any effect on the tariff structures which currently shield flag-carriers from competition - and which incidentally often also shield them from the legitimate demands of consumers who often have to bear the brunt of the harsh law of monopolistic supply which, although it may not do them any actual harm, certainly tries their patience.

Given this situation it is difficult to imagine how the Council can ever reach unanimous agreement on the proposals submitted by the Commission over the last few years which basically aim at deregulating air transport.

First of all, as in many other areas of Community policy, there are two conflicting attitudes here. On the one hand, there is the liberal approach favoured for many years by the United Kingdom - which, unlike the other Member States, has an Agency, the CAA, which like the CAB in the USA can effectively monitor and control the operations of carriers - and, for obvious reasons, by the Netherlands. On the other hand, there is the more conservative approach favoured by countries like France, Germany and Italy which for various reasons prefer dirigisme as a way of protecting their national airlines from the threat of competition.

---

[1] See N. Brough, 'Deregulation del trasporto aereo: la teoria, l'esperienza americana e le prospettive per l'Italia e per l'Europa', in *Einaudi Notizie,* 1983; N. Brough, 'Diritti di traffico vendonsi', in *Aviazione,* No 153 of April 1981, N. Brough, 'La giusta libertà' in *Turismo-Attualità,* No 18 of November 1980.

In France the Government has always imposed upon Air-France obligations which in many cases are hardly commercial but nevertheless relatively important within the framework of a policy designed to maintain the country's international prestige. It has therefore had to follow a broad policy of cross-subsidization which is difficult to reconcile with competitiveness.

The German airline, Deutsche Lufthansa, is extremely vulnerable to competition because of its high operating costs resulting from the number of routes covered, the frequency of flights, the quality of its aircraft and the high salaries of its staff. Lastly in Italy, where compared with other Member States it is often more difficult to discern a logical trend in the form of a specific basic strategy on policies governing air transport, a complex series of more or less pragmatic actions and reactions have served to maintain strict protection of Alitalia and its many privileges.

Two factors in particular serve to demonstrate Alitalia's dependence on the Italian Government.

The first is the extent to which Alitalia itself subsidizes routes which are bound to be uneconomic by charging fares which are much higher than actual costs on routes with heavy traffic. As Nick Brough recently pointed out in an interesting article, way back in 1973, when fares were not at all as they are now, Alitalia made a profit of over LIT 10 000 million on its four most profitable routes (the first being Rome-Milan) which it used to subsidize the other loss-making routes maintained because of their 'social' importance.[1] This cross-subsidization avoids the need for public subsidization of routes on which fares are kept excessively low, either because demand is too elastic or because it has been decided to support a particular service for social reasons. However, this convenient solution means that a small section of the public ends up subsidizing activities which should be paid for more equitably by society as a whole. Nevertheless, it is clear that as long as cross-subsidization remains the keystone of Italy's civil aviation policy the Government is bound to refuse any attempt at deregulation on individual routes or as part of air transport policy in general. Consequently, there is no way in which services will ever be tailored to meet the requirements and preferences of the general public.[2]

---

[1] Chamber of Deputies, Committee X: The situation of civil aviation in Italy. Fact-finding survey and documentation of legislation, Rome 1976, p. 385 quoted in N. Brough, *Deregulation del trasporto aereo,* op. cit., p. 4.

[2] While consumers on the few profitable routes will still have to pay not only the cost of the service they are using but also the costs of the services still provided on loss-making routes - a principle which is highly questionable in terms of public economic morality.

Another factor which causes such wide distortions between supply and demand because of the lack of competition on fares is the amazing number of discounts which Alitalia is obliged to give to a whole range of social categories.[1]

This unfair system, which means that the few 'ordinary' passengers have to pay over the odds, would obviously never be possible if there was proper competition between carriers.

Generally, therefore, we shall probably have to wait a long time before deregulation arrives in Europe. However, there is growing annoyance in certain countries about excessive bureaucratic interference with economic activities,[2] and the stagnation of demand on the air transport market seems to be continuing. Both these far from negligible factors may serve to limit today's excessive bilateralism and encourage airlines to adopt a more competitive attitude. However, as far as the Community's decision-making process on air transport is concerned, there are probably further disappointments in store since Article 84(2) of the Treaty states that provisions on sea and air transport have to be taken unanimously by the Council, although recently the European Parliament has voiced strong opposition.

Ultimately, therefore, only a solution at European Community level is likely to solve air transport problems within the Community once and for all.

Achievements with regard to Rhine navigation indicate that it would not be out of the question to associate non-member countries with any future Community air transport policy. This is provided, of course, that the Council overcomes its failure to establish a common transport policy and provided specifically in the air transport sector that, as suggested by the United Kingdom and the Netherlands, we can move away from the attitude held by most of the Member States in favour of maintaining structures that are designed to protect national flag-carriers from any form of competition and the consequent steadfast resistance to any Community attempt at harmonization that goes beyond matters of technical detail only. What is certain is that there is no chance of making progress with the common transport policy in general and European policy on air transport in particular with the 'step-by-step' policy, which is just a cover for lack of political will.

---

[1] These include, by way of example only, members of the CNR and the CONI, journalists, fire officers, inspectors of waterway engineering, the centre for the military applications of nuclear energy, all of which are entitled to a 30% discount; unionized journalists: 50%, and Ministers: discounts varying between 10 and 25%. For a full list - and some highly instructive information - consult Alitalia's manual of ticket procedures.

[2] The National Monetary Conference held in Italy in Genoa on 28 and 29 October 1983 showed that the time was now ripe for some measure of deregulation on monetary policy.

ANNEX E

Communication and proposals by the Commission to the Council of 15 March 1984

Annex VI

PROGRAMME OF COMMISSION'S INITIATIVES IN THE FIELD OF CIVIL AVIATION 1984-86

1984

Proposal on mutual recognition of certain licences and training in civil aviation

Modified proposal concerning air services for low-weight express air cargo

Proposal on facilitation of freight and passenger air transport and general aviation

Proposal on measures to facilitate market access

1985 and 1986

Extension to air transport of transparency rules for financial relations between Member States and public enterprises

Proposal on the widening of the field of activities of non-scheduled services

Review of the Directive on inter-regional air services

Airport efficiency criteria

Proposal on airport charges

8. Ports

From the very early days, before any interest was shown in sea and air transport, there were calls for Community action on ports. Moreover, as ports form the natural link between sea and inland transport, the provisions of Article 84(2), whose restrictive effects we have mentioned, constitute only a partial obstacle. In fact, although the EEC Treaty does not directly mention seaports, its provisions nevertheless apply under various headings to infrastructure, undertakings and various activities which may all concern ports. From a strictly legal point of view, the scope for Community action on ports should be considered not only on the basis of whether the general rules of the Treaty apply to transport, as settled in the judgment of the Court of Justice on Case 167/73 given on 4 April 1974, but also with regard to the provisions of Article 235 of the Treaty which states: 'If action by the Community should prove necessary to attain, in the course of the operation of the common market, one of the objectives of the Community and this Treaty has not provided the necessary powers, the Council shall, acting unanimously on a proposal from the Commission and after consulting the Assembly, take the appropriate measures.'

In any case, the application of Community law to the various modes of transport was bound to have a considerable affect on seaports because they constitute a strategic link in the transport chain, a link which has become even more essential with the accession of the new Member States.[1] Moreover, from an economic point of view, it was impossible to ignore the important regional development role played by ports since they determine the location of industry within the Community. Furthermore, in view of the economic circumstances at the beginning of the 1960s, namely intensive development of traffic through Community ports, it was feared that, unless there was a general programme for developing communication networks, bottlenecks might be created which would impede the development of industry in the Community.[2]

---

[1] Currently some 30% of trade within the Community and more than 85% of the Community's import and export trade with the rest of the world passes through Community ports. See in this connection Eurostat, *Statistical Yearbook - Transport, Communications, Tourism - 1981*, Luxembourg, 1983, Part 5 and Eurostat, *Monthly External Trade Bulletins* 1983.

[2] It is particularly interesting to note the terms used in the recent report on port policy (1982) submitted by Mr Angelo Carossino on behalf of the European Parliament's Committee on Transport: 'The aim of the common transport policy must be to provide low-cost, effective and rapid transport facilities for the internal market formed by the territory of the Community, but this cannot possibly be achieved without due consideration being given to seaports in every proposal submitted and every decision taken', or again: 'Ports are points of transition for the transfer of goods from sea to land transport and vice-versa. A transport policy which neglected seaports would be unthinkable. Modern developments towards the creation of an unbroken network of door-to-door transport stretching across continents and seas have meant that the role played by ports in switching goods from one mode of transport to another is becoming an increasingly significant factor in the price, quality and speed of services'. See EP Working Document No 1-844/82 of 15 November 1982, pp. 8-9.

It was the European Parliament which first drew attention to the port problem. In fact, back in 1960, its Transport Committee asked Paul J. Kapteyn to draft a report on transport policy.

The report[1] was adopted in 1961 and contains the first mention of the need to devise a common policy on ports at European level. Later, in 1961, the same Committee adopted another report by G. Garlato on a fact-finding study on the Rhine and the ports of Rotterdam and Amsterdam carried out by some of the members of the Committee.[2] Finally, on 29 November 1967 the Committee adopted the Seifriz report[3] on a common policy on port traffic, which was the first report devoted entirely to the common port policy. The main aim of this policy, it argued, should be to prevent factors like Community tariff policy, the coordination of the different modes of transport or the problem of infrastructure charging from distorting competition between seaports.

After a series of on-the-spot fact-finding visits to the major European ports by the Transport Committee over the next few years, on 12 April 1972 Horst Seefeld submitted to the European Parliament on behalf of the Committee a report on port policy in the European Community[4] which was adopted on 15 September 1972.

The report's conclusions, reached after intensive study and analysis, are embodied in a resolution adopted by the European Parliament on 17 April 1972.[5] Basically, it maintains that there is a close link between the lack of a port policy and failure to establish a coherent common transport policy within the Community. In calling for a common policy on port traffic, the report suggests that competition, combined to some extent with State aid and subsidies, is the motive force behind the expansion of the Community's ports. Community port policy should therefore follow the principle that ports should cover all their costs out of revenue and should therefore be placed on an equal competitive footing and that extensive cooperation between ports should be encouraged over investment policy. In order to devise a port policy, the resolution calls for the establishment of a Standing Committee chaired by the Commission of the European Communities and consisting of representatives of the different port activities. The Committee would have the task of compiling all the information required by the Commission before it can put proposals for a common port policy.

More recently, as we have mentioned, the Committee on Transport prepared a full report, which was presented by Angelo Carossino and is a very clear analysis of the role of port policy in the context of a common transport policy designed to meet the requirements prevailing some ten years after the Seefeld report.[6]

---

[1] 'Report by Paul J. Kapteyn on the problems concerning the common transport policy within the EEC', EP Working Document No 106/1961-62.

[2] EP Working Document No 108/1961-62.

[3] EP Working Document No 140/1967.

[4] EP Working Document No 10/1972.

[5] OJ C 46, 9.5.1972.

[6] 'Report drawn up on behalf of the Committee on Transport on the role of ports in the common transport policy', EP Working Document No 1-844/82, 15.11.1982.

Apart from levelling vigorous criticism against the lack of interest in ports shown by the Commission when devising a common transport policy, point B.VIII of the Carossino report lists the objectives of a common port policy:

'The main objective of a European port policy should be to ensure the competitiveness of our continent in international trade. This clearly means an economical and highly specialized and rapid system of port operations.

The ports must organize their own expansion independently. The Member States are responsible for determining national port policy, within the framework of their own legal systems. EEC policy should be limited to avoiding competition by aid and subsidies which might give rise to discrimination, by laying down common rules of conduct.

Another objective of the port policy should be to ensure that ports become humane places of work for all who work there.

The port policy of the EEC should contribute to the conservation or rehabilitation of the seas and coastlines of the world for mankind.

The major task of a Community port policy is the elimination of any form of discrimination in traffic between the ports and their hinterlands, through harmonization of the rail, road and inland waterway transport sectors.'

On the basis of these objectives, the report includes a motion for a resolution on the role of ports. In view of its importance it is given in full at the end of this chapter. The resolution calls for greater attention to ports than hitherto in the context of the common transport policy, especially competition between ports. It also calls for the introduction of an overall marine policy and in particular an environmental policy for the seas which surround the Community.

The Commission's approach to the port problem, on the other hand, was much more dilatory, and in some respects more hesitant.

Only three and a half years after publication of the Seifriz report, the Commission published its first communication on the subject in the form of a memorandum on the Community's port policy options[1] which it sent to the members of the Parliament's Transport Committee on 24 March 1971. The memorandum did not confine its analysis solely to port policy in connection with transport problems but considered ports within the broader economic context of the common market. Moreover, its aim was not so much to establish the principles and content of a port policy as to publish the conclusions of an extensive fact-finding survey carried out to determine how ports operate within the context of the Community's trade. It called for extensive consultation to be

---

[1] Doc. COM/16/VII/71.

followed by joint action to allow the Commission itself to compile the information it required to establish and implement a Community port policy.[1]

On 21 November 1972, the Commission, on the initiative of Mr A. Coppé, Member of the Commission responsible for transport, organized a first meeting with representatives of the 20 chief ports of the enlarged Community[2] to discuss the major topical problems regarding the development of ports within the EEC. This was followed by a second meeting in Brussels on 19 February 1974 chaired by Mr Le Goy, who was then the Commission's Director-General for Transport.

At the meeting it was decided to set up a Working Party of port representatives chaired by a Commission official. The idea of setting up a Standing Committee on Ports at Community level was abandoned, however, because of the steadfast opposition of the French and German representatives. The Working Party was given a highly circumscribed mandate which consisted principally of carrying out a fact-finding study on the institutional and administrative structure of the Community's ports.

The Working Party sent a detailed questionnaire to the main port authorities in Europe and on the basis of replies drafted a report on the current situation in the Community's seaports which was published in September 1977 (Catalogue No CB-22-77-863-EN-C). In 1980 it published an addendum[3] amending the fact-finding report and a second report by the Port Working Party compiled on the basis of the mandate it had been given at the first plenary meeting of the main ports of the Community held on 9 and 10 June 1977. Together with its annex this second report[4] examines in particular the problem of distortion of competition between the Community's ports.

However, a report prepared by the Commission on distortions of competition on routes linking ports with their hinterlands was not published.

At the first plenary seaports meeting it was decided that a second plenary session would take place at the end of 1980 to examine and draw conclusions from the results of the fact-finding studies carried out by the two sub-groups of the Port Working Party. These subgroups were to examine respectively the costs for ships calling at a port and the cost of cargo passing through a port in order 'to determine how differences between ports could cause distortions of competition'.[5] The ultimate aim was to draw up a list of priority measures to be taken on ports.

---

[1] The document is analysed in *Politique portuaire et politique maritime de la CEE*, published by the Studiecentrum voor de Expansie van Antwerpen, Antwerp, 1974, p. 5-8.

[2] Bremen, Hamburg; Antwerp, Ghent; Bordeaux, Dunkirk, Le Havre, Marseille; Genoa, Trieste, Naples, Venice; Rotterdam, Amsterdam; London, Liverpool, Southampton, Clyde; Copenhagen; Dublin.

[3] Doc. VII/440/80.

[4] Doc. VII/440/80.

[5] *La Politique commune des Transports de la CEE, Bilan de 1980-1981,* Studiecentrum voor de Expansie van Antwerpen, Antwerp, 1982.

This meeting actually took place in Brussels on 9 and 10 December 1980. It was chaired by Mr Richard Burke, the Member of the Commission then responsible for transport, and attended by representatives of 40 or so major seaports, the associated chambers of commerce and the port organizations of the eight maritime States of the Community, and observers from Greece. Most of the delegates at the meeting did not consider that any further action was necessary on the problem of distortion of competition and it was decided that any future cooperation between the ports and the Commission would be channelled through a working group set up by the ports themselves. From then on, the Port Working Group ceased to function and the Commission's General Reports stopped mentioning port activities.

There was already a sign that the Commission would abandon its plan to establish an EEC port policy in the answer given by Mr Burke, on behalf of the Commission, on 3 October 1980 to a written question from Mr Angelo Carossino on the state of advancement of the policy on ports. The answer included a statement to the effect that so far the need to take special measures for the application of the general rules of the Treaty to ports had not arisen.[1]

The Commission's abandonment of port policy is even clearer from Doc. EP 73.762 of 1 July 1981 in which it informed the European Parliament of the conclusions reached by the Port Working Group. It mentions that seven years of studies and close cooperation with the chief ports of the Community have demonstrated that there is no need for a specific Community policy on ports.[2]

One general consideration with regard to port policy is that ports cover a whole range of activities and services relating to ships and goods, all with extremely complex and very different problems and characteristics. The main differences between ports are the way in which they are organized, the different roles played by the public authorities in financing infrastructure and superstructure investment and maintenance expenditure, the operation of port authorities, taxation and manpower.[3]

---

[1] OJ C 322, 10.12.1980. In addition the answer states: 'The Commission's experience has tended to show that several of the features capable of affecting ports - landward infrastructure links and transport services and shipping services - relate directly to those fields of transport rather than falling into a separate classification of ports policy.'

[2] Although, as pointed out in the Carossino report, it later goes on to contradict this statement by stating: 'Since they are an important link in the Community's transport chain, seaports come within the framework of the general development of transport policy' (Doc. EP 73.762/Annex, p. 6).

[3] See A. Ventrella, 'Port management in the Community', a speech given to the Symposium on European Port Administration held at the University of Rome on 18 November 1982. This included the statistics on investment in port infrastructure given at the end of this chapter.

Moreover, opinions differ widely in port circles as to whether a Community port policy is in fact necessary. The idea of having Europe's ports specialize in different types of cargoes met with no success. Representatives of German ports have always been reluctant to see the establishment of a common port policy while France is totally opposed to any involvement by the Commission in port policy at all. Neither do the new Member States, with the exception of Greece, seem particularly keen on the idea of such a policy (and the opinion expressed by Mr Burke in 1980 is also very revealing).

It is basically the three Benelux countries and Italy which are most interested in further action on a Community port policy. There is a lot of ground to be made up, however, the first step being to reverse the Commission's decision to abolish the port policy division within the Directorate-General for Transport which was taken in 1981 when all Community interest in this sector was shelved.

However, in spite of all the difficulties we have mentioned, it is hard to see how a common transport policy can be established without including a common port policy, and this for many reasons. Above all, how can problems relating to ports be tackled within the context of a common policy on inland transport when, as the Commission itself maintains, ports form a link between sea transport and inland transport? Because of this role the operation of ports substantially affects the development of Europe's economy with all its various components, and these certainly include some aspects of sea transport and the special problem of ports.

Moreover, since the aim of the common market is to establish the free movement of capital, persons and goods as a means of ensuring that competition plays a fundamental role within the economy, this system must logically also include port undertakings and therefore must also follow the principle of non-discrimination. But if the rules on competition are also to form the basis of port policy, it necessarily follows that the Community should adopt a policy to harmonize the various aspects of port activities in the Member States. Furthermore, within a Community whose declared task it is to promote the harmonious development of economic activities, a continuous and balanced expansion, and an accelerated raising of the standard of living, ports should be seen as factors in the promotion of regional development since they play an important role in regional policy and land-use planning. It is difficult to see, therefore, how it is possible to do without a port policy in the context of policies designed to promote the balanced expansion of the Community's economy.

Finally, at a time when one of the central points at issue in respect of the establishment of a common transport policy is the coordination of transport infrastructure programmes and a Community mechanism to provide financial support for transport infrastructure projects of Community interest, how can the planning of inland transport infrastructure be dissociated from the planning of port infrastructure?

We can do no more, therefore, than express our full agreement with the arguments along these lines put forward by eminent Italian officials within the Commission's Directorate-General for Transport,[1] and by the European Parliament's Committee on Transport, a copy of whose resolution on the role of ports in the common transport policy is reproduced in the following pages.

---

[1] See A. Ventrella, op. cit.

Motion for a resolution submitted to the European Parliament by the Committee on Transport on 15 November 1982.

The Committee on Transport hereby submits to the European Parliament the following motion for a resolution, together with explanatory statement:

MOTION FOR A RESOLUTION
on the role of ports in the common transport policy

The European Parliament,
Having regard to the motion for a resolution by Mr Cottrell (Doc. 1-544/81) on a Severn Estuary port zone, and the motion for a resolution by Mr Pininfarina (Doc. 1-198/82) on the improvement of port and road infrastructures in Liguria and Piedmont in a European perspective;

Having regard to the report on the common transport policy by Mr Carossino (Doc. 1-996/81);

Having regard to the report by the Committee on Transport (Doc. 1-844/82),

A.   Whereas ports, as the link between sea transport and land transport, play an important role in transport policy;

B.   Noting with great disappointment that despite Parliament's resolution of 17.4.1972[1] there has been no progress at all in the common seaport policy;

C.   In view of the differences between the ports of the Community and the resulting difficulties for specific action on ports;

D.   None the less convinced that in the present situation it is necessary and possible to take some important steps in this direction,

1.   Calls on the Commission to pay greater attention to ports than hitherto, and particularly, when submitting any proposals connected with the common transport policy, to take greater account than in the past of their effects on competition between ports, with particular reference to the following:

     (i)   harmonization of specific taxes on transport (road taxes and taxes on mineral oils),

     (ii)   harmonization of social provisions in the transport sector,

     (iii)   harmonization of technical provisions, particularly of maximum permitted weights and dimensions in road transport,

     (iv)   a tariff system for infrastructure costs,

     (v)   infrastructures policy,

     (vi)   tariff policy for transport by rail, road and inland waterways,

     (vii)   policy on road transport and inland navigation capacity,

     (viii)   abolition of border formalities;

2.   Calls on the Commission, when allocating resources from the European Regional Development Fund or other Community funds for port investment, to take account of their effect on competition between ports and if necessary draw up an overall plan for these financial contributions in the context of proposals relating to all the ports either of a given region or coastline, or in the Community as a whole;

3.   Calls on the Commission to pay special attention, when drawing up the Community programme of financial contributions for infrastructure projects, to the individual ports themselves and their road, rail and waterway links with the hinterland;

---

[1] OJ C 46, 9.5.1972.

4. Reaffirms the principle it has upheld in the past that genuine competition between seaports should be maintained as a prerequisite for increased productivity;

5. Calls on the Commission, in view of the disparities between the administrative structures of ports, to continue to monitor the problem of contributions made to ports from the general fiscal revenue of the Member States and, where necessary, to initiate negotiations on the subject;

6. Reaffirms the call for the elimination of all discrimination in links between ports and the hinterland which is incompatible with the European Treaties;

7. Calls for account to be taken of the interests of ports and competition between ports when formulating the common shipping policy;

8. Calls for the introduction of an overall marine policy and in particular an environmental policy for the seas which surround the Community, with special reference to ports;

9. Calls on the Commission to set up a special service in its relevant directorate-general to study all aspects of port policy;

10. Instructs its President to forward this resolution and the attached report to the Commission and Council of the European Communities and the parliaments of the Member States.

ANNEX G

Investment in port infrastructure in the Community

TABLE 8.1

Member State	Cost of investment	Maritime access channels	
		Cost of maintenance	Remarks
Belgium	100% national government	100% national government	
Denmark	100% port authority	100% port authority	
FR of Germany	100% Federal Government outside port	100% Federal Government outside port	
	100% relevant territorial authority within the port	100% relevant territorial authority within the port	
France			
Autonomous ports	80% national government 20% port authority	} 100% national government	
Non-autonomous ports	30-50% national government balance Chamber of Commerce		
Ireland	100% port authority	100% port authority	
Italy	National government + port authority in varying proportions	Varies but in general the national government pays	
Autonomous ports			
State ports	80% national government 20% communes + provinces	100% national government	
Netherlands 'Havenbedrijven'	2/3 national government1/3 'Havenbedrijf'[1] (Rotterdam) or municipality (Amsterdam)	} 100% national government	'Havenbedrijf' in Rotterdam responsible for entire initial cost of access channel for ships drawing over 57'
'Havenschappen'	100% national government		
United Kingdom	100% port authority	100% port authority	

[1] See Mr Ventrella's speech of 1982.

TABLE 8.2

Lights, buoys and navigational aids

Member State		Cost of investment	Cost of maintenance	Remarks
Belgium	outside port	100% national government	100% national government	
	inside port	100% municipality/authority	100% municipality/authority	
Denmark	outside port	100% national government	100% national government	
	inside port	100% port authority	100% port authority	
FR of Germany	outside port	100% Federal Government	100% Federal Government	
	inside port	100% relevant territorial authorities	100% relevant territorial authorities	
France				
Autonomous ports	outside port	100% national government	100% national government	
	inside port	60-80% national government balance port authority		
Non-autonomous ports	outside port	100% national government		
	inside port	30-50% national government balance Chamber of Commerce	100% national government	
Ireland	outside port	100% Commissioners of Irish Lights[1]	100% Commissioners of Irish Lights	
	inside port	100 % port authority	100 % port authority	
Italy	outside port	100% national government	100% national government	Except at Genoa
	inside port			
Netherlands 'Havenbedrijven' 'Havenschappen'	outside port	100% national government outside the port - position within ports varies from port to port	100% national government outside the port - varying responsibility within the ports	Except radar
	inside port			
United Kingdom	outside port	Mostly Trinity House,[2] sometimes port authority or similar body	Mostly Trinity House, sometimes port authority or similar body	
	inside port	100% port authority	100% port authority	

[1] A statutory organization responsible for all navigational aids around the coast of Ireland other than those for which the port authorities are responsible.
[2] Trinity House is a non-statutory private guild responsible for the pilotage in the Thames estuary and in 40 other ports and for most lighthouses.

TABLE 8.3

Sea locks and exterior breakwaters

Member State		Cost of investment	Cost of maintenance	Remarks
Belgium	Locks	100% national government	100% municipality/authority	At Zeebrugge only
	Breakwaters	100%	100% authority	
Denmark	Locks	100% port authority	100% port authority	Only one small lock at Copenhagen
	Breakwaters	100%	100%	
FR of Germany	Locks	'Länder' and communes	'Länder' and communes	Only one sealock at Wilhelmshaven: responsibility of the Federal Government
	Breakwaters			
France Autonomous ports	Locks	80% national government 20% port authority	100% national government	
	Breakwaters	30-50% national government balance Chamber of Commerce		
Non-autonomous ports	Locks			
	Breakwaters			
Ireland	Locks	100% port authority	100% port authority	
	Breakwaters	100%		
Italy Autonomous ports	Breakwaters	National government and port authority in varying proportions	Varies but in general the national government pays	There are no locks in the Italian ports
State ports	Breakwaters	80% national government 20% communes + provinces	100% national government	
Netherlands 'Havenbedrijven'	Locks	2/3 national government 1/3 municipal (Amsterdam only) 2/3 national government 1/3 municipal (Amsterdam) or 'Havenbedrijf' (Rotterdam)	100% national government	Rotterdam has no sealocks
	Breakwaters	Varies from port to port		
'Havenschappen'	Locks	Varies from port to port	Varies from port to port	
	Breakwaters			
United Kingdom	Locks	port authority	100% port authority	
	Breakwaters	100% 100%	100%	

TABLE 8.4   Docks, quays, reclaimed land, etc.

Member State	Cost of investment	Cost of maintenance	Remarks
Belgium	60-100% national government balance municipality/authority	100% municipality/authority	
Denmark	100% port authority	100% port authority	
FR of Germany	100% 'Land' or commune	100% 'Land' or commune	
France Autonomous ports	Docks, quays etc. 60% national government, 40% port authority Reclaimed land - each case treated separately	100% port authority	
Non-autonomous ports	30-50% national government balance Chamber of Commerce	National government and Chamber of Commerce in varying proportions	
Ireland	100% port authority	100% port authority	
Italy Autonomous ports	National government and port authority in varying proportions	Port authority with an annual contribution from the State	At Genoa this figure is fixed at LIT 100 million p.a. by the Law of 1962
State ports	80% national government 20% communes + provinces	100 % national government	
Netherlands 'Havenbedrijven'	100% port authority	100% port authority	
'Havenschappen'	Cost shared by port authority, central government, province + commune	Cost shared by port authority central government, province + commune	
United Kingdom	100% port authority	100% port authority	

Note : This table does not cover jetties and specialized terminals or docks, quays and reclaimed land owned by the private sector.

9. Transport by pipeline

Because at the time of the negotiations transport by pipeline (in particular oil and gas pipelines) was relatively unimportant in economic terms, it is not mentioned in the Treaty. It is therefore governed by the Treaty provisions outside Title IV. In fact, from the very beginning, any attempt by the Commission to tackle the subject, particularly oil pipelines, in the context of the common transport policy met with the firm opposition of those governments particularly sensitive to lobbying by the oil industry. In terms of transport policy, there is no doubt that oil pipelines are a natural competitor to the transportation of crude oil by inland waterways. Not only did the Commission, at the beginning of 1963, put before the Council a proposal aiming to apply the consultation procedure introduced in 1962 concerning the development of transport policy measures by the Member States to transport by pipeline, but the Parliament even asked the Commission, in a resolution of 28 March 1963, to prepare a proposal for a Community regulation on transport by pipeline. However, at a meeting on 22 June 1964, the Council decided not to accept the proposal to apply the consultation procedure to transport by pipeline feeling that the time was not yet right for the Community to become involved in this mode of transport. However, reasoning that transport by oil pipeline principally concerned energy policy, the Council asked the Commission to set up a special Working Party on Energy and Transport to examine the problems involved.

This Working Party of government experts started work in 1965. It considered various matters, principally information on the development of oil pipeline networks within the Community, the application of the 'common carrier' principle to this mode of transport and the possible adoption of a Community regulation on the subject.

Unfortunately, because of lack of agreement in the Council, all this work was in vain. One thing is certain, however: transport by pipeline concerns not only transport policy but energy policy and regional policy as well. It therefore calls for a combined approach, which has so far been lacking, even though Article 235 of the Treaty is a perfectly suitable legal basis for Community action in this field and even though the economic and political importance of this sector is now beyond any dispute.[1] However, since Council decisions have to be taken unanimously and since there is a general reluctance to delegate to the Community executive energy policy decisions which are of importance to each Member State, there seems to be little chance of Community action on this mode of transport in the foreseeable future. There are currently no Commission proposals for legislative measures on pipelines before the Council, which speaks volumes on the current level of Community interest in transport by pipeline.

---

[1] See in this connection Eurostat figures, cit., part 9.

PART THREE

Special problems

1. The Community's external relations

1.1 Intergovernmental agreements and the European Communities

We have already seen that there are a number of bilateral agreements on road transport (e.g. bilateral quotas for the carriage of goods). We have already mentioned the main multilateral conventions signed by certain European countries. These include the International Convention concerning the Carriage of Goods by Rail (CIM) and the International Convention concerning the Carriage of Passengers and Luggage by Rail (CIV), which were signed in 1890, the 1956 Convention on the Contract for the International Carriage of Goods by Road (CMR), the TIR Convention on the International Transport of Goods by Road, which was introduced provisionally in 1949 and became permanent in 1958, the 1970 European Agreement concerning the Work of Crews of Vehicles engaged in International Road Transport (AETR), and the Agreement on the International Carriage of Passengers by Road by means of Occasional Coach and Bus Services (ASOR), which was signed in Dublin on 26 May 1982 and formally approved by the Council on 12 July 1982.[1] The 1868 Mannheim Convention governs inland waterway navigation.

In the context of the European Communities, it is obviously necessary to make a distinction between intergovernmental agreements concerning the ECSC and those concerning the EEC.

1.1.1 *Intergovernmental agreements and the ECSC*

In perfect concordance with the general principles of the ECSC and its institutional structure, the ECSC Treaty contains fairly precise provisions on relationships between the Community and third countries, as set out in Part Two of the Convention on the Transitional Provisions (Articles 14 to 17).

We have already noted the principle whereby commercial relations between the ECSC and third countries remain within the competence of the Member States (Article 71), and that, within limits precisely defined by the Community and under its control, this principle also applies to customs tariffs (Article 72), quantitative restrictions (Article 74) and commercial agreements (Article 75). On this legal basis, and by virtue of the legal personality vested in the Community by the Treaty (Article 6), the High Authority may enter into relations with

---

[1] OJ L 230, 5.8.1982. The Regulation concerning the implementation of the Agreement was adopted by the Council on 16 December 1982 (OJ L 10, 13.1.1983).

certain third countries. Particular mention should be made of agreements signed with Austria and Switzerland (and more recently with Yugoslavia) on the setting of international through tariffs for coal, steel and other ECSC products in transit through these countries, which now participate in the Community transit system for the carriage of goods by road.[1]

Furthermore, in 1954, the High Authority signed an association agreement with the United Kingdom in order to solve problems of common interest regarding coal and steel and trade relations. The agreement also covered transport problems, and of course had the same objectives as those set out in the Treaty.

1.1.2 *Intergovernmental agreements and the EEC*

The EEC Treaty contains a complex set of provisions governing relations between the Community and third countries. These can be subdivided into external relations under ordinary law, which are covered by Articles 228 to 236, and special external relations arising from the accession of other European countries to the Community (Article 237) and from the association of third States, unions of States or international organizations with the Community (Article 238), or the association of the overseas countries and territories (Articles 131 to 136 and the Implementing Convention annexed to the Treaty) which, since this Implementing Convention ceased to apply on 31 December 1962, now enjoy a status which is negotiated within the framework of regular agreements.

Certain of these Articles of the EEC Treaty give the institutions special responsibility for external relations in areas which may also include transport.

Thus, the first paragraph of Article 229 states: 'It shall be for the Commission to ensure the maintenance of all appropriate relations with the organs of the United Nations, of its specialized agencies and of the General Agreement on Tariffs and Trade.' The second paragraph states: 'The Commission shall also maintain such relations as are appropriate with all international organizations.' Accordingly, the Commission is represented in Geneva on the ECE's Inland Transport Committee and also participates in the GATT's work on transport. Pursuant to the second paragraph of this Article, the Commission has established firm links with the Central Commission for the Navigation of the Rhine. It is also interesting to note that Article 229 of the Treaty gives the EEC Commission direct powers which are not restricted by any special mandate which has to be given by the Council.

Again, under Article 231, whereby the Community is required to establish close cooperation with the Organization for European Economic Cooperation, the

---

[1] Council Regulation (EEC) No 222/77 of 13 December 1976 on Community transit, OJ L 38, 9.2.1977, and subsequent amendments.

Commission does cooperate with the OECD, as it is now known, on transport matters.

Article 234 states that rights and obligations arising from agreements concluded before the entry into force of the Treaty shall not be affected by the provisions of the Treaty, and lays down a procedure designed to eliminate any incompatibilities, based on the principle of unity of action by the Community *vis-à-vis* third countries which is clearly established by Article 228. Article 234 is important in connection with transport since the problem of compliance with agreements concluded before the entry into force of the Treaty and steps to eliminate incompatibilities established does arise with the Mannheim Convention. In the same connection, it is worth mentioning a Decision of 18 June 1973 authorizing the tacit extension of certain trade agreements concluded between the Member States and third countries.[1]

As already mentioned, under the association procedure provided for in Article 238, 'the Community may conclude with a third State, a union of States or an international organization agreements establishing an association involving reciprocal rights and obligations, common action and special procedures'.

On the basis of this Article, association agreements were signed with Greece (on 9 July 1961, coming into force on 1 November 1962) and Turkey (on 12 September 1963). These were designed to prepare for the entry of these countries into the European Economic Community - in the case of Greece on 1 January 1981 - and also covered transport. The two agreements state that the Treaty provisions on transport and measures adopted pursuant to these provisions may be applied to the two associate countries according to rules and a procedure to be adopted by the two Association Councils.[2] To date, no such measures have been adopted by Turkey and no action had been taken by Greece either until it became the Community's 10th Member State.

Of course, some measures already adopted or to be adopted under the common transport policy involve agreements with third countries on their implementation. We have already discussed the problems concerning the abolition of tariff discrimination, implementation of the bracket tariff system and the laying-up of inland waterway vessels. The main countries concerned are those which, because of their geographical position, carry transit traffic between the north and south of the Community, i.e. Austria and Switzerland to begin with and, since the accession of Greece, Yugoslavia. In addition, Switzerland, as a riparian State, also participates in Rhine navigation.

---

[1] OJ C 189, 11.7.1973, p. 47.
[2] Covered respectively in Article 65 and Article 22 and following of the two Association Agreements and consisting, on the one hand, of members of the governments of the Member States, the Council and the EEC Commission and, on the other, of members of the government of the associated State concerned.

We have mentioned that the Community has concluded an agreement on the application of the regulations on Community transit to Switzerland and Austria[1] in respect not only of the transit of goods but also of all problems connected with this issue. The Treaty also provides a solid legal basis for the solution of any problems affecting relations with third countries which arise in connection with the common transport policy. Finally, although the provisions of the Treaty are very clear on general problems concerning the Community's external relations and in fact Article 210 specifically recognizes the Community's legal personality,[2] it has very little to say specifically about the Community's competence in relations with third countries on specific matters like transport and says nothing about the allocation of responsibilities between the institutions of the Communities and the Member States.

As a result, the controversy which arose between the Commission and the Council with regard to the respective responsibilities of the Community and the Member States in respect of the European Agreement concerning the Work of Crews of Vehicles engaged in International Road Transport (AETR) led the Court of Justice to make a clear ruling on the basic principles governing the allocation of these responsibilities.

The judgment of the Court of 31 March 1971 is fundamental, particularly with regard to transport. It establishes the principle that the powers of the Community extend to relationships arising from international law, and hence involve the need in the sphere in question for agreements with the third countries concerned. In the grounds of its judgment, the Court held that 'although it is true that Articles 74 and 75 do not expressly confer on the Community authority to enter into international agreements, nevertheless the bringing into force, on 25 March 1969, of Regulation No 543/69 of the Council on the harmonization of certain social legislation relating to road transport necessarily vested in the Community power to enter into any agreements with third countries relating to the subject-matter governed by that Regulation'.[3] The Community is therefore deemed to be competent in the sphere of transport, whenever, under the common transport policy, measures are adopted under Community law which bind all the institutions of the Community. On the basis of this judgment, on 5 February 1973, the Commission forwarded to the Council a proposal for a Decision on the opening of negotiations with a view to concluding an agreement between the EEC and certain third countries - particularly those States partici-pating in the ECMT - on rules applicable to the international carriage of passengers by road by means of bus services, designed principally to solve

---

[1] Agreement of 23 November 1972, OJ L 294, 29.12.1972 for the Swiss Confederation and Agreement of 30 November 1972, OJ L 294, 29.12.1972 for Austria, which came into force on 1 January 1974, OJ L 337, 6.12.1973. To these two Agreements was added a Trilateral Agreement between the EEC, Austria and Switzerland, which came into force on 1 March 1978 (OJ L 44, 15.2.1978).
[2] Articles 6 and 184 of their respective Treaties make the same provisions in respect of the ECSC and the EAEC (Euratom).
[3] Case 22/70 *Commission* v *Council (AETR)* [1971] ECR 263.

transit problems. More recently, the Council approved a proposal for a Decision authorizing the Commission to negotiate an agreement between the Community and certain non-Community countries with a view to establishing uniform arrangements for international shuttle services by coach and bus.[1]

---

[1] Bull. EC 12-1982.

2. The inland waterways and the common transport policy

The idea of internationalizing the major rivers of Europe dates back to the French Revolution which set out to put an end to the absolute sovereignty exercised by States over the rivers running through them, which often, because of extortionate toll charges, amounted to prevention of or interference with navigation on these rivers. Already referred to in the Treaty of Paris of 30 May 1814, the international status of Europe's major rivers was confirmed by Articles 108 and 109, the Final Act of the Congress of Vienna of 9 June 1815 and the annexes on the Meuse, the Moselle, the Rhine and the Scheldt.

The Mainz Convention of 31 May 1831, which implemented the system laid down in the Final Act, accordingly established freedom of navigation on these rivers for trading purposes. Finally, the Mannheim Convention of 17 October 1868 established the Rhine Navigation System.

2.1 Rhine navigation

In its preamble, the Mannheim Convention states that its purpose is to maintain the principle of freedom of navigation on the Rhine for commercial purposes but does not define the relationship between freedom of trade and freedom of navigation. Nevertheless, the Convention does guarantee some basic principles, namely freedom of navigation, equal treatment and coordination of State intervention in related matters.

In fact there was some controversy over the actual concept of freedom of navigation as referred to in the Convention and this was the subject of conflicting interpretations at the time. Some argued that freedom of navigation was simply the technical freedom to navigate without any freedom of trade while others argued that it meant total freedom of navigation and trade. In fact a reasonable interpretation lies somewhere between the two, namely that freedom of navigation on the Rhine is the absolutely guaranteed right to transport goods and passengers.[1] This right includes commercial operations connected with these transport services, e.g. the signing of contracts of carriage and the right of entry into ports, as well as the right to use port facilities to load, unload and transship merchandise. However, freedom of navigation does not mean that the public authorities may not intervene to protect the transport market or the goods

---

[1] See W. Stabenow, *Die internationalen Konventionen über die Binnenschiffahrt im Lichte der wirtschaftlichen Integration Europas*, in Collection of papers presented at the Seminar of Advanced Studies on Transport Organization in European Economic Integration - 5th International Course, Università degli Studi di Trieste, 1967, pp. 529-557.

goods market from distortions of competition. In fact, under the system set up by the Mannheim Convention and even by the Treaty of Versailles, which we shall consider in a moment, the right to navigate a vessel on the Rhine was reserved to holders of a licence issued by the riparian States solely to their own citizens.

Article 356 of the Peace Treaty signed at Versailles on 28 June 1919 finally established the principle of freedom of navigation on the Rhine for the vessels of non-riparian States.

The Central Commission for the Navigation of the Rhine (CCR) set up by the Mannheim Convention originally consisted solely of representatives of the riparian States. It was later extended by the Treaty of Versailles to include Belgium, Italy, Switzerland and the United Kingdom.[1]

The Mannheim Convention was later revised by the Convention of 20 November 1963, but so far there has been no revision of the whole Convention system governing the Rhine as provided for in Article 354 of the Treaty of Versailles. The revision regularized the position of Switzerland, which since the Treaty of Versailles had been a member only of the Central Commission and now became a High Contracting Party to the Mannheim Convention.

After the revision the USA, which since 1945 had been a member of the Central Commission as an occupying power in Germany, ceased to participate.

2.1.1 *Rhine navigation and the EEC Treaty*

Clearly, as a result of the Mannheim Convention, there has always been the problem of the Community's responsibilities on Rhine navigation *vis-à-vis* EEC Member States and non-member countries. For instance, right at the beginning when thought was first being given to a common transport policy, the EEC Member States which also belonged to the CCR steadfastly refused to apply Council Regulation No 11/60 concerning the abolition of discrimination in transport rates and conditions to Rhine navigation, arguing that, because of the Mannheim Convention, they could not apply the checks referred to in the Regulation to Rhine navigation. It was not until 1970, following the action brought by the Commission under the infringement procedure provided for in Article 169 of the Treaty, that the Member States agreed to apply the Regulation to Rhine navigation.

As regards the scope of Article 234 of the Treaty, which governs the rights and obligations arising from agreements concluded before the entry into force of the Treaty between one or more Member States on the one hand, and one or more third countries on the other, a judgment handed down by the Court of Justice

---

[1] Italy left the CCR in 1938.

on 27 February 1962 stated that a Member State which, because of the entry into force of the EEC Treaty, enters into new obligations *vis-à-vis* other Member States, shall automatically cease to take advantage of rights deriving from agreements concluded previously between Member States which give rise to incompatibilities with these new obligations.[1]

There is still a possibility of conflict with non-member countries if, for example, under the Mannheim Convention in particular, Member States have contracted obligations towards such countries and there is a Community regulation which does not correspond to the principles of the Convention and does not acknowledge the guarantees provided by the Convention to the non-member countries. Apart from the clear possibility of legal conflict, it was rather because of the difficulties that it had encountered from the beginning with regard to the application of Community regulations to Rhine navigation that the Commission, on 8 April 1964, sent the Council a memorandum on the application of the EEC Treaty to Rhine navigation. In it the Commission concludes - although the Council has never taken note of these conclusions - that, referring to the judgment handed down by the Court of Justice, there is no legal obstacle which prevents the Community from exercising its own legislative and regulatory powers in respect of Rhine navigation.[2] However, if the non-member countries concerned considered that the new Community system was incompatible with the system embodied in the Mannheim Convention, the countries would be entitled to request that the Community regulation should not apply to their own citizens, a procedure which should cause no problems.

Switzerland in particular, which is directly concerned by the navigation of the Rhine (its only access to the sea), has always maintained that the CCR has sole responsibility for Rhine navigation, even though the Commission for the Navigation of the Rhine has no competence in the economic sphere. Since, on the other hand, the Community may not relinquish the responsibilities assigned to it by the Treaty, the EEC Commission has proposed opening negotiations with Switzerland to find solutions to the main problems concerning Rhine navigation.

One of the main problems, which affects not only the Rhine but inland waterway transport as a whole, is structural overcapacity. The general economic crisis combined with surplus capacity in the inland waterways sector, which carries a particularly high proportion of goods traffic within the Community, resulted in schemes like the temporary laying-up of inland waterway vessels surplus to requirements. In 1964 a plan was prepared along these lines (on a Union for the International Navigation of the Rhine) at an economic conference called by the CCR proposing the regulation of transport capacity, but in a referendum the boatmen concerned voted against the plan and it was then abandoned. At the end of 1967 the Commission came up with practical proposals including a

---

[1] Case 10/61 [1963] ECR pp. 21-23.
[2] For further details on the legal grounds for the Commission's position see Doc. VII COM(64) 140 of 8 April 1964.

scheme for the temporary laying-up of surplus vessels together with a system of financial compensation for the period the vessels remained out of service.[1] As it was clearly essential to reach an agreement with Switzerland on the proposal, negotiations began on the basis of Council Decisions and Directives of 28 December 1972 and 17 February 1975 which authorized the Commission to conduct these negotiations with the aim of setting up a Fund for the temporary laying-up of inland waterway vessels.

Article 1 of the draft Agreement on establishment of the Fund states that the aim is to help restore temporary imbalances between supply and demand which might seriously disrupt the market.[2] An unexpected obstacle arose, alas, in the shape of an opinion given by the Court of Justice on 26 April 1977[3] which, while recognizing the validity of the economic objective, rejected the terms in which the Agreement had been expressed since the statute of the Fund would impinge on the Community's freedom of action in external relations and would mean changing the Community's internal constitution. As a result the Council had to issue a new Decision amending the Directive for the negotiation of the Agreement with Switzerland, which caused considerable delays.[4] Subsequently, because of changes in the capacity situation, because the Dutch raised some objections and because of the organized opposition to the measures by European boatmen, the Community ultimately lost the advantage it had before the Court of Justice published its opinion, so that the national governments won the day.

2.2 Moselle navigation

The Convention of 27 October 1956 signed by France, the Federal Republic of Germany and the Grand Duchy of Luxembourg established an international Moselle Navigation System guaranteeing freedom of navigation on this tributary of the Rhine on the stretch between Metz and Koblenz, according to a statute very similar to that which applies to the Rhine.

The Convention also set up a Commission to control navigation on the Moselle (the Moselle Commission) on which the three riparian States are represented.

Since the three States which signed the Convention are Member States of the Community (which was not the case with the Rhine system), there are no conflicts of responsibility surrounding the application to the Moselle of the principles of the common transport policy.

---

[1] See J. Dousset, 'La navigation intérieure dans la politique commune des transports', in *Transports*, February-March 1973.

[2] *La Politique commune des transports de la CEE: bilan de 1974*, Studiecentrum voor de Expansie van Antwerpen, p. 25.

[3] OJ C 107, 3.5.1977, p. 4.

[4] Council Decision of 20 February 1978, based on the Commission's report to the Council of 19 July 1977, Doc. COM(77) 343 final.

3. Future Community relations with third countries and international organizations

According to the Commission's Communication to the Council of 11 February 1983 on inland transport,[1] which met with the broad approval of the ESC,[2] it is clear that the Community Executive is working hard on a policy on international transport and in particular on extending Community policies, especially those relating to transit problems, to the States bordering on the Community. It is also concerned with the Community's role within the Economic Commission for Europe, the European Conference of Ministers of Transport and the Central Commission for Navigation of the Rhine. Furthermore, the Commission is intending to conclude negotiations with Austria to solve the problem of transit through the Alps of traffic bound for Italy and Greece,[3] to speed up negotiations with Yugoslavia on Article 8 of the Cooperation Agreement,[4] and to continue the exchange of information and opinions with Switzerland further to the agreement signed in 1978. The Commission also intends to pursue negotiations with certain third countries on the deregulation of combined transport, as authorized by the Council in March 1981.[5] Another aim for the future is to achieve better coordination between bilateral agreements signed between Member States and third countries by amending the proposal already made on inland transport in the light of recent developments in Community law.[6]

As regards relationship with the international organizations, the Council should have another look, in the ECE context, at the question of accession by the Community to the AETR in accordance with the Commission's current proposal[7] and work towards the Community as such becoming a member of the ECMT by overcoming the difficulties raised, somewhat paradoxically, by the judgment handed down by the Court of Justice in 1971 on the subject of the AETR, a judgment which by establishing a link between the internal development of Community policy and its external policy re-awakened all the Freudian complexes of the Member States about the transfer of powers to the Community in respect of relations with third countries or international organizations. Never-

---

[1] OJ C 154, 13.6.1983, p. 1.
[2] OJ C 211, 8.8.1983, p. 34.
[3] The Council gave the Commission the necessary directives in Doc. 1164/81 Trans 18658 of 16 December 1981 (unpublished).
[4] Doc. COM(80) 109 final of 11 March 1980.
[5] Doc. 5606/81 Trans 45 of 24 March 1981 (unpublished). In October 1983 the Commission particularly asked the Council to sign the Agreement with Spain, which was initialled in July, on the international combined road-rail carriage of goods (Bull. EC 10-1983, point 2.1.183).
[6] OJ C 350, 31.12.1980, p. 23.
[7] Doc. COM(78) 767 final of 15 January 1979.

theless, the Commission will propose total or partial accession of the Community to the ECMT. Finally, there is an obvious need to improve cooperation between the Community and the Central Commission for the Navigation of the Rhine. Back in 1977, the EEC Commission proposed that the Community should sign the Mannheim Convention and Additional Protocol No 2.[1] Obviously, if negotiations on this matter can be brought to a successful conclusion this will have a very positive effect on the Community's transport policy by making it easier to control access to Rhine navigation by vessels of non-riparian States which are not members of the Community and by preventing further differences in interpretation of the Agreement with regard for example to exemption of river traffic from taxes, thus helping to solve the problem of charging users of the Rhine, and any other problems which may arise between the Community and the CCR, particularly regarding implementation of the Additional Protocol.

---

[1] Doc. COM(77) 518 final of 19 October 1977.

Conclusions

By now attentive readers will certainly have reached their own conclusions on the results achieved by Community transport policy in the 25 years since the signing of the Treaties of Rome. Although virtually all the provisions of the *lex specialis* on transport have been implemented through the adoption of some 170 Community measures (although not within the deadline set by Article 75(2)), thus making an important contribution towards the aim of establishing a common market in transport, there has nevertheless been a conspicuous failure to achieve the basic objective of a common transport policy. The 170 Commission proposals which have been adopted should be set against the 40 or more much more ambitious proposals which have been gathering dust in the Council of Ministers, in some cases for more than 10 years. There are many reasons for this state of affairs. On the one hand, Europe has been paralysed by the unfortunate combination (as regards the effects on Community decision-making) of the Gaullist principle of a Europe of nation States with the Thatcherite principle of fair returns (or haggling over the last penny as Sandro Pertini bluntly put it), which has been taken as a convenient justification for a marriage of convenience, rather than integration, between the United Kingdom and the rest of Europe. On the other hand, there are certain particular problems specific to transport. Chief among these is the fact that national transport has changed very little since the 1930s and is still basically interventionist. It is therefore difficult to achieve the full integration of the policies on the different national transport markets, which is an objective of the Treaty, but for which no clear rules are laid down.

Although there have been some extraordinarily passionate debates on various aspects of the different problems involved, any hope for the future lies in institutional change at European level such that the step-by-step approach, which often serves to disguise lack of political will, is no longer possible. The European Parliament is the place to watch, since this is where initiative is most likely to be taken. In fact, it is only by taking action against the Council for failure to act or, more generally, abolishing the Council's practice of taking decisions unanimously, or again by introducing a bicameral system as a way of changing the nature of relationships between the institutions that there may be progress on the transport policy. Moreover, the success of such action will also depend on public opinion within Europe. We may have to be prepared to accept the French idea of a 'two-speed Europe' which, by making a distinction between those Member States in the Customs Union and those which belong to the Economic Union, will put an end to all the ambiguity, and prevent lack of real political will in a small number of Member States resulting in total paralysis of the institutions, as it did in the 1960s.

These are the problems currently facing the Community, and they are becoming more acute day by day. It could not be in a worse position to cope with the delicate problems of the accession of Spain and Portugal.

At the transport policy level, the interaction between environmental aspects and transport growth will continue to intensify, whether or not Europe succeeds in solving its debilitating parochial problems. Therefore the Community's failure to establish a common transport policy is ultimately bound to result in an increasing number of measures taken at purely national level, like the Leber plan, which in turn will form an increasingly insurmountable barrier to the effective integration of national systems into a single transport market.

And Europe, even today politically straitjacketed in its inward-looking stance (and in this encouraged by the national bureaucracies), lacking the creative drive to overcome the grave problems of its structural crisis, having missed a thousand great opportunities in this half-century from the European Defence Community to a European technological research policy — Europe has less and less excuse (and cushioning resources) for allowing the common transport policy to fail as well.

Bibliography

M. Allais, M. Del Viscovo, L. Duquesne de la Vinelle, C. Oort and H.S. Seidenfus, *Options in transport tariff policy,* EEC, Studies collection, Transport series, No 1, Brussels, 1965.

N. Bellieni, 'I trasporti', in *Commentario al Trattato istitutivo della CEE*, Giuffré, Milan, 1965, Vol. I.

N. Bellieni, 'Verso una politica europea dei trasporti', in *Rassegna Economica*, Naples, 1966, No 1.

N. Bellieni, 'Titre IV - Transports', in *Droit des affaires - Marché Commun*, Ed. Jupiter, Brussels, 1973.

F. Berlingieri, *Il trasporto marittimo*, Fratelli Bozzi, Genoa, 1975.

W.A.G. Blonk (ed.), *Transport and Regional Development*, Saxon House, Farnborough, 1979.

W.A.G. Blonk, 'Het goederenvervoer tussen de EEG-landen in 1957 en 1963, omvang en beperkingen', in *Statistische en econometrische onderzoekingen*, The Hague, 1966, No 6.

V. Bodson, 'Le prospettive della politica comune dei trasporti', in *Automobilismo e Automobilismo Industriale*, No 5-6, 1970.

C. Bonet-Maury, 'Conséquences économiques et sociales des techniques nouvelles de navigation fluviale', in Collection of papers (1962) - Seminar of Advanced Studies on Transport Organization in European Economic Integration - 3rd International Course, Università degli Studi di Trieste, 1963.

N. Brough, 'Deregulation del trasporto aereo: la teoria, l'esperienza americana e le prospettive per l'Italia e per l'Europa', in *Einaudi Notizie*, 1983.

N. Brough, 'Diritti di traffico vendonsi', in *Aviazione*, No 153, April 1981.

N. Brough, 'La giusta libertà', in *Turismo Attualità*, No 18, November 1980.

H. Brugmans, *L'idée européenne*, 1918-1965, De Tempel, Bruges, 1965.

H. Brugmans, *L'Europe vécue*, Casterman, Paris-Tournai, 1979.

S.M. Carbone, *Il trasporto marittimo di cose nel sistema dei trasporti internazionali*, Giuffré, Milan, 1976.

S.M. Carbone, 'La ripartizione e la disciplina del traffico marittimo internazionale: la soluzione delle NU e le reazioni CEE' in *Il Diritto Marittimo,* October-December 1975.

L. Cartou, *Organisations Européennes*, Dalloz, Paris, 1967.

N. Catalano, *Manuale di diritto delle Comunità Europee*, Giuffré, Milan, 1965.

College of Europe, *Les chemins de fer et l'Europe* (2 volumes), De Tempel, Tempelhof, Bruges, 1969.

College of Europe, *Etude analytique des structures institutionelles des ports de la communauté européenne élargie*, De Tempel, Tempelhof, Bruges, 1972.

Commission of the European Communities, 'Memorandum sur l'orientation à donner à la politique commune des transports', Brussels, 10 April 1961 (Doc. VII/COM(61) 50 final).

Commission of the European Communities, *Options in transport tariff policy*, Studies Collection, Transport series, No 1, Brussels, 1965.

Commission of the European Communities, *Problems arising in the practical application of charges for the use of road infrastructures*, Studies Collection, Transport series, No 2, Brussels, 1970.

Commission of the European Communities, *Coordination of investments in transport infrastructures*, Studies Collection, Transport series, No 3, Brussels, 1973.

Commission of the European Communities, *The analysis of economic costs and expenses in road and rail transport*, Studies Collection, Transport series, No 4, Brussels, 1976.

Commission of the European Communities, *Etude de la structure de la navigation intérieure en Europe occidentale*, Studies Collection, Transport series, No 5, Brussels, 1978.

Commission of the European Communities, *Reference tariffs for goods transport*, Studies Collection, Transport Series, No 6, Brussels, 1982.

Commission of the European Communities, 'A transport network for Europe - Outline of a policy', *Bulletin of the European Communities, Supplement 8/1979*.

Commission of the European Communities, *Report on Scheduled Passenger Air Fares in the EEC*, Brussels, July 1981.

Commission of the European Communities, *The European Community's transport policy*, Luxembourg, 1980.

Commission of the European Communities, *Sixth General Report on the activities of the European Communities in 1972*, Brussels-Luxembourg, 1973.

Commission of the European Communities, *Thirteenth General Report on the activities of the European Communities in 1979*, Brussels-Luxembourg, 1980.

Commission of the European Communities, *Sixteenth General Report on the activities of the European Communities in 1982*, Brussels-Luxembourg, 1983.

Commission of the European Communities, *Report of an enquiry into the situation in the major Community sea ports drawn up by the Port Working Group*, Brussels, 1977, Catalogue No CB-22-77-863-EN-C.

Commission of the European Communities, *Report by the Port Working Group for carrying out the terms of reference given them by the plenary meeting of the major ports of the Community on 9 and 10 June 1977*, Doc. VII/440/80-EN.

Commission of the European Communities, *Addendum to the report by the Port Working Group for carrying out the terms of reference given them by the plenary meeting of the major ports of the Community on 9 and 10 June 1977, Revision of the fact-finding report (fourth assignment)*, Doc. VII/440/80-EN.

Commission of the European Communities, *Annex to the report by the Port Working Group for carrying out the terms of reference given them by the plenary meeting of the major ports of the Community on 9 and 10 June 1977, Revision of the fact-finding report (fourth assignment)*, Doc. VII/440/80-EN.

Commission of the European Communities, 'Communication from the Commission to the Council of 11 February 1983 on progress towards a common transport policy - Inland transport', OJ 154, 13.6.1983.

Commission of the European Communities, *List of pending proposals at 1 October 1983*, Doc. SEC(83) 1703 of 26 October 1983.

Commission of the European Communities, *Programme for Implementation of the Common Transport Policy*, Brussels, 23 May 1962, Doc. VII/COM(62) 88 final.

A. Coppe, *De uitvoering van de vervoerbepalingen in het EGKS - Verdrag in Nederland en het Europese Vervoerbeleid*, Rotterdam, December 1966.

Council of the European Communities, 'Council resolution of 15 December 1981 on Community railway policy', OJ C 157, 22.6.1982.

C. Delepiere-Nys, *Air Europe: La politique de coopération entre les compagnies aériennes de l'Europe des Six*, Editions de l'Université de Bruxelles, 1974.

N.S. Despicht, *Policies for transport in the Common Market*, Lambarde Press, London, 1964.

N.S. Despicht, 'Transport and the Common Market', in *Institute of Transport Journal*, London, 1966, Nos 8, 9 and 12.

F.D. Dominedò, V.D. Fiore, M. Iannuzzi, B. Minoletti, G. Renzetti and M. Scerni, *Conferences marittime e Mercato Comune*, Cedam, Padua, 1964.

J. Dousset, 'La navigation intérieure dans la politique commune des transports', in *Transports*, February-March 1973.

J. Dousset, 'Le programme d'action en matière de politique commune des transports', in *Transports*, Paris, 1962, No 69.

M. Duynstee, *Rapport sur certains aspects financiers et économiques des opérations de transport aérien*, Council of Europe, Strasbourg, 1964.

EIB, *Annual Report 1982*, Luxembourg, 1983.

EIB, *25 years - 1958-83*, Luxembourg, 1983.

ESC, *The problems currently facing Community shipping policy*, Brussels, 1979.

ESC, 'Opinion on the transport policy of the European Community in the 1980s', OJ C 326, 13.12.1982.

Euroffice, *The European Community's transport policy*, Luxembourg, December 1980.

European Parliament, *Rapport sur les problèmes concernant la politique commune des transports dans le cadre de la CEE*, Report by P.J. Kapteyn, Doc. 106/61.

European Parliament, *Report submitted on behalf of the Committee for Regional Policy, Land Use Planning and Transport on the present state and progress of the common transport policy*, Rapporteur H. Seefeld, Working Document No 512/78 of 5 January 1979.

European Parliament, *Report drawn up on behalf of the Committee on Transport on ways and means of effecting energy savings in the transport sector*, Doc. 1-249/81 of 25 June 1981.

European Parliament, *Report drawn up on behalf of the Committee on Transport on the common transport policy*, Rapporteur A. Carossino, Doc. 1-996/81 of 15 February 1982.

European Parliament, *Report drawn up on behalf of the Committee on Transport on the institution of proceedings against the Council of the European Communities for failure to act in the field of transport policy,* Rapporteur H. Seefeld, Doc. 1-420/82 of 1 July 1982.

European Parliament, *Report drawn up on behalf of the Committee on Transport on the role of ports in the common transport policy*, Rapporteur A. Carossino, Doc. 1-844/82 of 15 November 1982.

European Parliament, *Report drawn up on behalf of the Committee on Transport on the possibilities of providing Community support for a fixed link across the Channel*, Rapporteur M. Vandewiele, Doc. 1-372/83 of 30 May 1983.

European Parliament, *Report drawn up on behalf of the Committee on Transport on transport problems in the peripheral regions of the European Community* Doc. 1-755/83 of 28 September 1983.

European Parliament, *Report drawn up on behalf of the Committee on Transport on the creation of a European Foundation for Safety at Sea*, Rapporteur K. Kaloyannis, Doc. 1-773/83 of 10 October 1983.

Eurostat, *Statistical Yearbook: Transport, Communications, Tourism 1977,* Luxembourg, 1980.

Eurostat, *Statistical Yearbook: Transport, Communications, Tourism 1978-1979*, Luxembourg, 1981.

Eurostat, *Statistical Yearbook: Transport, Communications, Tourism 1980,* Luxembourg, 1982.

Eurostat, *Statistical Yearbook: Transport, Communications, Tourism 1981*, Luxembourg, 1983.

Eurostat, *Stock of fixed assets in industry in the Community Member States: towards greater comparability - Studies of national accounts*, No 2, Luxembourg, 1983.

Eurostat, *Monthly External Trade Bulletin*, Luxembourg, 1978-1983.

O. de Ferron, *Le problème des transports et le Marché Commun*, Droz, Geneva, 1965.

A. Frignani, M. Waelbroeck, *Diritto della concorrenza*, Jovene, Naples, 1983.

A. Frohnmeyer, 'Stand und Entwicklungstendenzen der gemeinsamen Verkehrspolitik in der Europäischen Wirtschaftsgemeinschaft', in *Zeitschrift für Verkehrswissenschaft*, Düsseldorf, 1965, No 4.

R. Goergen, 'Les problèmes généraux de l'économie européenne des transports', in *Transports*, Paris, 1965, No 99.

R.O. Goss, *Studies in Maritime Economics*, Cambridge Un. Press, Cambridge, 1968.

H. Gosse, 'Die Nachfolge der amerikanischen Verkehrspolitik und der Interstate Commerce Commission in den Europäischen Gemeinschaften', in *Europa-Verkehr*, Darmstadt, 1963, No 1.

H. Gosse, 'Aktuelle Fragen der Verkehrs- und Tarifpolitik in der EWG', in *Zeitschrift für Binnenschiffahrt*, Duisburg, 1967, No 8.

K.M. Gwilliam, S. Petriccione, F. Voigt, J.A. Zighera, *Coordination of investments in transport infrastructures*, Commission of the European Communities, Studies collection, Transport series, No 3, Brussels, 1973.

W. Isard, *Localizzazione e spazio economico*, edited by A. Riva, Istituto Ed. Cisalpino, Milan-Varese, 1962.

P.J. Kapteyn, 'L'intégration des transports,' in *Collection of papers (1960) - Seminar of Advanced Studies on Transport Organization in European Economic Integration - 1st International Course*, Università degli Studi di Trieste, 1960.

N. Kirchen, 'Le problème de la tarification des infrastructures', in *Les chemins de fer et l'Europe'*, De Tempelhof, Bruges, 1969.

W. Klaer, 'Direkte internationale Tarife-Studien zur Rechtsgrundlage, Entstehungsgeschichte und Einführung direkter internationaler Eisenbahngütertarife in der Europäischen Gemeinschaft für Kohle und Stahl', in *Archiv für Eisenbahnwesen*, Frankfurt, 1960, No 1.

G. Krauss, 'Die Leigedanken der Kommission der Europäischen Wirtschaftsgemeinschaft zur gemeinsamen Verkehrspolitik', in *Internationales Archiv für Verkehrswesen*, Frankfurt, 1961, No 8.

K. Kuhne,' Berechnung und Zurechnung der Wegekosten im Verkehr', in *Wirtschaftsdienst*, Hamburg, 1963, No 6.

H.C. Kuiler, *De ontwikkeling van de vervoerseconomie en die van de Europese vervoersintegratie*, Assen, 1963.

L. Lacoste, 'La tarification à fourchettes' in *Transports*, Paris, 1963, No 76.

J. Lemmens, 'Les aides dans le domaine des transports', in *Revue du Marché Commun*, Paris, 1966, No 89.

R. Malcor, *Problems arising in the practical application of charges for the use of road infrastructures*, Commission of the European Communities, Studies Collection, Transport series, No 2, Brussels, 1970.

M. Malderez, 'Les transports et l'intégration économique européenne', in *Revue de la Société d'Etudes et d'Expansion*, Liege, 1963, No 206.

Manuale delle Comunità Europee, see in particular Chapter VIII; A. Pappalardo, *Politica della concorrenza*, UTET, Turin, 1984.

U. Marchese, *Trasporti integrati terra-mare*, Istituto Int. Comunicazioni, Genoa, 1973.

U. Marchese, 'Sviluppi metropolitani nelle regioni marittime', in *Università degli Studi di Genova - Annali della Facoltà di Scienze Politiche*, Anno III, 1975, Giuffré, Milan, 1976.

U. Marchese, 'Progresso marittimo e porti', in Trasporti, Cedam, Padua, No 15, 1978.

U. Marchese, *Aspetti economici e territoriali del sistema dei trasporti*, ECIG, Genoa, 1980.

U. Marchese, 'I trasporti intermodali nel progresso marittimo e portuale', in *Porti Mare Territorio*, Giuffré, Milan, No 3, July-September 1981.

A. Meyer, 'Zur Frage der Anwendbarkeit des Vertrags zur Gründung der Europäischen Wirtschaftsgemeinschaft (EWG) auf die Luftfahrt', in *Zeitschrift für Luftrecht und Weltraumrechtsfragen*, Cologne, 1962.

B. Minoletti, 'Il cabotaggio marittimo nella Comunità Economica Europea' in *Collection of papers (1963) - Seminar of Advanced Studies on Transport Organization in European Economic Integration - 4th International Course,* Università degli Studi di Trieste, 1964.

J. Noël Mayer, 'Aperçu sur les problèmes que pose le financement de l'infrastructure routière dans les pays membres de la CEE', in *Reflets et perspectives de la vie économique*, Brussels, No 5.

Nord e Sud Europa: la sfida portuale degli anni '80, Ilres, Genoa, May 1981.

C.J. Oort, 'De margetarifering in het Europese goederenvervoer', in *Economisch-Statistische Berichten*, Rotterdam, 1962, No 2349.

F. Pocar, *Lezioni di diritto delle Comunità Europee*, Giuffré, Milan, 1979.

A. Rebhan, *Die Beseitigung und Verhinderung von Diskriminierung sowie Subventionen in den Verkehrstarifen Westeuropas*, Kirschbaum, Bad Godesberg, 1965.

R. Regul (editor), *L'avenir des ports européens,* College of Europe, Bruges Week 1970, De Tempel, Bruges 1971.

R. Regul, 'Transport policy in the Common Market for coal and steel', in *Legal provisions relating to transport in the Common Market*, The British Institute of International and Comparative Law, London 1963, No 2.

A.H. Reinarz, *Het vervoer in de EEG*, Nederlands Verkeersinstituut, s'-Gravenhage, September 1961.

A.H. Reinarz, *Algemene orientatie van het vervoerbeleid binnen de EEG*, Eigen Vervoerders Organisatie, The Hague, 1963.

G. Renzetti, 'La coordinazione dei trasporti', in *La Comunità Economica Europea*, Centro internazionale di studi e documentazione sulle Comunità Europee, Giuffré, Milan, 1960.

G. Renzetti, 'La politique des transports dans le cadre du Marché Commun', in *Annales suisses d'économie des transports*, Zürich, 1962, No 3.

P. Reuter, *Organisations Européennes,* P.U.F. 1965.

J. Robert, *Eléments d'une politique des transports maritimes*, Ed. Eyrolles, Paris, 1973.

F. Santoro, *La politica dei trasporti della Comunità Economica Europea*, UTET, Turin, 1974.

F. Santoro, *Politica dei trasporti*, Cedam, Padua, 1977.

L. Schaus, *Les transports dans le cadre de l'intégration européenne*, Bruylant-Oyez, Brussels-Louvain, 1977.

L. Schaus, 'Fragen der Auslegung und Anwendung des Vertrages zur Gründung der Europäischen Wirtschaftsgemeinschaft auf dem Gebiete des Verkehrs', Deutscher Industrie- und Handelstag, Bonn, 1960.

L. Schaus, 'Europäische Verkehrsintegration', in *Zeitenwende im Verkehr, Deutscher Verkehrs-Verlag*, Hamburg, 1963.

L. Schaus, 'Transportation Policy and the EEC', in *National Transportation Symposium* (1-6 May 1966), American Society of Mechanical Engineers, New York, 1966.

H. Schulze, 'Der Ausbau der grossen Verkehrsachsen innerhalb der EWG insbesondere der Haupt-Eisenbahnstrecken', in *Internationales Archiv für Verkehrswesen*, Frankfurt, 1962, No 5.

H.S. Seidenfus, 'Problemi di regolazione e deregolazione nell'economia dei trasporti della CEE', in *Collection of papers (1983) - Seminar of Advanced Studies on Transport Organization in European Economic Integration - 24th International Course*, Università degli Studi di Trieste, 1984.

F.P. Sgarro, *I trasporti marittimi nella futura politica comunitaria*, idem.

W. Stabenow, 'Les transports aériens dans le cadre de l'intégration européenne', in Wiffels-Stabenow-Van Huffel, *Gemeinsamer Markt und Verkehr - Marché Commun et Transport*, Antwerp, 1969, pp. 239-261.

W. Stabenow, 'Evolution of Transport Policy in the European Economic Community', in Studnicki-Gizbert (editor), *Issues in Canadian Transport Policy*, Toronto, 1983.

W. Stabenow, 'Die internationalen Konventionen über die Binnenschiffahrt im Lichte der wirtschaftlichen Integration Europas', in *Collection of papers (1964) - Seminar of Advanced Studies on Transport Organization in European Economic Integration - 5th International Course*, Università degli Studi di Trieste, 1967.

D. Strasser, *Les finances de l'Europe*, PUF, Paris, 1975.

Studiecentrum voor de Expansie van Antwerpen, *La politique commune des transports de la CEE de janvier 1967 à fin mars 1968,* Antwerp, 1968.

Studiecentrum voor de Expansie van Antwerpen, *La politique commune des transports de la CEE d'avril 1968 à fin août 1969*, Antwerp, 1969.

Studiecentrum voor de Expansie van Antwerpen, *La politique commune des transports de la CEE de septembre 1969 à fin août 1970*, Antwerp, 1970.

Studiecentrum voor de Expansie van Antwerpen, *La politique commune des transports de la CEE de novembre 1971 à fin décembre 1972*, Antwerp, 1973.

Studiecentrum voor de Expansie van Antwerpen, *La politique commune des transports de la CEE aperçu de 1959 à 1973*, Antwerp, 1974.

Studiecentrum voor de Expansie van Antwerpen, *Politique portuaire et politique maritime de la CEE*, Antwerp, 1974.

Studiecentrum voor de Expansie van Antwerpen, *La politique commune des transports de la CEE: bilan de 1974,* Antwerp, 1975.

Studiecentrum voor de Expansie van Antwerpen, *La politique commune des transports de la CEE: bilan de 1975*, Antwerp, 1976.

Studiecentrum voor de Expansie van Antwerpen, *L'action de la CEE en matière de transport maritime*, Antwerp, 1979.

Studiecentrum voor de Expansie van Antwerpen, *La politique commune des transports de la CEE: bilan de 1978-1979*, Antwerp, 1980.

Studiecentrum voor de Expansie van Antwerpen, *La politique commune des transports de la CEE: bilan de 1980-1981*, Antwerp, 1982.

J.P.B. Tissot van Patot and T.E. Rueb, *De navolging van de amerikaanse vervoerspolitiek en van de Interstate Commerce Commission in de Europese gemeenschappen*, Verkeerswetenschappelijk Centrum, Rotterdam, 1961.

Transportation Economics, Columbia University Press, London-New York, 1965.

R. Turvey, *Analysis of economic costs and expenses in road and rail transport*, Studies Collection, Transport series, No 4, Commission of the European Communities, Brussels, 1975.

Università degli Studi di Trieste, *Collection of papers - Seminar of Advanced Studies on Transport Organization in European Economic Integration - International Course*, Università degli Studi di Trieste, 1960-1984.

A. Vallega, *L'organizzazione delle regioni portuali nella CEE*, Fratelli Bozzi, Genoa, 1970.

A. Vallega, *I porti della CEE, attività motrici per processi di sviluppo economico regionale?*, Atti Secondo Convegno 'Aspetti geografici dell'integrazione europea', Naples, 22-23 May 1974, 1974.

L. van Huffel, 'Les influences de l'évolution maritime sur l'infrastructure portuaire', in *Collection of papers (1968) - Seminar of Advanced Studies on Transport Organization in European Economic Integration - 9th International Course*, Università di Trieste, 1969, p. 241-276.

L. van Huffel, *Proposte per la futura politica comunitaria dei trasporti*, idem, 1984.

F. Ventrella, *Esperienze comunitarie di gestione portuale,* report to the symposium 'Esperienze europee in materia di gestione portuale', Rome, 18 November 1982, organized by the Ist. di Diritto della Navigazione dell'Università di Roma.

E. Vittorelli, 'Les pipe-lines dans l'Europe des Six', in *Reflets et perspectives de la vie économique*, Brussels, 1962, No 5.

F. Voigt, *Verkehr*, Dunker & Humbolt, Berlin, 1973.

H. von der Groeben, H. von Boeckh and J. Thiesing (editor), *Kommentar Zum EWG-Vertrag*, Nomos Verlag, Baden-Baden, 1983 (3 ed.).

F. von Stackelberg, 'Il contributo dei trasporti multimodali nella futura politica comune dei trasporti', in *Collection of papers (1983) - Seminar of Advanced Studies on Transport Organization in European Economic Integration - 24th International Course*, Università degli Studi di Trieste, 1984.

M. Walbroeck, 'L'arrêt AETR et les compétences externes de la Communauté économique européenne', in *Intégration*, 1971.

H. Watermann, 'Die gemeinsame Verkehrspolitik auf Grund des Vertrages zur Gründung der Europäischen Wirtschaftsgemeinschaft, in *Zeitschrift für Verkehrswissenschaft*, 1969.

G.L. Weil, *Handbook on the EEC*, College of Europe, Bruges, 1966.

R. Wijffels, W. Stabenow and L. van Huffel, *Marché commun et transport - Gemeinsamer Markt und Verkehr*, Antwerp, 1969.

R. Willeke, H. Baum and W. Hoener, *Reference tariffs for goods transport*, Studies Collection, Transport series, No 6, Commission of the European Communities, Luxembourg, 1982.

C. Woelker, 'Il futuro della politica comunitaria dei trasporti dal punto di vista di uno Stato comunitario', in *Collection of papers (1983) - Seminar of Advanced Studies on Transport Organization in European Economic Integration - 24th International Course*, Università degli Studi di Trieste, 1984.

Community documents

1. *Official Journal of the European Communities:* legislation (L series), communications and information (C series).

2. Summaries of Community legislation
Commission of the European Communities, *Community legislation on transport* (published at irregular intervals).
Commission of the European Communities, list of pending proposals on 1 October 1983, Doc. SEC(83) 1703 of 26 October 1983.
R. Wijffels, W. Stabenow and L. van Huffel, *Marché Commun et Transport - Gemeinsamer Markt und Verkehr*, Antwerp, 1969.

3. Activities of the Commission and the other Community institutions
   (a) *Bulletin of the European Communities* (11 monthly editions a year).
   Information on official publications of the Commission and on documents published jointly by the Council and the Commission.
   (b) *General Report on the Activities of the European Communities* (published annually in February), Office for Official Publications of the European Communities (Euroffice), L-2985 Luxembourg.
   (c) European Parliament: *Working documents*, Euroffice, Luxembourg.
   (d) Economic and Social Committee: 'Opinions' published in the C series of the OJ; 'Reports' published by Euroffice, Luxembourg.
   (e) Court of Justice of the European Communities: *European Court Reports*.
   (f) Court of Auditors of the European Communities: various reports.

4. European Investment Bank (EIB): Annual reports, EIB, Bvd Konrad Adenauer, Luxembourg.

5. Statistics
Statistical Office of the European Communities (Eurostat): *Statistical Yearbook on Transport, Communications and Tourism* (published annually), Euroffice, Luxembourg.

Works published in English in the

european perspectives

Series

The European Community: How it works

Emile NOËL

CB-28-79-390-EN-C

The finances of Europe

Daniel STRASSER

CB-30-80-980-EN-C

The Community legal order

Jean-Victor LOUIS

CB-28-79-407-EN-C

The European Communities in the international order

Jean GROUX and Philippe MANIN

CB-40-84-206-EN-C

Thirty years of Community law

Various Authors

CB-32-81-681-EN-C

The Customs Union
of the European Economic Community

Nikolaus VAULONT

CB-30-80-205-EN-C

The European Monetary System

Origins, operation and outlook

Jacques van YPERSELE and Jean-Claude KOEUNE

CB-41-84-127-EN-C

Money, economic policy and Europe

Tommaso PADOA-SCHIOPPA

CB-40-84-286-EN-C

An ever closer Union

A critical analysis of the Draft Treaty establishing the European Union

Roland BIEBER, Jean-Paul JACQUÉ
and Joseph H. H. WEILER

CB-43-85-345-EN-C

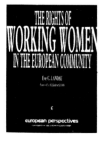

The rights of working women
in the European Community

Eve C. LANDAU

CB-43-85-741-EN-C

The professions
in the European Community

**Towards freedom of movement
and mutual recognition of qualifications**

Jean-Pierre de CRAYENCOUR

CB-33-81-061-EN-C

The challenges ahead - A plan for Europe

Various Authors

CB-28-79-827-EN-C

The old World
and the new technologies

Challenges to Europe in a hostile world

Michel GODET and Olivier RUYSSEN

CB-30-80-116-EN-C

The European Community –
The formative Years

**The struggle to establish the Common Market
and the Political Union (1958-66)**

Hans von der GROEBEN

CB-40-84-311-EN-C

In the same Series:

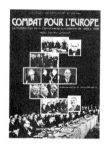

Combat pour l'Europe

La construction de la Communauté européenne de 1958 à 1966

Hans von der GROEBEN

CB-40-84-311-FR-C

Options européennes 1945-1985

Jacques van HELMONT

CB-44-85-064-FR-C

Further details of these publications and of the various language versions available are to be found in the catalogue of the Office for Official Publications of the European Communities.

European Communities — Commission

Transport and European integration
by Carlo degli Abbati

Luxembourg: Office for Official Publications of the European Communities

1987 - 229 pp. - 17.6 × 25.0 cm

The European Perspectives series

EN

ISBN 92-825-6199-2

Catalogue number: CB-45-86-806-EN-C

Price (excluding VAT) in Luxembourg

ECU 15.48   BFR 690   IRL 11.20   UKL 9.60   USD 14.00